Data Warehouse Designs

Achieving ROI with Market Basket Analysis
and Time Variance

Data Warehouse Designs

Achieving ROI with Market Basket Analysis and Time Variance

Fon Silvers

CRC Press
Taylor & Francis Group
Boca Raton   London   New York

CRC Press is an imprint of the
Taylor & Francis Group, an **informa** business
AN AUERBACH BOOK

CRC Press
Taylor & Francis Group
6000 Broken Sound Parkway NW, Suite 300
Boca Raton, FL 33487-2742

Printed in the United States of America on acid-free paper
Version Date: 20111107

International Standard Book Number: 978-1-4398-7076-1 (Hardback)

Visit the Taylor & Francis Web site at
http://www.taylorandfrancis.com

and the CRC Press Web site at
http://www.crcpress.com

This book is dedicated to Deborah,

my wife, my love, my best friend,

and my biggest fan.

Contents

Preface

This book is born of frustration. Early in our first data warehouse deliverable, we tried to deliver a Market Basket Analysis application. We also tried to deliver Type 2 time variant data. Neither effort succeeded. Since then, I continued to work on those two failed deliverables. First, I researched the root cause of our failures. Then, I designed solutions that resolved the root causes of the failure to deliver a Market Basket Analysis application and a time variant database design. Discovering that the Market Basket Analysis application and the time variant database design (both Type 1 and Type 2) fit together like a hand and glove was both lagniappe and serendipity.

The root cause of the failure to deliver a Market Basket Analysis application was the preconceived expectation that a Market Basket Analysis application was simply a table or view. Once I realized that Market Basket Analysis requires a full-fledged datamart with the supporting database design, ETL, and business intelligence infrastructure, the two-step ETL process and BI layer became obvious.

The root cause of the failure to deliver a Type 2 time variant application is the topic of Chapter 10. Once I understood the massive amount of nonoptimized work we'd been asking of the RDBMS, the solution became obvious. My only concern is that some will see the definition of the Instance_Key and Entity_Key and see only surrogate keys, which will cause those readers to misunderstand the purpose of an Instance_Key and Entity_Key. For them, the only alternative is brute force, which is very expensive.

This book presents the fruits of those efforts. Please read these chapters with the shared understanding that your data warehouse is different from every other data warehouse in some number of ways, and yet similar to every other data warehouse. Please take from these chapters the ideas that can help you now, and file away in your memory those ideas that seem less relevant. You may eventually come back to them later and find them helpful.

This book includes a CD-ROM containing sample data in an MS Access database. This sample data enables readers to work hands-on with the concepts and methods presented in the book.

Acknowledgments

I thank my family for their patience and understanding as I took time away from them to write this book. I thank my wife for taking the front-line parent job. The book is finished, and I'm back.

I thank my friends and colleagues for their help and contributions. Thank you to Brent Moser and Kishore Nagururu for your reviews and comments. I am grateful for your constructive criticism and patient guidance. Thank you to Dan Taylor and Pierre Guerrero for your help and direction in the database designs. Thank you to Sara Yeager and Ken Graham for explaining to me what I'd discovered. Let's do lunch again.

I thank God for making this book a reality. This has been a long journey of discovery, for which I am grateful. I thank Jack Rader, who gave me my first job. I thank Steve Olive, who taught me how to do my first job. Without their help, and the help of so many others, I would have accomplished nothing.

Finally, I thank Auerbach Publications for allowing me the opportunity to publish a second book.

The Author

Fon Silvers is a Data Warehouse ETL Analyst and Data Warehouse Support Team Lead in a Fortune 500 company. His first book was *Building and Maintaining a Data Warehouse*. Fon can be found at LinkedIn (http://www.linkedin.com/in/fonsilvers) and his Amazon Author page (http://www.amazon.com/Fon-Silvers/e/B001JRVJMG/ref=ntt_athr_dp_pel_pop_1).

1

Data Warehouse ROI

A DATA WAREHOUSE NEEDS A PURPOSE

When I was a boy growing up in rural Central Florida, the worst thing I could do on Saturday was nothing. Saturday was the day of the week reserved for chores around the house, such as weeding the garden, mowing the yard, and cleaning the cars and the house. If I was found doing nothing on Saturday, obviously I did not have a task assigned to me or I did not fully understand the task(s) already assigned to me. Either way, my parents would quickly help me by providing and clarifying tasks for me to do...immediately. To make matters worse, my newly assigned tasks would be the most onerous tasks of that Saturday. So, clearly the best way to avoid weeding the garden or cleaning the rain gutters was to volunteer for those tasks that were most tolerable, such as cleaning the house, which included working on the air conditioning.

For a data warehouse, every day is Saturday. A data warehouse without a purpose assigned specifically to that data warehouse will find itself with a new purpose. When Bill Inmon and Ralph Kimball pioneered the information factory and decision support concepts into the modern data warehouse, the genius of their designs and methods rendered the data warehouse an obvious value addition to any enterprise. The retention and juxtaposition of data in a data warehouse from various business units and business processes throughout an enterprise renders a data warehouse a unique collection of data that is found nowhere else in the enterprise. The benefits are obvious and the possibilities are almost infinite. With the addition of a data warehouse, data juxtapositions that were previously not available become standard tools of decision support. When Sales data that exists in an OLTP system can be joined with Product data that exists in an ERP system, and both Sales and Product data can both be joined with

Customer data that exists in a CRM system, what could possibly be a problem? The answer is simple, even for a data warehouse with Sales, Product, and Customer data: it is still Saturday.

A data warehouse with Sales, Product, and Customer information is a unique and valuable asset. But, even for unique and valuable assets in an enterprise, such assets must be able to answer the Purpose question: "Why are you here?" Implicit in the Purpose question are several other questions:

- Why is the enterprise funding the existence of a data warehouse?
- Why is the enterprise not directing that funding elsewhere?
- How long should the enterprise expect to continue to fund the existence of a data warehouse?
- What benefit does the enterprise derive from the existence of a data warehouse?
- Is the benefit of a data warehouse equal to or greater than the benefit of something else?

Consider all these Purpose questions in the context of a Five-Year Plan, a Ten-Year Plan, and a Fifteen-Year Plan.

These are not philosophical or aesthetic questions with little or no impact on the life of an enterprise or a data warehouse. To the contrary, for an enterprise with a finite budget and more opportunities than resources, the answers to these questions will help the management of an enterprise choose whether to create or maintain a data warehouse, automate a manufacturing operation, or expand into a new market segment. Why should management choose to (continue to) fund a data warehouse rather than automate a manufacturing operation or expand into a new market segment? The answer ("The genius of the data warehouse designs and methods render the data warehouse an obvious value addition to any enterprise") seems a rather weak answer when compared to the potential for a new market segment. Could the answer be that the retention and juxtaposition of data from various business units and business processes throughout the enterprise renders a data warehouse a unique collection of data that is found nowhere else in the enterprise? No, again although true, that answer seems rather weak. When the automation of a manufacturing operation promises an amazing ROI for the next ten years, and a new market segment is expected to achieve an ROI for the foreseeable future of the enterprise, a data warehouse must be able to identify and quantify the benefits returned by the continued existence of that data warehouse. Otherwise, such a data warehouse may never begin its existence, or may find itself repurposed to something other than decision support, such as weeding the garden.

A DATA WAREHOUSE NEEDS AN ROI

A purpose is no guarantee of success or survival in an enterprise. A purpose provides a focal point for the goals and objectives of a data warehouse. If the purpose for a data warehouse is perceived as weak, the data warehouse is perceived as weak. If the purpose for a data warehouse is perceived as strong, the data warehouse is perceived as potentially strong. If the purpose indicates a low ROI, that low ROI reflects on the data warehouse. If the purpose indicates a lofty goal, the data warehouse will be measured by the goal, even if it is measured by nothing else.

The Purpose of a data warehouse is not simply a restatement of the properties and qualities of a data warehouse. Those properties and qualities may include features, functionality, and response time as well as other properties and qualities.

- Features—For a data warehouse the features can be transaction and event data, business data, environment data, and join strategies, which join those sets of data within the data warehouse.
- Functionality—For a data warehouse functionality can be metrics and formulas that present information built from the data in the data warehouse, and delivery mechanisms that deliver that data.
- Response Time—For a data warehouse the response time is the wall clock time duration between the moments when a user requests and receives information from the data warehouse.

The purpose of a data warehouse is not a collection of these features, functionalities, and response times. Instead, these features, functionalities, and response times are the properties of a data warehouse by which it achieves its purpose. Similar to the tools of a carpenter, the hammer and saw are not the purpose; instead, the creation of furniture is the purpose. The hammer and saw are simply the tools by which the carpenter achieves the purpose of building furniture.

Why does this matter? Why pay such attention to the purpose of a data warehouse? Without a valuable yet feasible purpose that simultaneously expresses the value of a data warehouse, that data warehouse is vulnerable. The gravitational pull of data may cause a data warehouse to fail to achieve its purpose and goals. Admit it. Every data warehouse achieves value and ROI, which is neither published nor measured, and may be the "real" reason for the existence of a data warehouse. To continue to deliver its real, yet unpublished, purpose a data warehouse must be able to resist the influence of the gravitational pull of data.

GRAVITATIONAL PULL OF A DATA WAREHOUSE

A successful data warehouse that achieves its purpose and adds value and ROI can become its own problem. Well-organized, high-quality data with complete metadata in a data warehouse can attract a problem to itself—the gravitational pull of data. Oddly enough, if left unchecked, the gravitational pull of data will increase the probability that it will destroy the data warehouse as the data warehouse increases its size and success.

Gravity: Two objects, if they are close enough to each other, will be drawn toward each other. When one object is larger than the other, the small object (i.e., the apple) moves while the large object (i.e., the earth) remains stationary. The same is true for a data warehouse. Within an enterprise, a data warehouse can be the large object attracting other objects to it. In an enterprise this gravity occurs by the economies of scale presented by a data warehouse. For example, a data warehouse may have Sales, Product, and Customer data. That would mean that a data warehouse has spent and expensed the investment necessary to analyze the Sales, Product, and Customer data in operational source systems. That would mean that a data warehouse has spent and expensed the investment necessary to design and develop the ETL applications that capture and retain that Sales, Product, and Customer data. Finally, that also means that a data warehouse has spent and will continue to spend, expensed and will continue to expense, the overhead incurred by capturing and retaining Sales, Product, and Customer data. A new application needing Sales, Product, or Customer data can either replicate all those expenditures, expenses, and investments, which will expand the budget and reduce the ROI of the business unit sponsoring the new application, or that new application can get its Sales, Product, or Customer data from the data warehouse, which will allow the business unit sponsoring the new application to avoid the expenditures, expenses, and investments, reduce the budget, and increase the ROI of that new application and the business unit that sponsored it. Only one option is the obvious and preferred option: when data is available in a data warehouse, get that data from the data warehouse. That is the gravitational pull of data.

The data in a data warehouse will "pull" or "draw" applications needing data to itself. As a result, the ROI of the data warehouse will reflect the expenses necessary to provide data to applications without the benefit of that data; in addition, the ROI of the applications will reflect the benefit of that data without the expenses necessary to obtain that data. One application leveraging the data in a data warehouse is company. Fifty new applications per year is a crowd. Any data warehouse that draws that kind of a crowd will inevitably find that some portion of those applications, as they grow and change, will try to modify the data, structure, and architecture of a data warehouse to match their growth and change. Such modifications can convert an enterprise data warehouse into an application data warehouse. This is when a successful and growing data warehouse can become its own problem through the gravitational pull of its own data.

A data warehouse can also be the small object that is drawn to a larger object. When a ten-ton elephant wants to sit in your front yard, where does it sit? Your front yard. There's no stopping it. When a ten-ton business unit wants to use the data in a data warehouse…well, you can guess what is about to happen. That business unit is going to use the data in the data warehouse. The ten-ton business unit is going to require the data warehouse supplement the data already in the data warehouse with additional data; furthermore, the ten-ton business unit may want to design the additional data necessary to meet the purposes of the business unit, which may or may not be the purposes of the data warehouse. Data already in the data warehouse may be redesigned to meet the needs of the ten-ton business unit, possibly to the detriment of the data warehouse.

Why is the ten-ton business unit consuming the data warehouse in this way? The answer is the same for the ten-ton business unit as for the small single application. Any expense or investment that can be migrated from the ten-ton business unit to the data warehouse will increase the ROI of the ten-ton business unit. Any economy that robs Peter to pay Paul will continue to be supported by Paul. Likewise, an enterprise that allows a business unit to migrate its expenses to a data warehouse, but experience the benefits of the data in the data warehouse, will continue to be supported by all such business units. The data warehouse, however, is left holding the expenses, but none of the benefits, associated with the data.

The gravitational pull of the data in a data warehouse moves smaller applications toward itself so they can use the data in the data warehouse. The gravitational pull of the data in the data warehouse moves the data warehouse toward larger business units when a larger business unit has the clout necessary to exert control over the data warehouse. In both scenarios the success and growth of a data warehouse attracts forces that may, if left unchecked, destroy the data warehouse.

PURPOSE AND ROI

The solution to the gravitational pull of data is purpose and ROI. The purpose of a data warehouse is that set of features and functions it intends to deliver to the enterprise. The ROI of a data warehouse is the realized value caused by the data warehouse when the data warehouse delivers the features and functions of its purpose. The selection of a purpose should be decided as early as possible in the life of a data warehouse. For example, a data warehouse may produce Sales summary reports and Logistics exception reports every morning while an Operational Data Store sends low-inventory and late-shipment alerts in near real time to the PDA of Logistics staff managers. This is when a data warehouse makes itself part of the fabric of the enterprise. The data, reports, alerts, and analytics delivered by a data warehouse—delivered every hour, every day, sometimes in near real time—are collectively the purpose of a data warehouse. The ROI is benefit and value realized within the enterprise when the data warehouse delivers the features and functions included in its purpose.

The ROI of a data warehouse presents a cost to any effort that would change the data warehouse to fit the requirements of a ten-ton business application. In that way, a change to the data warehouse becomes a change to the enterprise. By delivering Sales reports every morning, Sales reports that are immediately consumed by all levels of management, a data warehouse inhibits any efforts that might abridge, interrupt, or delay the delivery of those Sales reports. By delivering near real time alerts from its operational data store to tactical managers throughout the enterprise, near real time alerts that help those tactical managers avoid expensive mistakes, a data warehouse inhibits any efforts that might interrupt or delay those near real time alerts. In that way, Sales reports and near real time alerts can be part of the purpose and ROI of a data warehouse.

Architected correctly, a data warehouse can do both. A data warehouse can maintain its own integrity and flexibility. The internal integrity of a data warehouse, including adherence to data warehousing principles, allows a data warehouse to continue being a data warehouse. The flexibility allows a data warehouse to continue to serve all parts of the enterprise. The purpose and ROI of a data warehouse presents just enough pause for thought to allow a data warehouse architect to achieve both goals—integrity and flexibility.

Bill Inmon and Ralph Kimball individually pioneered the modern data warehouse. Their genius was in their data warehousing principles. The data warehousing principles of Inmon and Kimball allow a data warehouse to assimilate new subject areas, new purposes, and new inertias. Rather than build a database and reporting application that can accommodate only one subject area and its data, the data warehousing principles of Inmon and Kimball allow a data warehouse to assimilate many subject areas with those subject areas already in the data warehouse. This is how a data warehouse is able to assimilate new subject areas throughout its lifetime. In the life of a data warehouse, adherence to data warehousing principles and achievement of data warehouse purposes form a symbiotic relationship. Adherence to data warehousing principles allows a data warehouse to maintain its integrity as a data warehouse while the data warehouse purposes justify adherence to the data warehousing principles. A data warehouse is able to continue its formula for success by achieving its purposes, and able to achieve its purposes because it follows the formula for success, which was pioneered by Inmon and Kimball.

NOT QUITE A VICTIM OF SUCCESS

A data warehouse without a focus and direction, without a purpose, is like a ship without a rudder—rather than choose its own path a ship without a rudder goes where the water takes it. A data warehouse is able to direct its path when it achieves its purpose and delivers ROI. A data warehouse directs its path as it is built in sections, which are subject areas. For example, Sales, Promotions, Logistics, and Customers are frequent subject areas in data warehousing. A data warehouse is not merely a collection of subject areas. The subject areas must be able to work as a cohesive whole within the data warehouse. But what are the symptoms that occur when a data warehouse is not quite a victim of its own success, a data warehouse that lacks focus and direction, that lacks a purpose? Three key indicators of a data warehouse provide a good clue as to the success or failure of a data warehouse. Those three key indicators are performance, relational integrity, and data quality.

Performance

The first clue that a data warehouse is not quite a success is the inability to return a result set. This may seem obvious. It should be obvious. Maybe that is why it is the first clue...because it is so obvious. When users run a report or a query and...and...and...and...they eventually go home for the night, performance is definitely an issue. My first data warehouse was described as "a rock" for its ability to remain motionless and yield absolutely nothing, including data. Performance was an issue.

When a data warehouse is unable to yield data the root cause can be many things. But the first root cause is a lack of purpose. A data warehouse that is built to look like a data warehouse will do exactly that: it will look like a data warehouse. But a data warehouse that is built to render a Sales report will do exactly that: it will render a Sales report. Why is that? If from the first planning meeting everyone understood that, regardless of what may or may not be in the data warehouse, it must be able to generate a Prior Day Sales report, then everyone will begin thinking of the data in terms of the Prior Day Sales report. First, the Sales subject area will be included. Second, Sales will be grained by the day, and maybe by other time grains. Third, the dimensional properties and attributes necessary to describe, quantify, and qualify data in the Prior Day Sales report will be included. In short, everything necessary to make the Prior Day Sales report a success will be included and optimized so that when the managers who decided to fund the data warehouse because they want their Prior Day Sales report ask for this report, that's exactly what they will get.

What was the purpose of the first subject area of that data warehouse? The purpose was the Prior Day Sales report. Now comes the fun part. When you hit the bull's-eye right in the center, what is within three inches in every direction? The answer is...more bull's-eye. By virtue of having a purpose (deliver the Prior Day Sales report) the data warehouse is able to deliver the Prior Day Sales report and a dozen other reports that are only slight variations of the Prior Day Sales report—for example, the Prior Day Department Sales report, the Prior Day Sub-Department Sales report, and the Prior Week Sales report. What about the Prior Day Logistics report? That's another subject area and another purpose. Remember, one subject area at a time.

Relational Integrity

Another good clue that a data warehouse is not ready for prime time is the multiplication and disappearance of data. When the Prior Day Sales report indicates that sales yesterday were $500,000, but the Prior Day Department Sales report indicates sales yesterday were $750,000, something is amiss in the data warehouse. Or, when the Prior Day Department Sales report indicates the Furniture department disappeared, something is not quite right in the data warehouse.

Again, this would seem to be rather obvious. That is why it is a good first indicator of less than stellar success. The dimension tables look like dimension tables. The dimension and fact tables join like dimension and fact tables. As individual elements of a data warehouse they all seem to fit the descriptions of a data warehouse. But, when joined together in the form of a report or query, they distort the data returned by the data warehouse. Why is that? Again, from the first planning meeting to the final report review the fact tables and dimension tables will be designed to correctly join to achieve the result set for a Prior Day Sales report if the Prior Day Sales report is the goal of that subject area. By using the Prior Day Sales report to guide the relational integrity of the Sales subject area, other reports and queries will also experience good relational integrity. In short, the relational integrity necessary to make the Prior Day Sales report a success will still be there for other reports. By achieving its purpose, which is the Prior Day Sales report, a data warehouse experiences the secondary success of achieving other ancillary purposes as well.

Data Quality

The third key indicator of the success or failure of a data warehouse is not quite so obvious. However, what it lacks in obviousness, it compensates for in simplicity. Why do less successful data warehouses not include a Data Quality program? The answer is simple: they don't know what bad-quality data looks like. A word looks exactly like a word; a non sequitur word looks exactly like every other word. But, when the only acceptable values for a data element are *north, south, east,* and *west* a data quality application can rather easily identify *yes* as a non sequitur word.

A Data Quality program is difficult. You can take that plain and simple statement to the bank. In a Data Quality program you programmatically lock your definitions of acceptable data values and bad data values in logic written into ETL code. To do so, you must know what acceptable and bad data look like, and you must be able to define them in terms of programmatic logic. That task, all by itself, is difficult. Typically, a Data Quality program is an iterative effort. Each iteration is a refinement of prior efforts.

So, the mere presence of an active and functioning Data Quality program is a key indicator of a successful or failing data warehouse. It's that simple. The presence of an active and functioning Data Quality program means that someone is validating some of the data in the data warehouse to verify that it is consistent with the logic and design of the data warehouse, which is much better than no one validating any of the data in a data warehouse.

How is a Data Quality program enhanced by the presence of a purpose? The purpose of a data warehouse provides a focus to the Data Quality program. If the purpose of a data warehouse is to produce a Prior Day Sales report, then the Data Quality program will begin by validating the data that contributes to the Prior Day Sales report. Even if the effort is incomplete, yet iterative, any attention to data validation is better than no attention to data validation; furthermore, validating the data delivered to the members of management who choose to fund the data warehouse is always a good choice.

PURPOSE

If you choose to aim at nothing, you just may hit the target.

A data warehouse, like every other enterprise asset, must have a reason for existing. If a data warehouse is not busy adding value as a data warehouse, it may soon begin adding value as something else. While ROI is thought to mean Return on Investment, for those operating a data warehouse ROI means Reason for Existing. The value added by a data warehouse contributes to the ability of a data warehouse to maintain its integrity in the presence of the gravitational pull of its own data. In that way, a data warehouse purpose can become its own self-fulfilling prophecy.

Build it and they will come. Yes, that often works, but to what level of success? Each subject area of a data warehouse must have its own purpose. Without a purpose to act as cohesive glue, a subject area of a data warehouse will eventually begin to spin out of control. After only a few subject areas experience this form of orbital decay, a data warehouse is already at risk.

The purpose of this book is to suggest and explain two purposes that can increase the value and ROI of a data warehouse. Specifically, those two purposes are Market Basket Analysis and Time Variant Data. Many enterprises aspire to include Market Basket Analysis in their set of analytics. Some enterprises pay marketing and consulting firms to provide Market Basket Analysis. Unfortunately, the results delivered often fail to meet the expectations, and sometimes fail to deliver at all. The following chapters will explain the obstacles to Market Basket Analysis and a design solution that overcomes those obstacles.

Time Variance is one of the concepts included in the pioneering works of Inmon and Kimball. The idea is that a data warehouse will present historical data in its historical context. For example, transactions in 1995 will be presented in their 1995 context while transactions in 2011 will be presented in their 2011 context. While the concept of Time Variant Data is intuitively easy to understand, it is also difficult to deliver each and every transaction in its historical context. An individual query may span a period of weeks, months, or years, which would require it to include the Time Variant context for each of those transactions. The solution design for Time Variant Data overcomes the obstacles of Time Variance, allowing a data warehouse to deliver Time Variant Data with a nominal degradation in performance.

Finally, the last chapter will combine these two purposes into one delivery. As stated earlier, when you hit the bull's-eye in the center, there is more bull's-eye in every direction. The combination of Market Basket Analysis using Time Variant Data is an example of such an ancillary benefit. By delivering the purposes of Market Basket Analysis and Time Variant Data, a data warehouse can achieve another deliverable—Market Basket Analysis of Time Variant Data.

A data warehouse that includes those three deliverables (Market Basket Analysis, Time Variant Data, and Market Basket Analysis of Time Variant Data) is a data warehouse with purpose. A data warehouse that delivers those three purposes is a data warehouse with an ROI.

2

What Is Market Basket Analysis?

Florida's 2004 hurricane season taught me to keep flashlights and batteries handy. You never know which hurricane will turn out the lights. Hurricane Charley left our electricity uninterrupted. Hurricane Frances, however, did such a spectacular job of knocking out electricity that we were without electricity, and lights, for a week. That's when I learned to find my way through my house by flashlight…all night long. Market Basket Analysis is similar to my experience after Hurricane Frances. Market Basket Analysis is a search for what you're looking for. You and your business are in a dark room with no light. You can shine a flashlight in the dark. Eventually, you use the information obtained by shining your flashlight into the darkness to operate your business. Your flashlight is Market Basket Analysis. The dark room is your business environment. And your business is not an allegory—it is very real.

ANALYSIS VERSUS REPORTING

Before exploring Market Basket Analysis, we need to establish a distinction between Business Intelligence Reporting and Business Intelligence Analysis. This distinction will guide the understanding of the activities and goals of Market Basket Analysis. Otherwise, we will be discussing two different sets of Business Intelligence methods and not realize we're having two different conversations, because they both use the same jargon. To understand the difference, we can go back to the flashlight in the dark room.

The Analysis Flashlight can shine on one spot at a time. You shine the Analysis Flashlight onto a corner of the room, another corner of the room, a couch, a chair, and eventually on every spot in the room. Having shown the flashlight onto a spot in the room, and recorded the observations of that area, there is no need to shine the Analysis Flashlight onto that area again. Rather than shine the Analysis Flashlight onto the same spot repeatedly, each time documenting the same observations, instead you shine the Analysis Flashlight onto a different spot, documenting the new observations in new spot each time. After a series of separate observations, you begin to create a map of what is in the darkness of the room. Eventually, the darkness is not so dark because your map tells you where everything is located. That is how you use the Analysis Flashlight.

The Reporting Flashlight, however, is used in a completely different manner. The map of the dark room provided by the Analysis Flashlight identified the location of a chair in the corner of the dark room. The Reporting Flashlight daily shines its light on the chair in the corner to verify the chair is still there. For days on end the Reporting Flashlight shines its light and for days on end the chair remains in the corner. Then one day, the Reporting Flashlight shines its light on the corner and the chair is no longer there. The chair has moved. You know where the chair has been for a long time, and that the chair has moved. That is how you use the Reporting Flashlight. The word *monitoring* has more of the connotation of the daily reports that watch the world within and around the enterprise. The Prior Day Sales report uses the word *report*, and for that reason we think of it as reporting. But what is really happening is that you are watching, or monitoring, your enterprise through the lens of Sales. When the same query generates similar data for two thousand consecutive days, you're monitoring, not analyzing. Then, when on a single day, the answer to the query in its two thousand and first iteration is an unusual and unexpected value (maybe very high, maybe very low) you close the Prior Day Sales report and begin to do the analysis to figure out what just happened.

When the chair in the dark room moves, and you know it moved via the Reporting Flashlight, you again use the Analysis Flashlight to again find the chair. Through a series of observations, the Analysis Flashlight maps the dark room until it finds the chair again. Once found, the Reporting Flashlight monitors the chair in its new location. Because the dark room is a changing world, this process repeats constantly. In a flexible and agile environment, the Analysis Flashlight and Reporting Flashlight look extremely similar, so similar in fact that they are sometimes confused with each other. The real distinction is not in the flashlight. The distinction is the methods by which they are used, and the goals they achieve. This confusion between analytics and reporting caused by a common toolset and jargon also applies to Market Basket Analysis and Market Basket Reporting.

Market Basket Analysis and Market Basket Reporting are flashlights that shine a light into the environment of your business. Market Basket Analysis is the exploratory method by which you come to understand patterns and natures of your business environment. This is when you learn to distinguish up from down, left from right, and forward from backward in your business environment. Market Basket Reporting is the monitoring method by which you verify up is still up, down is still down, and the chair is still in the corner of the room. In that way, Market Basket Analysis is the dynamic and iterative creation of an expectation based on a set of observations; meanwhile, Market Basket Reporting is the static and repetitive validation of the business environment based on periodic (i.e., daily, weekly, or monthly) observations.

ELEMENTS OF MARKET BASKET ANALYSIS

Market Basket Analysis is deceptively simple. That simplicity is a function of the spartan list of elements in Market Basket Analysis. Market Basket Analysis does not involve a complex set of tools and syntax that require years of training to understand. Instead, Market Basket Analysis does require an understanding of the enterprise and its business. Knowledge of the business will guide the questions posed by the analyst during Market Basket Analysis and facilitate an analyst's cognitive understanding of the answers. Market Basket Analysis can pose an almost infinite array of questions with only four elements—Itemset, Object, Affinity, and Statistics. The simplicity and depth of these elements of Market Basket Analysis allows the flexibility inherent in Market Basket Analysis.

Itemset

The name *Market Basket* came from the retail environment. In a retail environment, an interaction with a customer is documented by the shopping cart in which the customer places the items selected for a transaction because all the items chosen by a customer are in that customer's shopping cart. All the items, and only the items, chosen by a customer are in that customer's shopping cart. It is very easy to identify the contents of a

Market Basket—just look in that customer's shopping cart. This tangible and clear definition of a transaction, bounded by a shopping cart, led to a tangible and clear understanding of a transaction as a unit of work, known as a Market Basket. The analysis of the contents of all the shopping carts took the name Market Basket Analysis.

But language is a powerful tool. The words we use can both limit our thinking and expand our thinking. The analytic toolset honed in the retail environment as Market Basket Analysis can also be applied to any other environment wherein the unit of work is complete in and of itself. The term for that unit of work, which replaces the term *Market Basket*, is *Itemset*. An Itemset can be the contents of a shopping cart, the contents of a stock trade, the line items in an invoice, the products manufactured by the second shift, or the menu items selected by customers in a restaurant for dinner. In each of these cases, the contents of the activity are clearly bounded and known. They are, each of them, an Itemset. Because they are an Itemset they are all candidates for Market Basket Analysis. For the following examples, the Itemset would be bounded by the following:

- Shopping Cart
  - Enterprise: The retail store offering the products for purchase
  - Who: A customer selecting the products to be purchased
  - What: A retail sales transaction
  - When: The date and time when a customer visits the retail store
  - Where: All the selected products are located inside a shopping cart, which is inside a retail store.
  - How: The customer pays for, and takes possession of, the products in one transaction.

- Stock Trade
  - Enterprise: Brokerage firm
  - Who: A customer selecting stocks and/or bonds to be purchased
  - What: A stock and/or bond purchase transaction
  - When: The date and time when a customer pays for the stocks and/or bonds selected to purchase
  - Where: All the selected stocks and/or bonds are listed in a purchase agreement.
  - How: The customer pays for, and takes possession of, the stocks and/or bonds in one transaction.

- Invoice
  - Enterprise: Wholesale seller
  - Who: A retail seller selecting products to be purchased
  - What: A purchase transaction of pallets of product delivered via truck
  - When: A truck delivers the pallets of product at an agreed date and time.
  - Where: A truck delivers the pallets of product to a receiving dock.
  - How: A receiving clerk signs the invoice declaring the product matches the line items of the invoice, which then obligates the customer (i.e., the retail seller) to pay the price listed in the invoice.

- Manufactured Products during Second Shift
  - Enterprise: Manufacturing plant
  - Who: Laborers in the second shift
  - What: The manufacture of finished goods
  - When: A specific date during the second shift
  - Where: Inside the manufacturing plant
  - How: Laborers assemble raw goods and assembly parts into finished goods.

- Dinner in a Restaurant
  - Enterprise: A restaurant
  - Who: A customer selecting the menu items to be purchased
  - What: A restaurant sales transaction
  - When: The date and time when a customer visits the restaurant
  - Where: All the selected menu items are prepared and presented to the customer in the restaurant.
  - How: The customer eats the prepared menu items and then pays for them in one transaction.

In Market Basket Analysis, these bounded units of work are each an Itemset. This discussion of Market Basket Analysis would bog down to a repetitive and tedious discussion if each mention of an Itemset had to include each of the above examples. For a given enterprise transaction, the Itemset concept may apply, but not in the form of the examples listed above. Therefore, all subsequent discussions of Itemsets as the analytic focus of Market Basket Analysis will inherently assume we are discussing a unit of work, bounded and complete in and of itself, which is relevant to an enterprise transaction. If your enterprise perspective is that of a retail store, then the concept of an Itemset (i.e., a retail sales transaction) is already well established for you in the jargon of Market Basket Analysis. If, however, your enterprise perspective is that of a medical professional serving patients in remote locations via satellite, the concept of an Itemset (i.e., a provider/patient interaction) may require a bit more insight and consideration as you define the boundary of your Itemset. Be that as it may, an Itemset is the unit of work, bounded and complete in and of itself, which is the analytic focus of Market Basket Analysis; and, for every enterprise, an Itemset can be unique to that enterprise and different from the Itemset of all other enterprises.

Object

The items in an Itemset are Objects. The Objects of an Itemset can be the products in a shopping cart, the dinner selections in a restaurant, or the stocks and bonds purchased in a stock trade. In all these Itemsets, the Objects are clearly visible. They are in the shopping cart, on the dining room table, in the line items of the invoice, and so on, and clearly visible for both the enterprise and the customer to see. In its simplest form, Market Basket Analysis can be performed using these visible Objects. In that simplest Market Basket Analysis, the analyst seeks to find those permutations of Objects that occurred simultaneously in an Itemset. After finding those permutations of Objects that occurred simultaneously, an analyst can then calculate the frequency of occurrences of permutations of Objects. Some permutations of Objects occur very often. Other permutations of Objects occur very seldom. Some permutations of Objects never occur at all in an Itemset.

There is a class of invisible Objects in an Itemset. These invisible Objects can be shared by multiple Market Baskets. You cannot see them. That is why they are invisible. Regardless, they are in the Market Basket and may be the focus of investigation during Market Basket Analysis. For example:

- The Four P's of Marketing (Product, Price, Place, and Promotion)—The price of a product influences a customer's decision to include or exclude products from a set of products purchased during a transaction. Likewise, the product and its functions and features are also in the Market Basket. The promotion of that product and its placement before the customer influence a customer's decision to purchase, or not purchase, that product.

- Weather—Seasonal products are seasonal because the sale of such products is influenced by the weather. Winter clothes are typically sold in the winter. Likewise with summer clothes. Weather phenomena such as hurricanes, snowstorms, and cold fronts can change the preference and decision of a customer.
- Cost of Living and Employment Rate—The economic context present at the time of an Itemset influences the selection of Objects. When times are hard customers choose differently from when times are easy. As such, the economic context surrounding the Itemset influences the Objects in the Itemset.

These and other conditions are inherently included in every Market Basket and are part of the Itemset. So, while the collection of tangible Objects in an Itemset are unique to an individual Itemset, the collection of invisible Objects in an Itemset are shared by, or at least available to, a group of Itemsets. The weather outside surrounds all the Itemsets on a given day, as does the cost of living and the televised commercials that provide price and product description. All these factors are the invisible Objects that influence a customer's decision to include and exclude Objects from an Itemset. As such, all the available invisible Objects are in all the Itemsets, regardless of other Objects in the Itemset. An invisible Object can influence a customer to choose to include one Object and simultaneously choose to exclude another Object in the same Itemset.

Affinity

Affinity is the probability that one Object will occur simultaneously in an Itemset with another Object. For example:

- What is the probability that an oil filter will occur in an Itemset that also includes a quart of motor oil?
- What is the probability that hot dog buns will occur in an Itemset that also includes hot dogs?
- What is the probability that a customer will request racing stripes and a spoiler on the same car?

The first calculation is a count of the number of Itemsets that include the first Object (i.e., a quart of motor oil, a hot dog, or racing stripes). The second calculation is a count of the number of Itemsets that include the first

Object that also include a second Object (i.e., an oil filter, hot dog buns, or a spoiler). The final calculation is the quotient of the number of Itemsets including the first and second Objects divided by the number of Itemsets that include only the first Object. If 50% of the Itemsets that include hot dogs also include hot dog buns, then the probability of hot dogs coinciding with hot dog buns is 50%. If 25% of the Itemsets that include a quart of motor oil also include an oil filter, then the probability of motor oil coinciding with an oil filter is 25%. Knowing that an oil change includes multiple quarts of oil (in my car, four quarts of oil), you can alter the calculation slightly to look for "oil change" Itemsets—in other words, to look for the portion of Itemsets that include four quarts of oil and that portion of Itemsets that include four quarts of oil and an oil filter.

Affinity is calculated as a percentage or probability. When calculated as a percentage, that percentage is the proportion of past occurrences of two Objects occurring simultaneously in an Itemset. The probability that those two Objects will coincide in the future varies directly with the percentage of past Itemsets wherein the two Objects coincided. No set of two Objects will always occur in an Itemset. Regardless of the strength of correlation between two Objects in an Itemset they will not occur simultaneously every time. Therefore, the Affinity between two Objects is expressed as a probability. As that probability approaches 100% (i.e., the "always" condition), the correlation becomes stronger. A set of two Objects will very rarely reach 100% correlation. Also, as that probability approaches 0% (i.e., the "never" condition), the correlation becomes weaker and possibly nonexistent (i.e., the two Objects never coincide). The "never" condition (i.e., two Objects coincide in 0% of the Itemsets) is not so rare. Therefore, the proportion of a set of two Objects coinciding relative to the total number of Itemsets containing one of the two Objects can be expressed as a percentage value between 0% (i.e., never) and 100% (i.e., always). In addition, the probability of future occurrences of the two Objects in the same Itemset is based on past occurrences of the two Objects in the same Itemset.

Statistics in Market Basket Analysis

Clearly, Market Basket Analysis draws heavily from statistics. Itemsets correspond to Sample Sets. Affinity, Correlation, and Probability are almost synonymous. So, it stands to reason that a strong background in statistics would serve a Market Basket Analyst well. An important distinction between Itemsets of Market Basket Analysis and Sample Sets of a Multiple Linear Regression is the flexibility of data. Market Basket Analysis found its first best application in retail marketing. Cash registers in the retail environment are able to capture transaction data in granular detail for each and every transaction. As such, transaction processing systems produce a volume and wealth of data that feed into Market Basket Analysis. Today, the software used in manufacturing, communications, supply chains, transportation, Web-based applications, and any other application that can capture and log activity produce large volumes of data used in Market Basket Analysis. The logged activity varies based on the activity in the Itemset. One Itemset may contain one object and another may contain one thousand objects. This variability is not found in Multi-Linear Regression, which has a predefined set of variables, each containing one and only one value at a time. Regardless, the statistical nature of Market Basket Analysis is still found in the calculations of Affinity between Objects in an Itemset.

Market Basket Analysis distinguishes itself from statistics in the goals and methods applied during the processes of Market Basket Analysis. Despite any altruistic claims to the contrary, the ultimate goal of Market Basket Analysis is to make money. Either through improved marketing, streamlined manufacturing, more efficient customer interactions, or anything else that increases revenue and/or decreases expenses, Market Basket Analysis is expected to improve the bottom line of the enterprise. As such, the language of Market Basket Analysis diverts from its statistical background toward language that is more actionable within the business operations of the enterprise. Specifically, the language of Market Basket Analysis includes the following concepts, which may coincidentally resemble statistics but are functional business concepts.

- Complementary—The probability of two Objects occurring in the same Itemset is strong. The strong correlation of simultaneous occurrences of the Objects suggests the two objects have some connection. That connection may be direct or indirect. For instance, in an auto parts hardware store motor oil and an oil filter have a direct connection. The direct connection is that both are involved in an oil change, which is the most frequent automotive maintenance. The most famous indirect connection is that between beer and diapers. In the "beer and diapers" anecdote of Market Basket Analysis lore, husbands and fathers who go by their local store to buy diapers on their way home from work are also susceptible to the suggestion to buy beer by simply placing the beer near the diapers. In that way, motor oil and oil filters are complementary through a direct connection and beer and diapers are complementary through an indirect connection.

- Independent—An object occurs independently of all other factors when occurrences of that object are evenly distributed among the Itemsets. Impulse purchases are typically independent of other factors. That is why they are impulse purchases. An independent Object, such as a candy bar at the cash register, can seem to be confusing. No matter how you stratify or group the data, it always occurs with approximately the same frequency. That happens when an Object will occur in an Itemset regardless of the other Objects in the Itemset. Therefore, that Object occurs independently of all other Objects.

- Substitution—Two objects are substitutes for each other when they (almost) never occur in the same Itemset, and yet both have a similar affinity to the same set of Objects. The most common form of substitution occurs when different brands of the same product are available—Brand X and Brand Y. Typically, a customer will purchase Brand X or Brand Y, but not both. Of course, there will be those occurrences when a store does not have a sufficient quantity of a single brand. In those circumstances a customer may supplement the purchase of a single brand with the purchase of another brand of the same Object. However, the strong correlation of the two objects rarely occurring together, but almost always correlating with similar objects, would indicate that Brand X and Brand Y are substitutes for each other. Common examples of substitutes include soft drinks (typically people prefer one brand) and clothes (typically people prefer one style).

- Driver Object—If this were a book on statistics, the Driver Object would be defined as the independent variable because the Driver Object is the variable that is manipulated by the analyst. That being the case, the Driver Object exists independently of any other variables—hence, the independent variable. Market Basket Analysis, however, has a goal of actionable knowledge. The business of the enterprise, that group of people approving the funding for the data warehouse and Market Basket Analysis, is interested in knowing how best to apply its resources to the advantage of the enterprise. In other words, the enterprise wants to know how to manipulate the Four P's of its own marketing plan (Product, Price, Promotion, and Placement) to its greatest profit. The Driver Object can be any combination of the Four P's of the marketing plan. In a manufacturing plant, the Driver Object can be any single element, or combination of elements, that can be manipulated within the manufacturing process. In general, the Driver Object is that part of the Itemset that is controlled by the enterprise. The enterprise can offer a product at a price. In that way, the enterprise drives the Driver Object.

- Correlation Object—If this were a book on statistics, the Correlation Object would be defined as the dependent variable because the Correlation Object varies according to the effect of the Driver Object. That being the case, the outcome in the Correlation Object varies dependent on the Driver Object. Again, Market Basket Analysis has a goal of actionable knowledge. The enterprise that funds the Market Basket Analysis is interested in understanding the potential outcome as it manipulates the Driver Object. For example, when the price of a product goes up, sales goes _____. When the pace of manufacture goes down, the quantity of rework goes _____. In general, the Correlation Object is that part of the equation where the enterprise measures the affinity between the presence of a Driver Object and simultaneous occurrences of a Correlation Object via Market Basket Analysis.

While Market Basket Analysis may not use the statistical or forecasting models found in a college statistics textbook, Market Basket Analysis does lean heavily on the knowledge and skills associated with a strong statistical background. Even though Market Basket Analysis is not textbook statistics, it does use the concepts in the statistics textbook.

LOGIC OF MARKET BASKET ANALYSIS

Market Basket Analysis measures two events. The first is an action by the enterprise, that is, the Driver Object. The second is the response to that action, that is, the Correlation Object. Data from past occurrences of action and response provide the level of affinity. That level of affinity can then be used to predict future occurrences of action and response. Your knowledge of your enterprise and the business environment surrounding your enterprise can allow application of the affinity between action and response beyond just the predicted probability. Viewed through the lens of your knowledge of your enterprise and the business environment surrounding your enterprise, you can apply the affinity and probability discovered in Market Basket Analysis to the business of your enterprise.

Enterprise Relationships

An enterprise is in a relationship. A retail enterprise has a relationship with its customers. A restaurant enterprise has a relationship with its customers. A manufacturing enterprise has a relationship with its laborers. In all these relationships, the enterprise acts first. That action is represented in Market Basket Analysis as the Driver Object. The response from the people on the other side of that relationship is captured in Market Basket Analysis as the Correlation Object. Over multiple iterations of action and response, the enterprise can use Market Basket Analysis to study and learn the preferences, likes, and dislikes of the customers, laborers, and others on the other side of that relationship. In that way, Market Basket Analysis is a search for responses, or specifically, a search for a pattern within the responses it receives. Do customers prefer a two-for-one deal on dry cleaning? Do employees become more productive under various compensation packages, management styles, or work environments? These are all patterns. Market Basket Analysis is a search for such patterns.

The world is made of recurring patterns. The key to a self-determinant future is a pattern. If you know your own goal, and the pattern that achieves that goal, then you can work toward that goal by choosing the pattern that achieves that goal. So many people and organizations fail to achieve their goal because they chose only the goal, and not the patterns that achieve that goal. For that reason, we study the lives of great achievers, in the hope that by learning patterns that led to achievement, we might someday be able to repeat a pattern and that achievement. Likewise, if an enterprise can learn the patterns that lead to success and failure, then that enterprise can create its own future by following the path that leads to its goals. A goal of Market Basket Analysis is the discovery of the patterns of the enterprise, and a goal of an analyst is to discern the outcome of the patterns of the enterprise.

Patterns, and the search for patterns, are not a justification in and of themselves for the investment expended to facilitate Market Basket Analysis. No, there has to be an ROI at the end of the day. Market Basket Analysis, if left to academic curiosity, would be a collection of object correlations with no purpose, meaning, or application. While that might provide excellent fodder for white papers and research grants, it does not provide an ROI sufficient to convince the keepers of funds that the Market Basket Analysis effort should continue. To that end, Market Basket Analysis must provide actionable information. So, rather than simply find five objects that coincidentally happen to occur simultaneously more frequently than other collections of five objects, Market Basket Analysis is organized by two classes of objects—Driver Objects and Correlation Objects.

In its best application, Market Basket Analysis can identify those actions by the enterprise that will have a strong probability of achieving a desired response. For example:

- If you desire that a cat be chased, release a dog from the leash.
- If you desire that an object fall to the ground, drop a hammer.
- If you desire that an object float in the air, release a helium balloon.

Once you know the patterns of your business environment, you know your options and their probability of achieving the desired response. The Correlation Object is the answer to the question "What is the response to the Driver Object?"

- How do customers respond to a product offering?
- How do customers respond to a price?
- How do customers respond to a service offering?
- How do employees respond to a compensation package?
- How do employees respond to a management method?
- How much re-work occurs when an assembly line moves faster or slower?
- What clothes sell best in the winter?
- Where would Tampa Bay Buccaneers gear sell well?

The Correlation Object is that part of the pattern that is beyond the control of the enterprise.

Market Basket Analysis discovers patterns. The logic of those patterns, shown in Figure 2.1, isolates the actions of the enterprise, the response to those actions, and the probability of that response occurring.

If the enterprise desires a specific response (e.g., increased sales, increased productivity, increased product quality), the logic of Market Basket Analysis identifies the actions that lead to that response and the probability that response will occur. The enterprise can use that information to consider its options. For all available actions, what are the probable

---

Driver Object leads to Correlation Object with an Affinity qualifier.

FIGURE 2.1
Market basket scope analysis logic.

responses and outcomes? For all the desired responses and outcomes, what are the available actions?

The logic of Market Basket Analysis is a pattern. The three parts of that pattern are a Driver Object, a Correlation Object, and their Affinity (i.e., probability to occur simultaneously). The purpose of the Market Basket Analysis pattern is to provide actionable information to the enterprise. The Driver Object identifies the actions of the enterprise or the environment variables known by the enterprise. The Correlation Object identifies the response or outcome. The Affinity identifies the probability the Correlation Object will occur. These three parts of the Market Basket Analysis logic statement provide the enterprise information to help improve its understanding of the interactions between the enterprise and the business environment. Market Basket Analysis cannot replace the decision-making process of the enterprise. Rather, Market Basket Analysis can identify the probable response by others in the business environment to each option available to the enterprise. The decision-making process is not replaced; rather it is enhanced by Market Basket Analysis.

Outside the Basket

The concept of thinking outside the basket can be seen in recent changes made to restaurant menus. A recently adopted practice in restaurant menus is that of suggesting a wine that best accompanies a specific entrée. From a marketing perspective, this is simultaneously product placement and genius. It is product placement because the menu places a wine selection in front of the customer. It is genius because most restaurant customers are not wine connoisseurs and do not know how to match a wine with an entrée. By suggesting a specific wine for a specific entrée, a customer is able to choose that wine, which has a much higher profit margin than beer or a soft drink, with complete confidence in the chosen wine selection.

How is this thinking outside the basket in Market Basket Analysis? Obviously, someone examined the meals purchased, noting the entrée and wine permutations. For the number of entrée selections that would have matched well with a wine selection, a disproportionately small number of entrée selections were purchased in conjunction with a wine selection. In other words, the sale of all entrée selections had a lower than expected affinity with the sale of all wine selections. If this thinking were "in the basket," then the measured affinity would be between a filet mignon and a Burgundy wine. But, by thinking outside the basket a restaurant owner noted that filet mignon, lobster, and all entrées in general were not correlating well with wine in general.

Market Basket Analysis occurs outside the basket by incorporating hierarchical groupings, geographic groupings, functional groupings…any grouping that applies to the objects in an Itemset. Objects can be grouped by the time of day the Itemset occurred, by the marketing campaign or promotion in effect at the time of the Itemset, by the temperature of the room of the Itemset, by the location at which the Itemset occurred, and so on. These are the invisible objects in a market basket. You don't see them. But they are there. Any property, attribute, group, or designation associated with an object can be included with that object in the Itemset. By doing so, that property, attribute, group, or designation can be included in the Itemset during Market Basket Analysis.

An object, property, attribute, group, or designation can be correlated with any other object, property, attribute, group, or designation. By doing so, the invisible becomes visible in an Itemset. This level of abstraction also has an interesting interaction. If an enterprise is operating in balance, all levels of abstraction should approach its equilibrium affinity with all other levels of abstraction. For example, in a grocery store each aisle should have the same level of affinity for all other aisles. The aisle containing slow-moving products that constitute a small portion of overall sales should have an affinity with all other aisles of the store that corresponds to that overall portion of sales. If, however, that slow-moving aisle has an unexpectedly high affinity for an aisle on the other side of the store, that would be an opportunity to investigate that unexpectedly high level of affinity. Likewise, an aisle of a grocery store that carries staple products, some of which you expect to find in every grocery cart, should have an affinity with all other aisles of the store that corresponds to that higher portion of sales. If, like the affinity of wine in a restaurant, an aisle of that grocery store has an unexpectedly low affinity with the fast-moving staples aisle, that would also be an opportunity for investigation.

Of course, the Complement, Substitute, and Independent relationships found in a market basket can also be found outside the market basket. The levels of abstraction, however, soon render such observations less action-able. The actionable observations, however, can be found by juxtaposing an object in the Itemset with an object from outside the same Itemset. This method allows the Market Basket Analysis to compare an individual object with the enterprise as a whole. The fabled story of beer and diapers is a good example of thinking outside the market basket. Beer and wine were found to behave as complements on Friday afternoon, but no other time of the week. That conclusion incorporated hierarchical groupings of beer and wine, time groupings of both, and the Complement and Independent concepts (Complement on Friday afternoon and Independent the rest of the week).

The concept of thinking outside the basket is simply the use of an Object's property, attribute, group, or designation during Market Basket Analysis. It allows the analyst to calculate the affinity between all beers and all dia-pers, or all entrées and all wines. Then, the analyst can compare the affin-ity between individual members of such a group to find those individual items with more or less affinity than the affinity between the two groups.

WHAT MARKET BASKET ANALYSIS IS NOT

Market Basket Analysis is a powerful marketing tool. The power of that tool has generated more discussion than experience. The result of cycles of discussion sans experience is expectations run amok. So, before we get any further into a discussion of what is included in Market Basket Analysis, we need to perform some expectations management by discussing what is not included in Market Basket Analysis. Otherwise, readers will be disap-pointed throughout this book because the paragraph on how to achieve world peace and universal harmony via Market Basket Analysis never appeared. The two most common misconceptions about Market Basket Analysis are that it can discern causality and personal intent.

Affinity Is Not Causality

The relationship between a Driver Object and a Correlation Object can appear to be a causal relationship. In a causal relationship between two objects, the action of the first object causes a result in the second object. In such a relationship, the active agent has control over both the cause and the effect. The active agent initiated the causal action. Because the initiated action caused the effect to occur, the active agent is actually in control of both the cause and the effect.

While the Objects in Market Basket Analysis may appear to be cause and effect, they are not. An Object may experience causality. That level of analysis into the causal relationship between two objects can only occur outside the Market Basket Analysis. An investigation of causality between two objects may be directed by the affinity discovered during Market Basket Analysis. However, the investigation within a Market Basket Analysis cannot be confused with an investigation of a causal relationship. The perception of Market Basket Analysis as causality analysis will cause the Market Basket Analysis thought process to digress from the investigation of affinity and probability, which will cause the analysis to miss object affinities that exist while finding object affinities that do not exist.

Affinity Is Not Intent

A frequent goal of marketing is to influence consumers to purchase products or services. Marketing is often seen as the process of knowing and manipulating the needs and desires of consumers. As such, two goals of marketing are to know what consumers want so the enterprise can provide what consumers want or to convince consumers to want what the enterprise is selling. Either way, the goal of marketing can be to know and manipulate the minds of consumers.

The leap of logic from Market Basket Analysis to knowing the minds of consumers is an impassable chasm. Regardless, some manage to make that connection despite obvious differences between the two. When that occurs, an analyst may believe that the results of Market Basket Analysis reveal the intent of consumers. While some marketing analysts may be so gifted in their craft as to truly know and manipulate the desires and intentions of consumers, Market Basket Analysis is not so gifted. To the contrary, Market Basket Analysis is not able to identify any desires or intentions. Instead, Market Basket Analysis merely identifies a statistical probability that two Objects will simultaneously be in the same Itemset. Like the causality faux pas, to think of Market Basket Analysis as an understanding of the desires and intentions of consumers will cause the analysis to miss object affinities that exist while finding object affinities that do not exist.

MARKET BASKET ANALYSIS AS AN ACTIVITY

Market Basket Analysis occurs in the two activities identified at the beginning of this chapter—Analysis and Reporting. Market Basket Analysis as an iterative analytic exercise explores data to find statistical relationships within the unit of work of an enterprise. That unit of work within Market Basket Analysis is known as an Itemset. But, within the enterprise, that unit of work may be a single sales transaction, service work order, or manufacturing shift. For that unit of work in the enterprise, some of the identified affinities may be key to the success of the enterprise.

When an affinity between two objects is key to the continued success of the enterprise, the enterprise may choose to monitor that affinity. For that situation, Market Basket Analysis can also occur as a repeated batch application that monitors the affinity of key objects as Key Performance Indicators. A Key Performance Indicator is a measurement that can predict or confirm the health of the enterprise. By including Market Basket Analysis as a batch reporting application to monitor key affinities, the enterprise will increase its ability to monitor itself more effectively.

BACK TO THE BASKET

You may be slightly disappointed that Market Basket Analysis is not all you thought it was. If you were looking for a silver bullet that would answer all your questions and give you the keys to success, then the purpose of this chapter was to bring your expectations more in line with the reality of Market Basket Analysis. Market Basket Analysis can provide helpful insights into your enterprise and your business environment. If your expectations of Market Basket Analysis now match the reality of Market Basket Analysis, then the benefits of Market Basket Analysis have increased because you now know what to expect.

You may now begin to understand why the Market Basket Analysis effort in your enterprise has not delivered the promised benefits. The promised benefits were never stated, because no one knew what to expect. You've simply heard that Market Basket Analysis is a powerful tool and you thought you'd try it. Hopefully, somewhere in that process someone would figure out what to expect. Now that you know what to expect, you realize your expectations did not match the reality of Market Basket Analysis. In addition, you realize the Market Basket Analysis effort never delivered because Market Basket Analysis, not Market Basket Reporting, is an iterative analytic tool and not a report to be approved by management.

Finally, you may be realizing that Market Basket Analysis is entirely feasible within your enterprise. You may already have thought of ways to apply Market Basket Analysis within your own department and ways to suggest it to other departments. If you are excited about the possible observations and insights to be gained by Market Basket Analysis within your enterprise, then the purpose of this chapter was to introduce you to a powerful tool that will help you understand your enterprise and its relationships with the business environment within and around the enterprise.

3

How Does Market Basket
Analysis Produce ROI?

Numerous articles, journals, books, and experts agree that Market Basket Analysis is a good idea. Data mining books include Market Basket Analysis. Podcasts explain the need for Market Basket Analysis. Marketing textbooks explain Market Basket Analysis as an analytic method. So, all in all, everyone agrees that Market Basket Analysis adds value to an enterprise. But, when the budget meeting occurs and the decision is about to be made whether to invest in a new market expansion or Market Basket Analysis, broad generalities of approval of Market Basket Analysis just do not quite carry the day. So, before we suggest the expenditures and investments required to make Market Basket Analysis happen, we need to consider some of the specific benefits of Market Basket Analysis.

ANALYTIC STRUCTURE

Market Basket Analysis is perceived as being difficult, as an advanced branch of analytics. For that reason, many analysts who need Market Basket Analysis feel they don't have the oversized database or the high-powered analysis engine that is misunderstood to be key to Market Basket Analysis. Misconceptions such as these indicate the first obstacle to success is a lack of structure. Only when an analysis effort has a structure can knowledge and experience be attached to that effort via the structure.

The first ROI of the Market Basket Analysis solution design outlined in the following chapters is that it breaks this cycle. The solution design in the following chapters is based on generally available technologies and methods.

The table definitions and join strategies in the solution design leverage structures and techniques that are already standard fare in the information systems industry. The information that is new is a set of concepts that can be applied to any enterprise. As such these concepts provide a structure to the analysis. The structure created by these concepts is well defined and can, therefore, be repeated; and, when repeated, the concepts can be applied to various subject areas and hierarchical levels within the enterprise.

The second ROI of analytics is the by-products of analytics. Market Basket Analysis is a search. Every search reveals more than the intended answer. When searching for a report or document, invariably you find reports and documents other than what you were looking for. In the process of searching for one document, you find ten others in addition to the one. There is an old saying about searching: "You find it in the last place you look." That is of course true because once you find what you're looking for, you stop looking. So, of course you find what you're looking for in the last place you look. Implicitly, that means that you also looked in other places and found other things. This also happens with Market Basket Analysis. You find other patterns and affinities you weren't looking for. In this way, an analysis effort such as Market Basket Analysis will discover knowledge about the enterprise, knowledge that extends beyond the answer to the question at hand. These are the hidden gems and jewels that are the by-product of analysis.

ANALYTIC SKILLS

Sir Francis Bacon stated that "knowledge is power." The ability to generate knowledge is even more powerful. The third ROI of the solution design in the following chapters is that it renders available analytic skills, which were previously unavailable to analysts. The original genesis of the Market Basket Analysis solution design in this book was the unavailability of such analytic skills. The knowledge generation process in the Market Basket Analysis solution design is oriented first around the need for an analytic method. This Market Basket Analysis solution design allows an analyst to manage the knowledge and the process and skills that created them.

Ownership of the analytic process and skills leads to the fourth ROI. Thinking is a difficult activity. The scientific process provides a structure that renders thinking a tangible process. A hypothesis is expressed in terms of Affinity. A permutation of Driver and Correlation Objects is hypothesized to achieve a level of affinity. Then, through multiple sets of Itemsets that hypothesis is tested and refined. At the end, a hypothesis that has been tested and validated through the scientific process becomes knowledge. If that knowledge is actionable, the enterprise can implement the actions implicit in that knowledge.

ACTIONABLE KNOWLEDGE

The ROI of analytic skills is a valuable addition to any enterprise. However, it will not carry the day without the ROI we all came to see. The knowledge-generating processes, the by-products of those processes, and the metaknowledge underlying that knowledge represent an investment in the future of the enterprise. Wonderful as that may be, the bills have to be paid today. Otherwise the investment in tomorrow will never be allowed to mature.

The ROI of Market Basket Analysis is actionable knowledge. That actionable knowledge comes in three forms—Complements, Substitutes, and Independents. Each of these three forms of actionable knowledge can also provide KPIs that can be used to monitor the enterprise. By acting on the actionable knowledge provided by Market Basket Analysis the enterprise is able to engage in activities that increase revenues or decrease expenses, or the reverse, that is, avoid activities that reduce revenues or increase expenses. These activities may include business processes that are already occurring, missed opportunities that have yet to be leveraged, or business processes that are currently occurring and disadvantageous to the enterprise.

Complements

Complements are two objects in an Itemset that have a strong affinity for each other. They tend to occur simultaneously in the same Itemset. The knowledge that two objects have a strong tendency to occur simultaneously is a golden opportunity for any enterprise. If the simultaneous occurrence of the two objects is advantageous to the enterprise, then the enterprise need only expend resources to cause one of the two objects. The enterprise does not need to expend the resources to cause both to occur.

If the second object is going to simultaneously occur with the first object, then any incremental expense or opportunity missed to cause the second object to occur is unnecessary. Instead, the enterprise should expend its resources to make the first object occur, and then let the second object occur simultaneously with the first object. In other words, if it's good, and it will happen, let it happen.

If, however, the simultaneous occurrence of the two objects in an Itemset is disadvantageous to the enterprise, the enterprise is equipped with the knowledge that a disadvantageous scenario has a strong tendency to occur. The enterprise can then choose to either prevent the simultaneous occurrence of objects or leverage the simultaneous occurrence of objects. If the enterprise is able to prevent the second object from occurring, but at an incremental cost, then the enterprise can choose to either expend the resources necessary to prevent the second object from occurring simultaneously with the first object or the enterprise can choose to absorb the simultaneous occurrence of the second object. The question is, Which has the higher cost, the prevention or the problem? Problems do exist that cost more than their prevention. So, in the case of a disadvantageous Complement, an action can be to either tolerate the co-occurrence of the objects in an Itemset or prevent the co-occurrence of the objects in an Itemset.

Another action to be taken in the case of a disadvantageous Complement is to leverage one of the two objects. An example of the leverage of a disadvantageous Complement is a tariff, that is, a tax on imported products. A tariff is levied on imported products to increase the price of those products when they sell in a retail store. In this situation, the two objects are (1) imported products and (2) reduced sales of domestic products and the Itemset is a fiscal period (e.g., fiscal quarter, fiscal year), which is measured by the GDP of the fiscal period. The disadvantageous Complement is caused when an imported, rather than domestic, product sells in the retail market. The domestic government prefers that domestic products sell as much as possible. A tariff works to prevent the presence of imported product in retail stores, which is expected to cause the sale of domestic products to increase. The use of a tariff also has the added benefit of increasing the revenues of the domestic government.

In an enterprise disadvantageous Complements will occur. If the disadvantageous Complement cannot be prevented, and the cost is intolerably high, then it should be leveraged. Like the tariff, the enterprise can respond to the disadvantageous Complement by modifying the situation to generate, or minimize the disadvantage, as much as possible. Finding the leverage to apply in such a situation may require creativity and ingenuity. The actionable knowledge is the awareness that the Complement is disadvantageous to the enterprise, and that the cost of preventing it is too high, and that it should be leveraged in some way.

Substitutes

Substitutes are two objects in an Itemset that have a strong affinity to not occur in the same Itemset, that is, they avoid each other. The knowledge that the two objects have a strong tendency to avoid each other is another opportunity for the enterprise. Knowing that two objects avoid each other, the enterprise can choose to let the two objects always remain separate, or try to join them together in an Itemset.

If the co-occurrence of two objects is advantageous to the enterprise, yet expensive to facilitate, then the question is, Which is more expensive, the missed opportunity when the two objects avoid each other or the cost of facilitating the co-occurrence of the two objects? This may be a quantitative question that can be answered in fiscal numbers, or this may be a value judgment that can only be measured in the intangible asset of the enterprise. Either way, the awareness of the two objects that are Substitutes, and the opportunity it creates, is an actionable knowledge delivered by Market Basket Analysis.

The more ubiquitously understood manifestation of Substitutes is cannibalism. This occurs when an action that increases the occurrence of object A also decreases the occurrence of object B. This is called cannibalism because the enterprise eats away from one part of itself to feed another part of itself. The eating away is the decreased occurrence of object B. The feeding is the increased occurrence of object A. The awareness of two Substitutes (e.g., objects A and B) helps the enterprise understand the consequences of its own actions. This awareness is the opportunity to choose between the two options. If the advantage of increased occurrences of object A compensates for the decreased occurrences of object B, then the enterprise can tolerate the increased occurrence of object A. If, however, the advantage of increased occurrences of object A is not sufficient to compensate for the decreased occurrences of object B, then the enterprise can choose to take no actions on objects A and B, allowing them to achieve their natural equilibrium.

Independents

An Independent object is a single object that has no strong affinity to co-occur or avoid any other object in an Itemset. An Independent object occurs in an equilibrium proportion of Itemsets, regardless of what else is in the Itemsets. An Independent object is going to occur as often as it occurs because, for some reason that may or may not be known, it is natural for that Independent object to occur. The knowledge that an object naturally occurs in Itemsets with, and without, the intervention of the enterprise is yet one more opportunity discovered by Market Basket Analysis. If an Independent object is advantageous to the enterprise, the enterprise cannot increase the occurrence of the Independent object by increasing the occurrence of a correlating object because there is no correlating object. The enterprise can, however, increase the opportunity for the Independent object to occur.

A good example of the increased opportunity of an Independent object to naturally occur is all the "impulse buy" products conspicuously displayed immediately in front of every cash register in every grocery store. Impulse buying activity occurs because...well, because the impulse to buy candy bars and soft drinks naturally occurs. Usually the impulse buyer is a child. A parent has been shopping for groceries with a child in the grocery cart. Throughout the entire store the child has been asking for one thing, wanting another thing, grabbing something else, and on and on it goes...until they get to the cash register. At the cash register the child finds a cornucopia of candy and goes berserk. At that moment, the parent can buy two minutes of peace and quiet for the price of a candy bar. Neither the parent nor the child equates the candy bar with the contents of the grocery cart. No, instead the candy bar is purchased simply to appease the child. That is a naturally occurring Independent object.

If, however, the occurrence of an Independent object is disadvantageous to the enterprise, then the enterprise can attempt to reduce the opportunities for that Independent object to occur. A good example of reduced opportunities is safety equipment. Accidents naturally occur. Rather than present a naturally occurring accident with a soft piece of human flesh to rip, cut, smash, or tear, we wear safety equipment. A carpenter wears safety goggles to reduce the opportunity for wood chips to fly into an eyeball and cause blindness. Wood chips occur regardless of the kind of wood being cut, and the equipment performing the cut, and the environment surrounding the cut, and...well, wood chips just have a natural tendency to fly. Rather than present two eyeballs as an opportunity for an accident, a carpenter wears safety goggles. A butcher wears safety gloves to reduce the opportunities to cut off a finger. A construction worker wears a hard hat to reduce the opportunities to catch a falling bolt with a skull. These examples show how an enterprise can respond to an Independent object by reducing the opportunity for that Independent object to occur.

An enterprise cannot discourage the occurrence of a disadvantageous Independent by inhibiting a strongly correlated object from occurring because no strongly correlated object exists. In such cases the enterprise is left to deal directly with the Independent object. The enterprise can choose to either discourage the occurrence of the Independent object by removing the opportunities for it to occur, or the enterprise can attempt to shield itself from the effects of the Independent object. Despite how bad this may seem, the ROI in this situation is the awareness that the enterprise is dealing directly with an Independent object, that only a direct approach will work because there is no correlating object to attack. Instead, the enterprise can be aware that an end-run gambit is a waste of time and resources, and that a direct approach is necessary.

KPIs

Complement objects, Substitute objects, and Independent objects are the actionable knowledge most frequently associated with Market Basket Analysis. The discovery of such objects and their affinities provides insight into the equilibriums within and around the enterprise. These affinities demonstrate the equilibrium between objects. For example, four quarts of motor oil and one oil filter would be a natural Itemset for an oil change. For that Itemset, the equilibrium between quarts of motor oil and oil filters is four to one—that is, four quarts of oil to one oil filter.

Some of the object affinities will probably be key indicators of the life and health of the enterprise. Such indicators may be able to predict the upcoming health of the enterprise. Others may only confirm the current state of the enterprise. Either way, the KPIs can be predefined and executed daily in a batch environment. That way, the KPIs can be monitored passively by reviewing the output when an analyst is available to review the results of the Market Basket Reporting.

Market Basket Reporting operates in a batch environment so that it can monitor KPIs with no manual intervention. The KPIs can themselves be monitored to raise awareness when the affinity, or lack of affinity, of an object or group of objects changes. The problem may be caused by misplaced product or incorrectly labeled product, expired product or too much product, or any of any almost infinite number of causes that could influence affinities within the enterprise. The causes of a fluctuation in the affinities of an enterprise, however, will never be found unless someone knows to look for them. No one will know to look for those affinities within and around the enterprise until an automated KPI notices that something has changed.

That is the final ROI of Market Basket Analysis—affinity KPIs in Market Basket Reporting. Even if no actions arise from the Market Basket Analysis, the enterprise will be able to monitor via automated jobs the affinities between objects inside and outside the enterprise.

ROI

Market Basket Analysis provides business analysts the opportunity to dig into the data of the enterprise, to get data under their fingernails, to really get hands-on and hands-in the data. The problem with many BI Reporting tools is that they are well packaged and GUI-operated. The BI Reporting tool actually insulates a business analyst from the data. Market Basket Analysis, however, draws a business analyst into the data to experience the data.

Market Basket Analysis also discovers affinities and relationships between the elements of the enterprise. The actions of the enterprise occur in units of work known as Itemsets. The elements of the enterprise appear within those units of work, that is, the Itemsets. The proportions and affinities for those enterprise elements to co-occur, never occur, or independently occur within an Itemset are found via Market Basket Analysis. Each of these relationships presents an opportunity to the enterprise. Some of these relationships may be so key to the success of the enterprise that Market Basket Reporting may monitor them via automation.

These are the deliverables of Market Basket Analysis. Together they constitute the ROI of Market Basket Analysis and Market Basket Reporting.

4

Why Is Market Basket Analysis Difficult?

Charades is a game where a single person tries to communicate with a group of people, usually three to five people, without using any words. That person is assigned a secret word or phrase. The goal of the game is to communicate that word or phrase to the group of people until finally someone in the group is able to correctly guess the word or phrase. What can that person use to communicate to the group? Basically, the person can use his/her body and that's about it. A common method is to tug at your ear, which means "sounds like..." and then you try to communicate a word that is different from the word assigned to you but sounds like the word assigned to you. Sometimes you have to do that when the word or phrase is very difficult to act out with your body. For instance, *nuclear holocaust*, *World Series*, and *Antietam* are much more difficult to communicate than *dog*, *cat*, or *run*.

Imagine a game of charades that has one person trying to communicate *hamburger meat goes with hamburger buns*, and then another game of charades that has two million people trying to communicate *hamburger meat goes with hamburger buns*. It's not going to look like an Olympic synchronized swimming team. No, in fact it's going to look like two million people waving their arms and legs and tugging at their ears. It's going to look like chaos on a grand scale. Then, imagine that some of them are really trying to communicate *hamburger meat goes with hamburger buns but without cheese*, and others are trying to communicate *hamburger meat goes with hamburger buns and blue cheese*, and still others are trying to communicate *tofu meat goes with hamburger buns*. Then, imagine that they aren't trying to communicate with you at all. No, they are just going about living their lives and you are trying to interpret their actions, hoping to discern some sort of consistent pattern to their actions. Add in the people who were just buying hamburger meat, the people who were just buying

41

hamburger buns, and the people who are going to come back after they get home and realize they bought hamburger meat rather than turkey meat and you're close to appreciating the difficulties of Market Basket Analysis.

NOISE

The first and most noticeable difficulty with Market Basket Analysis is the noise—not the kind of noise you hear, but rather the kind of noise you query. When looking for an affinity between hamburger buns and something else, you find that hamburger buns correlate with a thousand other objects, each with its own affinity. At a different time of day hamburger buns correlate with a slightly, but not exclusively, different set of a thousand objects. However, on the weekend all that changes and hamburger buns correlate to only a few hundred objects.

The chaos in all that noise is neither chaos nor noise. Rather, it is the presence of layers upon layers of various patterns. The data prepared for a college class in statistics or forecasting presents an intended pattern. The student is able to apply a statistical method recently learned in class to find the single pattern that pervades the data. The data from your enterprise has not been prepared by a college professor and does not demonstrate a single pattern. No, the data from a real enterprise has multiple patterns. You will probably have to discover the patterns one at a time.

Some of the data will have no pattern at all. The lack of a pattern is a manifestation of randomness. Randomness is an essential element of any statistical model. As a statistical model is able to explain the pattern of the data, the remaining random variance decreases to an acceptable level. No statistical model will be able to explain 100% of the data. Market Basket Analysis is no exception. Therefore, while Market Basket Analysis can find objects that have a strong positive affinity for each other, it cannot identify objects that correlate at 100%, because no such correlation exists. Objects that correlate near 100% would be considered complementary objects because they seem to complement each other. Objects that correlate near 0% would be considered substitutes because they seem to never occur simultaneously in an Itemset. But, even in the case of substitutes, randomness indicates that substitute objects will occasionally occur simultaneously in the same Itemset. An object that correlates equally with all other objects is considered to be an independent object. An independent object will correlate a little higher or lower with a specific group or during a specific time of day or through a specific channel for a day and then will correlate a little lower or higher on another day. In that way, randomness indicates that the lack of correlation in an independent object will fluctuate. In general, randomness will cause the correlation, be it positive, negative, or neutral, between two objects to fluctuate.

Conversely, fluctuations in correlation may not be randomness. Rather, fluctuations in correlation may be the presence of multiple patterns overlaid on each other. For most retail stores the two largest patterns are period of the week (i.e., weekday and weekend) and period of the day (i.e., morning before the workday begins, daytime during school, after school and before the workday ends, and after the workday ends). A wonderful example of such an apparent fluctuation dates back to the days before cable television and digital video recorders. A municipal water works department noticed unusual fluctuations in their water pressure. After significant investigation, they found the source of the fluctuation in water pressure. When a popular sporting event or movie was broadcast on network television, members of that city were delaying a trip to the bathroom so they could see the end of the television show. The fluctuation appeared first as a spike in water pressure as fewer citizens were consuming water and then as a drop in water pressure as an usually large number of citizens ran to the bathroom and flushed their toilets. Eventually, that water works department came to rate the popularity of television shows by the drop in water pressure that occurred at the conclusion of that television show. In this example, two patterns overlap the normal consumption of water. The first overlapping pattern is the tendency to wait until a television show is over to go to the bathroom. The second overlapping pattern is the popularity of the television show, which influences the number of citizens willing to delay their trip to the bathroom. In this way, fluctuations in correlation may not be randomness but rather may be the presence of multiple simultaneous patterns not yet discovered.

Randomness is not actionable. The goal of Market Basket Analysis is to produce actionable information. Significant fluctuations in correlation between two objects indicate a pattern of randomness that can be neither leveraged nor avoided. If the enterprise cannot forecast the correlation between two objects, then the enterprise is left to the whims of chance. For this reason, randomness is an indicator of a future area of investigation. Only when the overlaying patterns of correlation are each identified can they become actionable information for the enterprise.

LARGE DATA VOLUMES

The best way to reduce the effect of truly random fluctuations in correlation is by incorporating large volumes of data. In statistical analysis this is the concept of statistical significance. In general, a larger sample set generates a result with higher statistical significance and a smaller sample set generates a result with lower statistical significance. Higher statistical significance occurs as an increasing portion of the randomness in a sample set is explained. This does not mean that a large sample set will by its own power and volume explain away all randomness. If that were the case, Market Basket Analysis would have been reduced to an exercise in data gathering, rather than data analysis. Instead, larger data volumes (i.e., large sample sets) simply increase the scope and perspective of the world as viewed through the data, like seeing the forest rather than the trees.

To illustrate the effect of sample size on the conclusions drawn during Market Basket Analysis, consider an investigation into the correlation between two objects—milk and cookies. Recognizing the wonderful experience of dunking a cookie into a glass of milk and then eating that cookie, you would expect milk and cookies to have a high affinity for each other. In a sample set of two Itemsets you find the following:

- Milk and no cookies
- Cookies and no milk

In this abbreviated sample set milk and cookies seem to be substitutes as they never occur simultaneously in the same Itemset. However, recognizing the brevity of the sample set you include another Itemset. Now the sample set includes the following three Itemsets:

- Milk and no cookies
- Cookies and no milk
- Milk and cookies

A conclusion drawn from this second sample set would indicate that two-thirds of the time, milk and cookies are substitutes, and one-third of the time milk and cookies are complementary. Not until you increase the number of Itemsets in the sample set does the picture become a bit more clear:

- Milk and no cookies
- Cookies and no milk
- Milk and cookies
- Milk and cookies
- Milk and cookies
- Milk and cookies
- Milk and cookies
- Milk and cookies
- Milk and cookies
- Milk and cookies
- Milk and cookies
- Milk and cookies
- Milk and cookies

The increased sample set allows the large number of *milk and cookies* Itemsets to demonstrate the true affinity between milk and cookies. In this way, the *milk and no cookies* and *cookies and no milk* Itemsets decrease in significance as the volume of data grows. Interestingly, they also prevent milk and cookies from ever achieving a perfect affinity, that is, 100% correlation.

The same illustration can be drawn for two objects that are substitutes. For example, fifteen Itemsets wherein the two objects occur simultaneously would seem to indicate that those two objects are complements. But then another fifteen thousand Itemsets wherein the two objects occur exclusively of each other indicate that the two objects are actually substitutes. Likewise, an independent object when investigated myopically may seem to have an affinity for a specific object. Only when the scope of that investigation is expanded do you realize that the affinity you discovered was between the time of day and the second object. The first object was maintaining its independence while the second object was increasing its occurrence during that time of day. For the reasons shown in these examples, a large sample set can be expected to generate conclusions that are more significant than those generated by a small sample set.

The data gathered for Market Basket Analysis can be "large" in multiple ways. These manifestations of a large sample set include the following:

- Time—The span of time included in a sample set. A sample set that spans fifteen years is larger than a sample set that spans fifteen days.
- Groups—The number of enterprise regions, divisions, channels, and so on, included in a sample set. A sample set that spans all areas of the enterprise is larger than a sample set that spans only the mid-Atlantic region or the aeronautics division.
- Completeness—The portion of the universe of Itemsets represented in a sample set. A sample set that includes the entire universe of Itemsets is larger than a sample set that includes half the universe of Itemsets.

These are the three dimensions along which a sample set can increase in scope. Each of them has its own distinct impact on the significance of the conclusions drawn from the Market Basket Analysis.

Time

Time in a Market Basket Analysis refers to the span of hours, days, weeks, months, and years included in the sample set. If a sample set includes only one day, then all the conclusions drawn from that sample set carry the implicit understanding that all days are like that day. If a sample set includes a week of days, then all conclusions drawn from that sample set carry the implicit understanding that all Mondays are like that Monday, and all Tuesdays are like that Tuesday, and so on. Some patterns follow the pattern of a week wherein the weekdays and weekend have patterns distinct from each other. Expanding a sample set to include a full month, a set of contiguous months, or a full calendar year increases the time-based patterns that can be discovered. The discovery of seasonal patterns requires multiple contiguous years of data. The data points in contiguous years allow the analysis to compare the months of January, the Fourths of July, the Twenty-fifths of December, and any other periodic pattern that repeats each year.

Time-based patterns have multiple patterns beyond the date (e.g., July 4, December 25). The attributes of dates hold their own set of patterns. The date of August 27 can be a weekday one year and then fall on the weekend in the next year. That would make one August 27 different from another August 27, even though they are both August 27. Time-based patterns such as weekdays, weekends, and holidays are time-based patterns that are based on the attributes of dates rather than the dates themselves. Time and the attributes of time, therefore, contribute to the scope and perspective of Market Basket Analysis.

Groups

An enterprise expansive enough to have a data warehouse probably has multiple groups within itself. Those groups can be geographic (e.g., north, south, east, west, north-central), operational (e.g., distribution routes, broadcast areas, contracted affiliates), demographic (e.g., urban and inner city, rural and agricultural, DMA), governmental (e.g., city limits, state lines and national boundaries), or lines of business (e.g., retail sales, service and repair, online sales). The groupings of the enterprise can influence the data available to, and included in, the Market Basket Analysis. The groups themselves are attributes of the data they present to the analysis and should stay connected to the data during analysis.

Combining all groups of the enterprise in the data available to the analysis should have the effect of enhancing the statistical significance of the conclusions drawn during analysis. For the reasons mentioned above in the milk and cookies example, a large set of data obscures the outliers as it highlights patterns in the data. Unfortunately, combining all groups of the enterprise can have the reverse effect. A holiday in Norway may not be a holiday in France and vice versa. So, the attributes associated with the groups of the enterprise may be needed to stratify the data, separating Norway from France. By including data from groups within the enterprise and the attributes of those groups, the analysis can leverage the large data volumes to increase the statistical significance of conclusions drawn by the analysis and simultaneously identify patterns that are distinct to each group.

Completeness and Data Sampling

Television news programs in the United States report election results on the night of an election based on a sample of the voting precincts, possibly as few as 1% of the total precincts. The statistical insignificance of such a small sample set renders the predicted outcome completely irrelevant. The most famous such occurrence is the 1948 presidential election wherein the *Chicago Tribune* printed and distributed newspapers declaring Thomas E. Dewey the winner of the presidential election. The irony was that Harry S. Truman won that presidential election. Apparently, the data sample used by the *Chicago Tribune* was a bit small, premature, and eventually embarrassing.

The cost of gathering data is the reason for data sampling. Statistics includes the standard practice of data sampling because statistical practices are best employed where the 80/20 rule applies. The 80/20 rule tells us that 80% of the value can be achieved with 20% of the cost, and that the remaining 20% of the value can be achieved with 80% of the cost. Statistics also includes the concept of statistical significance to help a statistician monitor the value of the statistical results relative to the cost of gathering data. When the cost of measuring an entire universe of data values (e.g., chemical content of the grains of sand on the beach, number of fish in the ocean, chemical parts per million of the water in the Mississippi River) is prohibitively high, a sample of that universe of values is statistically extrapolated to represent the entire universe of values.

Contrast that with a universe of values that is relatively low in cost to gather. For example, a schoolteacher measures the academic progress of all the students in a class, rather than just the front row, by administering a test to all the students. In that case, the value derived by sampling is extremely low and the cost of measuring the entire universe of values is even lower. So, the teacher measures the academic progress of all the students, rather than a sample of the students.

For Market Basket Analysis the same concepts apply. A data sample, rather than the whole universe of data, is used when the 80/20 rule indicates that 80% of the value of the Market Basket Analysis can be achieved with 20% of the cost. In other words, when the cost of including all the data is prohibitively high, and the value of the analysis can still be delivered with a sample of the data, then a sample set of data can be used in the Market Basket Analysis. In most Market Basket Analysis applications, the data to be analyzed is internal to the enterprise. The data, therefore, is available to the data warehouse and to the Market Basket Analysis. In that scenario, the majority of the cost is the disk storage and CPU throughput to process the data. For an enterprise with ten years of data available in electronic form, the whole universe of data may reasonably be considered too costly to be included in the analysis.

Like any statistical analysis, the data provided to the Market Basket Analysis application may be only a sample of the whole universe of data. If the sample is large enough to provide statistically significant results, the use of data sampling can provide the benefits of analysis without excessive overhead. In the iterative world of Market Basket Analysis wherein an iteration of analysis will lead to another iteration of analysis which will lead to yet another iteration of analysis, the delivery of value without excessive overhead in each iteration can quickly become a key to the success of a

Market Basket Analysis application. In that way, a complete set of data can be good but not always best, and a sample set of data can be incomplete but not always worst.

Data Sample Integrity

The Achilles' heel of data sampling is the integrity of the data sample. A data sample can represent a universe of values only when the data sample is evenly distributed throughout the universe from which it is a sample. If a data sample is skewed such that it misrepresents the universe of values, the results drawn from that data sample will be equally skewed. The creation of a data sample, therefore, falls under the axiom of all information systems—"garbage in…garbage out."

In the event a complete universe of data is not a feasible option, then utmost care must be taken to ensure that the sample data provided to the analysis truly has no bias or skew and is a true representation of the universe of data values. Statistical practices include random sampling methods, which provide a sample of data with no bias or skew. While it may be tempting, and even seem reasonable, to use a sample set of data that comes from a group or section of the enterprise already understood by the analyst, or at least handy and already available, data sampling based on such convenient methods will deliver skewed and questionable results at best. If a data sample must be used rather than the complete universe of values, statistical random sampling is the best way to generate a sample set of data.

DATA WAREHOUSE DATA STRUCTURES

The tables and views in a data warehouse have been optimized for query performance. The queries for which they have been optimized are the BI Report queries, which occur frequently and can generate a high cost to the data warehouse when not optimized. You already know that the tables in your data warehouse have not been optimized for Market Basket Analysis; otherwise you would not be reading this book right now. That lack of optimization is caused by aspects peculiar to Market Basket Analysis that do not occur in normal BI Reporting. Those aspects include the flexibility of the Itemset, lack of control, and the recursive nature of Itemsets.

Flexibility of the Itemset

An Itemset can hold an almost infinite number of permutations of objects. The minimum number of objects in an Itemset is one. Without at least that first object, the Itemset does not exist. The maximum number of objects in an Itemset is limited only by the application that created the data and the application that stores the data. If the application that created the data has a limit of two thousand items in a transaction, then the maximum number of objects in an Itemset is that limit—two thousand. As such, an Itemset is an array. The procedural logic of a stored procedure or Cobol *occurs* statement works well with an array. Procedural logic is able to read through the array, each time cataloging each object in the array until it reads the end of the array. While reading through the array, procedural logic can keep a log of the other objects in the array and a tally of the number of times those other objects occurred in the array. Then, procedural logic can repeat that process beginning with the second object in the array. The third time through the array can begin with the third object in the array. The algorithm for reading through an array is to let the nth object be the Driver Object in the nth iteration through the array and let all other objects be the Correlation Object. In this way, procedural logic can read through the objects in an Itemset by treating the Itemset as an array.

Set logic, the basis of relational SQL, lacks the flexibility of procedural logic because set logic is based on a recurring set of rows of data. This works well if the rows of data fit in the same set definition. The flexibility of an Itemset, however, causes the data of an Itemset to not fit in a single set definition, as one row will have data in only one column while another row will have data in two hundred columns. Therefore, the set logic inherent in SQL does not work well due to the flexible number of objects in each Itemset.

The Market Basket Analysis solution design in Chapter 5 uses relational tables and SQL. However, the solution design in Chapter 5 breaks the array of an Itemset into a defined pattern of a Driver Object and a Correlation Object. That way, the solution design does not need to know how many objects are in the array. In the solution design the array is broken into pairs of objects and then the array completely disappears. In this way, the flexibility of the array of an Itemset is replaced by a predetermined definition of pairs of objects. Once the array of an Itemset is converted into a set of rows of data, each containing a pair of objects, the advantages of set logic and relational SQL are leveraged by the most basic of SQL statements—SUM and GROUP BY.

Lack of Control

The flexibility of an Itemset is an issue for Market Basket Analysis because the analyst cannot control the number of objects in an Itemset. An analyst cannot ask everyone who interacts with the enterprise to please limit their activity to five objects, no more, no less. On the contrary, the people who interact with the enterprise, each of them generating an Itemset, are simply going about their business with no thought of the Market Basket Analysis about to be performed on the data they are generating. So, an analyst seldom has any reliable way to influence the number of objects included in an Itemset.

Any attempt to force an Itemset to fit into a predefined Itemset definition will modify the data so significantly as to render any conclusions fallacious at best. The only way to discern the patterns of the enterprise is to first let those patterns happen, to release control of the Itemsets to the people who, by their interaction with the enterprise, generate the Itemsets of the enterprise.

Only after the Itemsets are allowed to occur naturally can those Itemsets be studied in earnest. The solution design in Chapter 5 is able to handle this lack of control because it first converts the Itemset with an undefined number of objects into a predefined set of rows. Each row contains a pair of objects. One object is the Driver Object. The other object is the Correlation Object. Because the relational SQL logic knows the recurring format of the rows of data, each containing two objects, the set logic of relational SQL is able to handle an undefined number of rows, each in a predefined format.

Recursive Nature of Market Basket Analysis

When studying an Itemset to discern the patterns surrounding the occurrence of Item X, the analyst does not know where in that Itemset Item X occurs. Unfortunately, the enterprise was not able to ask all the people who interacted with the enterprise to please use Item X first. Then, when the analyst is ready to study Item Y, the enterprise is not able to ask everyone to please come back and repeat their Itemset, but this time beginning with Item Y. So, again the analyst has no idea where in all the Itemsets the focal Item Y will occur. Then, when the analyst is ready to study Item Z…well, the problem continues.

In this way, Market Basket Analysis would pick up the first object in an Itemset and consider all the other objects in the context of that first object, but only if that first object is the focal object. If not, then the Market Basket Analysis would skip the first object and pick up the second object and consider all the other objects in the context of that second object, but only if that second object is the focal object. This process continues for every object in the Itemset, even if the focal object is found somewhere in the middle of the Itemset. The search for the focal object in the Itemset continues because the person generating the Itemset may have chosen to include an object twice. Logically then, Market Basket Analysis juxtaposes each object, one at a time in its own turn, against all the other objects in the Itemset. This is a recursion of the Itemset, juxtaposing each nth object in the Itemset with all other objects in the Itemset. By the way, an individual object may occur multiple times, and not in contiguous order, within a single Itemset. The logic that juxtaposes a Driver Object with all Correlation Objects must be able to resolve all the multiple occurrences of each object into a single occurrence of that object.

As mentioned previously, procedural logic in a stored procedure is able to perform a recursion by considering one Driver Object at a time. In each pass through the logic, procedural logic can keep a tally of the Correlation Objects as having occurred in the context of a Driver Object. Once that recursion is complete, procedural logic can then move on to the nth object until it reaches the end of the Itemset.

The solution design in Chapter 5 is able to accomplish the recursion between a Driver Object and all the other objects in an Itemset by first capturing each recursion as a row of data. Each row of data juxtaposes a Driver Object with a single Correlation Object. Then, the set logic of relational SQL is able to use a SUM and GROUP BY statement to count the number of occurrences of each Correlation Object that occurred in an Itemset within the context of a Driver Object. The same relational SQL is also able to sum any metrics or measurements (e.g., quantity, currency, points) associated with each Correlation Object.

ON YOUR MARK...GET SET...GO!

The solution design in Chapter 5 cannot change the laws of data sampling. Unfortunately, the need to maintain the integrity of the data sample and simultaneously achieve statistical significance cannot be removed. However, the large data volumes necessary to deliver statistically significant and actionable information can become feasible by the solution design in Chapter 5. Rather than allow itself to become mired in recursions of arrays containing an undefined number of members, the solution design first converts the Itemset array into a set of rows. From that point on, the Market Basket Analysis application is able to achieve its results by summing the metrics and measurements in the columns and rows of that table. So, unless there are any questions before moving on…it's on to the solution design for Market Basket Analysis.

5

Market Basket Analysis Solution Definition

Chapter 2 identified the elements of Market Basket Analysis, which included the Itemset, Objects, and Affinity. In that discussion, these elements were presented as definitions, concepts, and examples. The information included in that discussion is key to creating a working and value-adding Market Basket Analysis application. For that reason, if you skipped past the first chapters of this book to go directly to the solution design, please go back and read Chapter 2. The information provided in Chapter 2 will not be repeated here in Chapter 5; the information in Chapter 2 will be assumed to be a shared common understanding of the elements of Market Basket Analysis. So, if you have not read Chapter 2, please stop here and read Chapter 2 before continuing with Chapter 5. Also, you will eventually need the information in Chapter 3 and Chapter 4 as you build a working Market Basket Analysis application. So, please keep a bookmark in those chapters. Later on when you start to ponder such questions as "What is my goal? What am I trying to achieve?" and "Why do the results of my analysis not come out quite right?" that's when you're ready for Chapters 3 and 4. If, however, you did read all the prior chapters, get ready to have some fun with Market Basket Analysis.

MARKET BASKET SCOPE STATEMENT

The Market Basket Scope Statement, shown in Figure 5.1, is the guiding question that will help an analyst stay focused on the pursuit of actionable information. The odd bits of data, information, conclusions, and

> When Driver Object A is in an itemset, what Correlation Object B is in, or not in, the itemset?

FIGURE 5.1
Market Basket Scope Statement.

conundrums discovered during Market Basket Analysis will tempt any analyst inherently curious enough to engage in Market Basket Analysis to veer away from the goal and ROI of Market Basket Analysis. So, rather than wander off in investigation of curious distractions, we start with the Market Basket Scope Statement.

This scope statement is intentionally simple. The simplicity of this scope statement will allow an analyst an extreme amount of latitude, only so long as an analyst is answering the question in the scope statement. But, whenever an analyst allows curiosity to divert the focus of the analysis from the scope statement to "I wonder...?" and "What if...?" questions, the analysis will lose its ability to deliver actionable information and its ROI.

The scope statement directly references the three elements of Market Basket Analysis. So, the first task is to define those three elements in the context of a single analysis. As you perform iterations of analysis to discover layers of patterns in the enterprise, you will begin by first defining the three elements in the context of that analysis. So, keep in mind that the definition of an Itemset at 9:00 a.m. may not be the definition of an Itemset at 3:00 p.m. As you cycle through iterations of analysis and layers of patterns, these definitions may change from one iteration to the next.

Definition of the Itemset

Your enterprise probably already has a transaction that is the lowest-level, most granular unit of business activity. If you're not sure what that transaction would happen to be for your enterprise, you will probably find it at the point when money changes hands, either literally or as an agreement to pay money on credit or terms. For most businesses, the moment when money changes hands is the transaction that defines the business. Your enterprise might happen to cut wood, spread stain with a brush, drive nails with a hammer, and rotate screws with a screwdriver, but you can tell your enterprise sells furniture when someone buys your product with the intent to use your product as a dining room table. Having identified a transaction of your enterprise, the Itemset is defined as the agreement on which that transaction is based. For example:

- In a restaurant, that unit of business activity is the meal documented on a check. A customer says, "Waiter, check please," and the waiter hands the customer a check. That check is the lowest-level, most granular transaction in the enterprise. Let the checks be the Itemset.
- In a retail store, that unit of business activity is the sales transaction documented on a receipt. The customer presents products for purchase. The cashier records the products in a cash register. Once all the products have been entered into the cash register, the cash register prints a receipt. The cashier presents the receipt to the customer, who then pays for the products listed on the receipt for the price listed on the receipt. That receipt is the lowest-level, most granular transaction in the enterprise. Let the receipts be the Itemset.
- In a contract service company, that unit of work is the work order. A customer requests services to be performed. The contract service company and the customer negotiate the services and price, which are documented in a work order. That work order is the lowest-level, most granular transaction in the enterprise. Let the work orders be the Itemset.

It's that simple. For your first attempt at Market Basket Analysis (or maybe your first attempt at this Market Basket Analysis solution design) there is no need to make it more complex than necessary. The lowest-level transaction in the enterprise has the advantages of being ubiquitously understood in the enterprise, well defined within the enterprise, and usually well documented. That being the case, the lowest-level transaction is the most intuitive Itemset and the most tangible Itemset, and therefore, the most obvious initial definition of an Itemset.

Alternatively, your enterprise might have numerous points of interaction with customers wherein your enterprise exchanges something for money. A single shop might, for a price, sell hard goods, which have a physical form that can be touched. That same shop might sell, for another price, a warranty on the hard goods. Again that shop might sell, for yet another price, service and maintenance on the hard goods it sells. All these moments wherein the enterprise exchanges money for something are the transactions of the enterprise. All those transactions can be defined as the Itemset; or, each kind of transaction can be its own Itemset definition separate from the others. If the options presented by your enterprise seem confusing, then opt for simplicity by choosing only one kind of transaction...at least for your first attempt at Market Basket Analysis. Later on, as you become more knowledgeable of the data of your enterprise and Market Basket Analysis, you will have a better understanding of the feasibility of combining types of transactions. Depending on your enterprise and the data of your enterprise, combining transactions may work wonderfully and provide amazing insights…or fail miserably. But, for the first analysis iteration, simple is best.

Definition of the Driver Object

Having defined an enterprise transaction as the Itemset, the next definition is the Driver Object. The Driver Object is the first half of the scope statement: "When Driver Object A is in an Itemset…" The Driver Object is the thing that is the focal point of the analysis. To be able to study the effects of various objects as they occur in an Itemset the analysis must be able to uniquely identify each and every one of those various objects as they occur in the Itemset. For example:

- In a restaurant, the check presented to the customer is the Itemset. The Driver Object would then be a menu item listed on that check. All the menu items, therefore, must be uniquely and consistently identifiable. Omelets must always be identified as omelets, never as any other menu item, and no other menu item can be misidentified as an omelet. If that is true for all menu items, then the Driver Object can be defined as the menu items listed on the check that was presented to the customer.

- In a retail store, the receipt presented to the customer is the Itemset. The Driver Object would then be the products listed on that receipt. All the products, therefore, must be uniquely and consistently identifiable. The 64-inch red wool blanket by Ashcroft Mills must always be identified as the 64-inch red wool blanket by Ashcroft Mills, and never confused with the 102-inch red wool blanket by Ashcroft Mills or the 64-inch red wool blanket by Wellington, or any other product offered by the enterprise. If that is true for all products offered by the enterprise, then the Driver Object can be identified as the products listed on the receipt that was presented to the customer.

- In a contract service company, the work order is the Itemset. The Driver Object would then be the services and work listed on that work order. All the services therefore must be uniquely and consistently identifiable. The two-day audit must always be identifiable as the two-day audit, and never confused with the office consultation. If that is true for all the services offered by the enterprise, then the Driver Object can be identified as the services listed on the work order that was signed by the customer.

In each of these Itemsets, the Driver Object is a uniquely and consistently identifiable object within the enterprise.

Definition of the Correlation Object

The Correlation Object is in the same class of entity as the Driver Object and completes the scope statement "…what Correlation Object B is in, or not in, the Itemset?" The Correlation Object definition should mirror the Driver Object definition. If the Driver Object is the menu items in a restaurant, then the Correlation Object is also the menu items in a restaurant. Likewise, the Correlation Object can be the same products, services, and so on, that are defined to be the Driver Object. The reason is very simple. You're going to use the Driver Object and Correlation Object interchangeably. For example.

- When French silk pie is in an Itemset, what is the affinity for filet mignon?
- When filet mignon is in an Itemset, what is the affinity for French silk pie?
- When a dessert is in an Itemset, what is the affinity for a steak?
- When a steak is in an Itemset, what is the affinity for a dessert?

Like the example in Chapter 1 of a flashlight, you're trying to view the interactions within your enterprise from multiple vantage points. Each time you ask a question you are looking at your enterprise from the perspective of that question. The interchangeable Driver and Correlation Objects allow the analyst to consider each affinity from two vantage points:

- Does Object A somehow lead to Object B? Object A is the Driver Object while Object B is the Correlation Object.

- Does Object B somehow lead to Object A? Object B is the Driver Object while Object A is the Correlation Object.

Chapter 2 warned of the dangers of perceiving Market Basket Analysis as a study in the cause-and-effect relationship within the enterprise. The relevance of this warning is shown here in the definitions of the Driver and Correlation Objects. The relationship between a Driver Object and Correlation Object may have the look and feel of cause and effect. Regardless, you must continue telling yourself it is not a study in cause and effect. Ordering the filet mignon does not somehow cause you to order the French silk pie. The reverse of that is also not true. The cause may be something so mundane as they are listed on facing pages of the menu. If that's the case, then the affinity between filet mignon and French silk pie may stop when a new version of the menu separates them by three pages. If that were to happen, Market Basket Reporting would show that something changed the affinity between filet mignon and French silk pie.

The definition of the Correlation Object, therefore, has already been achieved by the definition of the Driver Object. Because they are interchangeable, both are defined as the same object. The definition of the Driver and Correlation Objects, therefore, can be simplified to the definition of the Objects (both Driver and Correlation) in the Itemset. If you think of the two objects as one object definition, the two objects (Driver and Correlation) will truly be interchangeable.

KEY DEFINITIONS

At this point the Itemset has been defined. The Driver Object and Correlation Object have been defined. Thus far, all these definitions have been business definitions within the source systems that hold these objects. To facilitate the analysis of the Itemsets and Objects they must have keys compatible with the Market Basket Analysis application. Chapter 6 will discuss the definition of keys in greater detail as that discussion includes the relational platform in which the analysis is performed. For the purpose of defining the Market Basket Solution, the definition of keys can be discussed here in a broad generic form.

Itemset Key Definition

The Itemset is the unit of work, the unit of business activity. To discuss what Objects are in, or not in, an Itemset the Itemset must have the identity properties that allow each Itemset to be uniquely and consistently identified such that each Itemset will always be distinct from, and never confused with, all other Itemsets. In other words, each Itemset must have a key unique to itself. The source system that is the system of record for the Itemset transactions may, or may not, have within itself a feasible key that can uniquely identify each and every Itemset. If that source system has a key that maintains the identity properties of the Itemset and performs well in the relational platform of the analysis, then that source system transaction key may be defined as the Itemset key. If the source system does not have a key that simultaneously maintains the identity properties of the Itemset and performs well in the relational platform of the analysis, then the ETL application (ETL will be discussed in Chapter 7) that presents data to the Market Basket Analysis application will generate a key that does maintain the identity properties of the Itemset and performs well in the relational platform of the analysis.

For the examples listed later in this chapter, the Itemset key will be defined as an integer data type. This should not be interpreted to mean that an Itemset key must be an integer data type. Instead, this use of integers simply means that integers make acceptable sample data.

Object Key Definition

The Driver Object and Correlation Object are interchangeable. Both objects should therefore share the same key structure. The Market Basket Analysis application receives its data from a data warehouse. Assuming the data warehouse already has a defined key structure for the objects in the Itemset, the Market Basket Analysis application should be able to leverage those keys already in the data warehouse.

If the data warehouse does not have a defined key structure for the objects in the Itemset, then the Market Basket Analysis application will not be able to identify occurrences of the individual objects in an Itemset. If that is the case, then the data warehouse is not able to support a Market Basket Analysis application. The entity definitions and key structures of the data warehouse must be remediated before the Market Basket Analysis application can leverage data from the data warehouse.

If the data warehouse does have a defined key structure for the objects, but that key structure does not perform well in a relational platform, then you may need to define a surrogate key structure that does perform well in a relational platform. While defining a key structure that does perform well in a relational platform, you might consider backfilling the new key structure you created for the Market Basket Analysis application back into the data warehouse. If that key structure did not perform well in the relational platform of the Market Basket Analysis application, it is probably not performing well in the relational platform of the data warehouse. Replacing a suboptimal key structure with an optimized key structure may singlehandedly improve the performance of the data warehouse. Then, you might consider backfilling optimized key structures throughout the data warehouse.

In general, the preferred method is to leverage the key structures of the data warehouse as the objects are used in the Market Basket Analysis application. There should be no reason to make this difficult. Let Product 0010 continue to be Product 0010, and let Service 1234 continue to be Service 1234. You've spent years learning these keys and key structures. Members of your staff probably speak in terms of key values, rather than ten-word descriptions, because the key values are so much more precise and semantically efficient. Bringing that data into a Market Basket Analysis application should not cause you to dispose of those keys and key structures. Let the object keys in the Market Basket Analysis application be what they are in the data warehouse, unless there is an overwhelming and compelling reason against the use of those object keys.

Attribute Definitions

The Itemset and Objects also have attributes. These attributes qualify and clarify the enterprise transaction represented by each row of Market Basket Analysis data. Those attributes, however, do not yet incorporate into the Market Basket Analysis data. The object definitions of the Itemset and Objects and the key definitions of the Itemset and Objects will be used specifically to build a narrow and lean Market Basket Table. The Market Basket Table must be narrow and lean because the Market Basket Analysis application will use the Market Basket Table to do the heavy lifting. The keys of the Itemset and Objects will later be used to incorporate the attributes. But, for the moment, the Market Basket Analysis application would be significantly suboptimized by including the attributes of the Itemset and Objects.

Itemset Metric Definitions

The Itemset is an enterprise transaction. An enterprise transaction includes metrics that measure the activity in that transaction. Typical transaction metrics include quantity (e.g., how many occurrences of an object occurred in the Itemset) and dollars (e.g., the dollar value of the objects in the Itemset). These metrics may mean the quantity and purchase price of the menu items listed on a restaurant check, or the quantity and sales price of the products listed on a sales receipt or work order.

These Market Basket Analysis metrics should be the same metrics used to measure activity in your enterprise. The feedback delivered by the Market Basket Analysis may be somewhat useless if the metrics incorporated in the Market Basket Analysis application are not the metrics used by, and understood by, those who already measure the activity of the enterprise. If, for example, the enterprise measures transaction activity in terms of sales quantity and sales dollars, then analysis of those same transactions should include the same sales quantity and sales dollars metrics. Otherwise, the data delivered by the Market Basket Analysis application will seem to be less actionable. To deliver the maximum possible ROI, the Market Basket Analysis should be able to report its findings and conclusions in terms of the metrics used, and understood by, the enterprise. To analyze and report using those metrics, they should be included in the data incorporated in the Market Basket Analysis application.

MARKET BASKET TABLE

Now that the Market Basket objects, keys, and attributes have been defined, all the elements necessary to create the Market Basket Table are ready. The first column in the Market Basket Table is the Itemset_Key. The Itemset_Key uniquely identifies a single transaction. All rows directly associated with a transaction have the Itemset_Key value that uniquely identifies that transaction. If a transaction has one object (e.g., only one menu item, only one product, only one service), then only one row in the Market Basket Table will have the Itemset_Key value for that transaction. If, however, a transaction has two thousand objects, then two thousand rows in the Market Basket Table will have the same Itemset_Key value for that transaction.

The second column holds the Object_Key. The Object_Key uniquely identifies each individual object. If a single object (e.g., small french fries, chair, or 16 oz. can of beans) occurs in a single transaction three times, those three occurrences within a single transaction will be summarized to one row of data, marked by the Itemset_Key that uniquely identifies the transaction and the Object_Key that uniquely identifies the object. For every Itemset wherein that object occurs, in each Itemset that object will be identified by the same Object_Key value. So, the object *small french fries* is identified by the same Object_Key every time it occurs. Likewise, every object is identified by the same Object_Key every time it occurs.

The remaining columns hold the metric measurements of the transaction that is the Itemset. In Table 5.1, the metric measurement columns are Quantity and Dollars. These columns should be defined to fit the transaction of your enterprise. Your enterprise transaction may include a different set of transaction metrics. If so, then rather than Quantity and Dollars the Market Basket Table should include columns that reflect the transaction metric measurements of your enterprise transaction.

Chapter 6 will discuss the physical structure of the Market Basket Table. Chapter 7 will discuss the ETL application that will populate the Market Basket Table, including the curious-looking first row for

TABLE 5.1

Market Basket Table

Itemset_key	Object_key	Quantity	Dollars
1	0	0	$0.00
1	15	1	$15.31
2	16	2	$24.42
2	43	1	$14.32
2	57	2	$18.18
2	64	1	$12.37
3	15	2	$30.62
3	16	1	$12.21
3	64	1	$12.37
3	78	4	$53.76
3	98	1	$2.45
4	43	3	$42.96
4	57	1	$9.09
4	78	1	$13.44
4	87	1	$16.87
4	98	1	$2.45

Itemset_Key = 1 wherein all the other values are set to zero. Details of this row will be provided in Chapter 7. For the purposes of this discussion, we can assume the Market Basket Table has been created and populated.

MARKET BASKET QUERY

Once a batch of Itemsets has been loaded into the Market Basket Table, the data is ready to be queried into a usable form. The SQL that will perform this query is in Figure 5.2. The indexing of the Market Basket Table, explained in Chapter 6, makes the Market Basket Query feasible. The batch cycles of the Market Basket Query, explained in Chapter 7, control the execution of the Market Basket Query. The Market Basket Query selects data from only the Market Basket Table in a recursive join that juxtaposes all the objects within a single Itemset.

```
INSERT INTO MARKET_BASKET_BI_TABLE
( ITEMSET_KEY
, DRIVER_OBJECT_KEY
, DRIVER_QUANTITY
, DRIVER_DOLLARS
, DRIVER_COUNT
, CORR_OBJECT_KEY
, CORR_QUANTITY
, CORR_DOLLARS
, CORR_COUNT)
SELECT
A.ITEMSET_KEY
, A.OBJECT_KEY      AS DRIVER_OBJECT_KEY
, A.QUANTITY       AS DRIVER_QUANTITY
, A.DOLLARS        AS DRIVER_DOLLARS
, 1                AS DRIVER_COUNT
, B.OBJECT_KEY     AS CORR_OBJECT_KEY
, B.QUANTITY       AS CORR_QUANTITY
, B.DOLLARS        AS CORR_DOLLARS
, 1                AS CORR_COUNT
FROM MARKET_BASKET_TABLE A
INNER JOIN MARKET_BASKET_TABLE B
       ON A.ITEMSET_KEY = B.ITEMSET_KEY
WHERE A.OBJECT_KEY <> B.OBJECT_KEY
       AND A.OBJECT_KEY <> 0  ;
```

FIGURE 5.2
Market Basket Query.

The Market Basket Query provides all the elements of Market Basket Analysis—Itemset, Driver Object, and Correlation Object. The Market Basket Query is used to populate the table that will be used for analysis. The good news about that development is that the recursive Market Basket Query, which performs the heavy lifting in Market Basket Analysis, is performed only once for each Itemset and under controlled and optimized conditions. However, before we discuss the output from the Market Basket Query, we need to understand the underlying logic that provides the elements of Market Basket Analysis.

Itemset

The Itemset_Key value that was included in the Market Basket Table is preserved, as shown in Figure 5.3, without modification in the Market Basket Query.

The Itemset_Key is the linchpin around which all this Market Basket Solution Design revolves. The Itemset_Key must be identical for all rows representing a transaction. The Itemset_Key must be unique to each and every transaction such that each and every Itemset has its own unique Itemset_Key. If two transactions share the same Itemset_Key, they will be perceived to be the same transaction by the Market Basket Analysis. If rows within a single transaction do not have the same Itemset_Key, they will be perceived to belong to separate transactions by the Market Basket Analysis. So, the success or failure of the Market Basket Solution Design rests first on the integrity of the Itemset_Key.

Driver Object

The Driver Object is represented by the columns that begin with DRIVER_, as shown in Figure 5.4.

The DRIVER_OBJECT_KEY identifies the object that performs the function of a Driver Object. In the context of the Market Basket Scope Statement, the DRIVER_OBJECT_KEY refers to "When Driver Object A

```
SELECT
A.ITEMSET_KEY
```

FIGURE 5.3
Itemset.

```
, A.OBJECT_KEY      AS DRIVER_OBJECT_KEY
, A.QUANTITY        AS DRIVER_QUANTITY
, A.DOLLARS         AS DRIVER_DOLLARS
, 1                 AS DRIVER_COUNT
```

FIGURE 5.4
Driver Object.

is in an Itemset." An object can be both the Driver and Correlation Object. When an object is represented by the DRIVER_OBJECT_KEY, that object is the Driver Object.

The DRIVER_QUANTITY and DRIVER_DOLLARS are metric measurements for the transaction captured in the Itemset row. The metric measurements in Figure 5.2 and Figure 5.4 are representative examples. For any given Market Basket Analysis, the metric measurements could be any that are applicable to the transactions being studied. The metric measurements must be additive. They will be created by a summing operation. They will be used within a summing operation. If a required metric is not additive, such as a Yes/No or numeric, but nonadditive, code value, then that measurement should be presented as a count of the occurrences of the possible values of that metric. For example, a Yes/No metric would be represented by a count of the occurrences of *Yes* and a count of the occurrences of *No*.

The DRIVER_COUNT will be used to count the number of occurrences of the DRIVER_OBJECT_KEY. Rather than ask the Market Basket Query to sum and count records, the DRIVER_COUNT field provides the number 1 in each row, which allows the Market Basket Query to only sum the numeric, additive value of the DRIVER_COUNT, which is 1. By summing the DRIVER_COUNT, the Market Basket Query is counting occurrences of the DRIVER_OBJECT_KEY.

Correlation Object

The Correlation Object is represented by the columns that begin with CORR_, as shown in Figure 5.5.

The CORR_OBJECT_KEY identifies the object that performs the function of a Correlation Object. In the context of the Market Basket Scope Statement, the CORR_OBJECT_KEY refers to "what Correlation Object B is in, or not in, the Itemset?" An object can be both the Driver

```
, B.OBJECT_KEY      AS CORR_OBJECT_KEY
, B.QUANTITY        AS CORR_QUANTITY
, B.DOLLARS         AS CORR_DOLLARS
, 1                 AS CORR_COUNT
```

FIGURE 5.5
Correlation Object.

```
FROM MARKET_BASKET_TABLE A
INNER JOIN MARKET_BASKET_TABLE B
ON A.ITEMSET_KEY = B.ITEMSET_KEY
WHERE A.OBJECT_KEY <> B.OBJECT_KEY
AND A.OBJECT_KEY <> 0  ;
```

FIGURE 5.6
Recursive join.

and Correlation Object. When an object is represented by the CORR_OBJECT_KEY, that object is the Correlation Object.

The CORR_QUANTITY and CORR_DOLLARS metric measurements have the same purpose and properties as the DRIVER_QUANTITY and DRIVER_DOLLARS metric measurements. Within an Itemset the quantity and dollar values are the same when an object is the Driver Object and when that same object is the Correlation Object. The CORR_COUNT will be used to count the number of occurrences of the CORR_OBJECT_KEY.

Recursive Join

The Driver and Correlation Objects are juxtaposed by the recursive join, shown in Figure 5.6, which is where the real heavy lifting of the Market Basket Query occurs.

The Market Basket Table is referenced twice. This SQL method loads the Market Basket Table into memory twice. The aliases A and B allow the relational SQL engine to give each of the copies of the Market Basket Table an identity unique from each other. The first copy of the Market Basket Table is named *A*, and the second Market Basket Table is named *B*. Those two tables, because they are copies of the same Market Basket Table, are identical to each other.

The join clause "A.OBJECT_KEY <> B.OBJECT_KEY" prevents an Object_Key from being both Driver Object and Correlation Object. If an Object_Key were allowed to be both Driver Object and Correlation Object, that would present results that would be rather circular in logic: Object A is in an Itemset when Object A is in the Itemset. So, rather than allow the results of the Market Basket Analysis to be circular, the join clause "A.OBJECT_KEY <> B.OBJECT_KEY" prevents an Object_Key from being both Driver Object and Correlation Object.

Chapter 6 will explain how a database design will optimize the recursive join in Figure 5.6. Chapter 7 will explain the use of the recursive join in the flow of data through the Market Basket ETL. A common misperception of Market Basket Analysis is that this recursive join will be performed against the whole body of data every time a Market Basket Analysis query is executed. In this Market Basket Solution Definition, the recursive join is performed on an Itemset only once. The result set is stored in another table. Also, the recursive join is performed against only a subset of the data. Because the recursive join considers each Itemset only within the context of that Itemset, the recursive join is not enhanced by including many Itemsets. For a given Itemset, the result set is the same regardless of the number of Itemsets involved in a single iteration of the recursive join.

Single Object Itemset

The join clause "A.OBJECT_KEY <> 0" resolves the special case of an Itemset with only one object, shown in Table 5.2.

The Driver Object in Itemset 1 has no Correlation Object. This is a case wherein nothing is something. The analysis must be able to see when nothing occurred. Specifically, the analysis must be able to see when a Driver Object has no Correlation Object. This matching of something to nothing is achieved by creating a "nothing" object, which will be the Correlation Object when none exists. In this example, the key of the nothing object is zero. In the recursive join that juxtaposes all objects as both Driver and Correlation Objects, the nothing object can become a Driver Object. To let a nothing object be a Driver Object would, of course, be complete nonsense. To prevent the nonsense of a nothing Driver Object, the join clause "A.OBJECT_KEY <> 0" explicitly excludes all such nothing Driver Objects. The result is shown in Table 5.2. The two rows in the top of Table 5.2 include the row with a nothing Driver Object (i.e., Drive_Object_Key = 0) and the row with a nothing Correlation Object (i.e., Correlation_Object_Key = 0). By eliminating the row with a nothing

TABLE 5.2

Single Object Itemsets

Itemset Key	Driver Object Key	Driver Quantity	Driver Dollars	Driver Count	Corr Object Key	Corr Quantity	Corr Dollars	Corr Count
1	15	1	$15.31	1	0	0	$0.00	1
1	0	0	$0.00	1	15	1	$15.31	1

Itemset Key	Driver Object Key	Driver Quantity	Driver Dollars	Driver Count	Corr Object Key	Corr Quantity	Corr Dollars	Corr Count
1	15	1	$15.31	1	0	0	$0.00	1

Driver Object (i.e., Driver_Object_Key = 0), only the row with a nothing Correlation Object (i.e., Correlation_Object_Key = 0) is included in the result set from the Market Basket Query. That one row with a nothing Correlation Object (i.e., Correlation_Object_Key = 0) is shown in the bottom of Table 5.2.

MARKET BASKET BI TABLE

The Market Basket Query populates the Market Basket BI Table. Once the data is in the Market Basket BI Table, the data in the Market Basket Table is no longer needed. The recursive SQL is only used as an ETL application from the Market Basket Table to the Market Basket BI Table. This means the recursive SQL that converts the data from a vertical form (all objects in an Itemset vertically arranged in multiple rows) to a juxtaposed form (all objects in an Itemset arranged as Driver and Correlation Objects) need run only once for each Itemset. Chapter 7 provides details on the use of the Market Basket Query as a batch ETL application. For the purposes of the solution design, the Market Basket Query can be assumed to have populated the Market Basket BI Table. The data from Table 5.1, converted to a juxtaposed form, will look like the data in Table 5.3.

Once the Market Basket data is loaded into the Market Basket BI Table, the recursive nature of Market Basket Analysis has been realized into the juxtaposition of objects in an Itemset. Within a single Itemset, each object will occur as a Driver Object once for every other object in the Itemset as all the other objects take their turn as the Correlation Object; in addition, each object will occur as a Correlation Object once for every other object in the Itemset as all the other objects take their turn as the Driver Object. This is the juxtaposition of objects as Driver Object and Correlation Object. This juxtaposition also causes an explosion of data as each object within an Itemset occurs in $2*(n-1)$ rows, where n equals the number of unique objects in an Itemset. An object will occur $n-1$ times as the Driver Object, and $n-1$ times as the Correlation Object.

An Itemset will never change. A transaction that has completed will never happen again. Another transaction may occur such that the second transaction is identical in every possible way to the first transaction. However, that second transaction is still the second transaction and not

TABLE 5.3

Market Basket BI Table

Itemset Key	Driver Object Key	Driver Quantity	Driver Dollars	Driver Count	Corr Object Key	Corr Quantity	Corr Dollars	Corr Count
1	15	1	$15.31	1	0	0	$0.00	1
2	16	2	$24.42	1	43	1	$14.32	1
2	16	2	$24.42	1	57	2	$18.18	1
2	16	2	$24.42	1	64	1	$12.37	1
2	43	1	$14.32	1	16	2	$24.42	1
2	43	1	$14.32	1	57	2	$18.18	1
2	43	1	$14.32	1	64	1	$12.37	1
2	57	2	$18.18	1	16	2	$24.42	1
2	57	2	$18.18	1	43	1	$14.32	1
2	57	2	$18.18	1	64	1	$12.37	1
2	64	1	$12.37	1	16	2	$24.42	1
2	64	1	$12.37	1	43	1	$14.32	1
2	64	1	$12.37	1	57	2	$18.18	1
3	15	2	$30.62	1	16	1	$12.21	1
3	15	2	$30.62	1	64	1	$12.37	1
3	15	2	$30.62	1	78	4	$53.76	1
3	15	2	$30.62	1	98	1	$2.45	1
3	16	1	$12.21	1	15	2	$30.62	1
3	16	1	$12.21	1	64	1	$12.37	1
3	16	1	$12.21	1	78	4	$53.76	1
3	16	1	$12.21	1	98	1	$2.45	1
3	64	1	$12.37	1	15	2	$30.62	1
3	64	1	$12.37	1	16	1	$12.21	1
3	64	1	$12.37	1	78	4	$53.76	1
3	64	1	$12.37	1	98	1	$2.45	1
3	78	4	$53.76	1	15	2	$30.62	1
3	78	4	$53.76	1	16	1	$12.21	1
3	78	4	$53.76	1	64	1	$12.37	1
3	78	4	$53.76	1	98	1	$2.45	1
3	98	1	$2.45	1	15	2	$30.62	1
3	98	1	$2.45	1	16	1	$12.21	1
3	98	1	$2.45	1	64	1	$12.37	1
3	98	1	$2.45	1	78	4	$53.76	1
4	43	3	$42.96	1	57	1	$9.09	1
4	43	3	$42.96	1	87	1	$16.87	1
4	43	3	$42.96	1	98	1	$2.45	1

(Continued)

TABLE 5.3 (CONTINUED)

Market Basket BI Table

Itemset Key	Driver Object Key	Driver Quantity	Driver Dollars	Driver Count	Corr Object Key	Corr Quantity	Corr Dollars	Corr Count
4	57	1	$9.09	1	43	3	$42.96	1
4	57	1	$9.09	1	78	1	$13.44	1
4	57	1	$9.09	1	87	1	$16.87	1
4	57	1	$9.09	1	98	1	$2.45	1
4	78	1	$13.44	1	43	3	$42.96	1
4	78	1	$13.44	1	57	1	$9.09	1
4	78	1	$13.44	1	87	1	$16.87	1
4	78	1	$13.44	1	98	1	$2.45	1
4	87	1	$16.87	1	43	3	$42.96	1
4	87	1	$16.87	1	57	1	$9.09	1
4	87	1	$16.87	1	78	1	$13.44	1
4	87	1	$16.87	1	98	1	$2.45	1
4	98	1	$2.45	1	43	3	$42.96	1
4	98	1	$2.45	1	57	1	$9.09	1
4	98	1	$2.45	1	78	1	$13.44	1
4	98	1	$2.45	1	87	1	$16.87	1

the first transaction. For that reason, once an Itemset has been added to a Market Basket BI Table, that Itemset will never change. So, that Itemset can remain in the Market Basket BI Table indefinitely. In that way, a Market Basket BI Table becomes a datamart with a very long life. The retention period, therefore, becomes a relevant requirement for a Market Basket Analysis application as the Market Basket BI Table grows and ages. The requirement would be specific to each individual Market Basket Analysis effort, but eventually the Itemsets in a Market Basket BI Table will lose their relevance.

MARKET BASKET ANALYSIS BI VIEW

The Market Basket Analysis BI View presents each Driver Object juxtaposed against each Correlation Object in a cumulative form. The Itemset_ Key is not present because the result set of the Market Basket Analysis BI View considers the behaviors of Driver Objects and Correlation Objects across the Itemsets in the Market Basket BI Table.

The SQL of the Market Basket BI View, shown in Figure 5.7, has three main sections. The three sections are marked by the horizontal lines in Figure 5.7.

The first section of the Market Basket BI View presents the Market Basket Analysis keys and metrics. The keys should always be present in

```
SELECT
DRIVER.DRIVER_OBJECT_KEY
, CORR.CORR_OBJECT_KEY
, DRIVER.DRIVER_QUANTITY_SUM
, DRIVER.DRIVER_DOLLARS_SUM
, DRIVER.DRIVER_COUNT_SUM
, CORR.CORR_QUANTITY_SUM
, CORR.CORR_DOLLARS_SUM
, CORR.CORR_COUNT_SUM
, CORR.CORR_QUANTITY_SUM/DRIVER.DRIVER_QUANTITY_SUM AS QUANTITY_RATIO
, CORR.CORR_DOLLARS_SUM/DRIVER.DRIVER_DOLLARS_SUM AS DOLLARS_RATIO
, CORR.CORR_COUNT_SUM/DRIVER.DRIVER_COUNT_SUM AS COUNT_RATIO
FROM
━━━━━━━━━━━━━━━━━━━━━━━━━━━━━━━━━━━━━━━━━━━━━━━━━━━━━━━━━━━━━━━━━━━━
(SELECT
DRIVER_OBJECT_KEY
,SUM(DRIVER_QUANTITY) AS DRIVER_QUANTITY_SUM
,SUM(DRIVER_DOLLARS) AS DRIVER_DOLLARS_SUM
,SUM(DRIVER_COUNT) AS DRIVER_COUNT_SUM
FROM(SELECT
ITEMSET_KEY
,DRIVER_OBJECT_KEY
,DRIVER_QUANTITY
,DRIVER_DOLLARS
,DRIVER_COUNT
FROM MARKET_BASKET_BI_TABLE
GROUP BY
ITEMSET_KEY
,DRIVER_OBJECT_KEY
,DRIVER_QUANTITY
,DRIVER_DOLLARS
,DRIVER_COUNT)
GROUP BY
DRIVER_OBJECT_KEY)DRIVER
INNER JOIN
━━━━━━━━━━━━━━━━━━━━━━━━━━━━━━━━━━━━━━━━━━━━━━━━━━━━━━━━━━━━━━━━━━━━
(SELECT
DRIVER_OBJECT_KEY
,CORR_OBJECT_KEY
,SUM(CORR_QUANTITY) AS CORR_QUANTITY_SUM
,SUM(CORR_DOLLARS) AS CORR_DOLLARS_SUM
,SUM(CORR_COUNT) AS CORR_COUNT_SUM
FROM MARKET_BASKET_BI_TABLE
GROUP BY
DRIVER_OBJECT_KEY
,CORR_OBJECT_KEY)CORR
ON DRIVER.DRIVER_OBJECT_KEY = CORR.DRIVER_OBJECT_KEY
ORDER BY
DRIVER.DRIVER_OBJECT_KEY
, CORR.CORR_OBJECT_KEY
```

FIGURE 5.7
Market Basket Analysis BI View.

the Market Basket Analysis BI View. Without the keys, analysts using the view will not be able to know the objects presented by the view. The metrics, however, can be customized to suit the needs of a specific data warehouse. The metrics provided in Figure 5.7 are fairly representative of a common set of metrics. They can be modified to meet the source data available in a data warehouse, or requirements of a Market Basket Analysis application. The metrics of a Market Basket Analysis BI View will be either additive or relative in nature. The relative metrics are built using the additive metrics. When modifying the metrics of the Market Basket Analysis BI View, metrics must be handled according to their additive or relative properties. Otherwise, the results of the Market Basket Analysis will be incorrect.

The second section of the Market Basket BI View isolates the Driver Object and its metrics. The Market Basket Analysis BI View operates against the Market Basket BI Table, which is an exploded representation of each Itemset so that the Market Basket BI Table can juxtapose every occurrence of the Driver Object against every occurrence of the Correlation Object. To reverse the exploded representation of the Itemset, the Market Basket Analysis BI View retrieves the Driver Object in a sub-select that includes a GROUP BY clause. Because an individual object that can be the Driver Object can be the Driver Object in multiple Itemsets, the ITEMSET_KEY is included in that GROUP BY statement. The result is that the juxtaposed, and therefore repeated, statements of the Driver Object are reduced to one statement of the Driver Object, which allows the metrics of the Driver Object to represent only one iteration of the Driver Object in an Itemset rather than $n - 1$ iterations of the Driver Object.

The third section of the Market Basket Analysis BI View joins the Correlation Object to the Driver Object. This is where the Driver Object finally gets to drive. The join between the Driver Object and the Correlation Object in the third section of the Market Basket Analysis BI View places the Correlation Object into the context of the Driver Object. This also multiplies again the number of rows containing the Driver Object to $n - 1$ number of rows (where $n =$ the total number of objects in an Itemset). However, this join occurs without the recursive join of the Market Basket Query in Figure 5.2.

The result set of the Market Basket Analysis BI View using the sample data in this chapter is presented in Table 5.4.

TABLE 5.4

Driver Object and Correlation Object Result Set

Driver Object Key	Corr Object Key	Driver Quantity Sum	Driver Dollars Sum	Driver Count Sum	Corr Quantity Sum	Corr Dollars Sum	Corr Count Sum	Quantity Ratio	Dollars Ratio	Count Ratio
15	0	3	$45.93	2	0	$0.00	1	0.0000%	0.0000%	50.0000%
15	16	3	$45.93	2	1	$12.21	1	33.3333%	26.5839%	50.0000%
15	64	3	$45.93	2	1	$12.37	1	33.3333%	26.9323%	50.0000%
15	78	3	$45.93	2	4	$53.76	1	133.3333%	117.0477%	50.0000%
15	98	3	$45.93	2	1	$2.45	1	33.3333%	5.3342%	50.0000%
16	15	3	$36.63	2	2	$30.62	1	66.6667%	83.5927%	50.0000%
16	43	3	$36.63	2	1	$14.32	1	33.3333%	39.0936%	50.0000%
16	57	3	$36.63	2	2	$18.18	1	66.6667%	49.6314%	50.0000%
16	64	3	$36.63	2	2	$24.74	2	66.6667%	67.5403%	100.0000%
16	78	3	$36.63	2	4	$53.76	1	133.3333%	146.7649%	50.0000%
16	98	3	$36.63	2	1	$2.45	1	33.3333%	6.6885%	50.0000%
43	16	4	$57.28	2	2	$24.42	1	50.0000%	42.6327%	50.0000%
43	57	4	$57.28	2	3	$27.27	2	75.0000%	47.6082%	100.0000%
43	64	4	$57.28	2	1	$12.37	1	25.0000%	21.5957%	50.0000%
43	78	4	$57.28	2	1	$13.44	1	25.0000%	23.4637%	50.0000%
43	87	4	$57.28	2	1	$16.87	1	25.0000%	29.4518%	50.0000%
43	98	4	$57.28	2	1	$2.45	1	25.0000%	4.2772%	50.0000%
57	16	3	$27.27	2	2	$24.42	1	66.6667%	89.5490%	50.0000%
57	43	3	$27.27	2	4	$57.28	2	133.3333%	210.0477%	100.0000%

57	3	$27.27	2	$12.37	1	1	33.3333%	45.3612%	50.0000%
57	3	$27.27	2	$13.44	1	1	33.3333%	49.2849%	50.0000%
57	3	$27.27	2	$16.87	1	1	33.3333%	61.8629%	50.0000%
57	3	$27.27	2	$2.45	1	1	33.3333%	8.9842%	50.0000%
64	1	$12.37	1	$30.62	2	1	200.0000%	247.5344%	100.0000%
64	1	$12.37	1	$36.63	3	2	300.0000%	296.1196%	200.0000%
64	1	$12.37	1	$14.32	1	1	100.0000%	115.7639%	100.0000%
64	1	$12.37	1	$18.18	2	1	200.0000%	146.9685%	100.0000%
64	1	$12.37	1	$53.76	4	1	400.0000%	434.5998%	100.0000%
64	1	$12.37	1	$2.45	1	1	100.0000%	19.8060%	100.0000%
78	5	$67.20	2	$30.62	2	1	40.0000%	45.5655%	50.0000%
78	5	$67.20	2	$12.21	1	1	20.0000%	18.1696%	50.0000%
78	5	$67.20	2	$42.96	3	1	60.0000%	63.9286%	50.0000%
78	5	$67.20	2	$9.09	1	1	20.0000%	13.5268%	50.0000%
78	5	$67.20	2	$12.37	1	1	20.0000%	18.4077%	50.0000%
78	5	$67.20	2	$16.87	1	1	20.0000%	25.1042%	50.0000%
78	5	$67.20	2	$4.90	2	2	40.0000%	7.2917%	100.0000%
87	1	$16.87	1	$42.96	3	1	300.0000%	254.6532%	100.0000%
87	1	$16.87	1	$9.09	1	1	100.0000%	53.8826%	100.0000%
87	1	$16.87	1	$13.44	1	1	100.0000%	79.6680%	100.0000%
87	1	$16.87	1	$2.45	1	1	100.0000%	14.5228%	100.0000%
98	1	$2.45	1	$30.62	2	1	200.0000%	1249.7959%	100.0000%
98	1	$2.45	1	$12.21	1	1	100.0000%	498.3673%	100.0000%
98	1	$2.45	1	$42.96	3	1	300.0000%	1753.4694%	100.0000%

(Continued)

TABLE 5.4 (CONTINUED)

Driver Object and Correlation Object Result Set

Driver Object Key	Corr Object Key	Driver Quantity Sum	Driver Dollars Sum	Driver Count Sum	Corr Quantity Sum	Corr Dollars Sum	Corr Count Sum	Quantity Ratio	Dollars Ratio	Count Ratio
98	57	1	$2.45	1	1	$9.09	1	100.0000%	371.0204%	100.0000%
98	64	1	$2.45	1	1	$12.37	1	100.0000%	504.8980%	100.0000%
98	78	1	$2.45	1	5	$67.20	2	500.0000%	2742.8571%	200.0000%
98	87	1	$2.45	1	1	$16.87	1	100.0000%	688.5714%	100.0000%

The Market Basket BI View metrics are general in nature, but specific to the SQL in Figure 5.7 and the result set in Table 5.4. These data definitions are intended to present the concepts of the Market Basket Analysis BI View that you might use in your Market Basket Analysis application. For any given Market Basket Analysis application, the keys and metrics will probably be slightly different from the keys and metrics defined below. The important aspect of these definitions is the understanding of their concepts, how they are created, and how they are used. Once those concepts and principles are understood, they can be applied to any other Market Basket Analysis application.

DRIVER_OBJECT_KEY

DRIVER_OBJECT_KEY in the Market Basket BI View performs the same function it performed in the preceding Market Basket Table and Market Basket BI Table. The context is still the first half of the Market Basket Scope Statement. The DRIVER_OBJECT_KEY identifies the Driver Object for each individual row. That Driver Object provides the context of each individual row, so that the keys and metrics in that row can be understood to answer the question of the Market Basket Scope Statement in Figure 5.1.

CORR_OBJECT_KEY

CORR_OBJECT_KEY in the Market Basket BI View performs the same function as performed in the preceding Market Basket Table and Market Basket BI Table. The context is still the second half of the Market Basket Scope Statement. The CORR_OBJECT_KEY identifies the Correlation Object for each individual row. That Correlation Object provides the answer, within the context of the Driver Object, to the question of the Market Basket Scope Statement in Figure 5.1.

DRIVER_QUANTITY_SUM

DRIVER_QUANTITY_SUM is an additive metric that presents the total number of Driver Objects in an Itemset. This value is calculated by summing the Quantity values from the Market Basket Table. The Market Basket Analysis BI View, however, operates against the Market Basket BI Table, which is an exploded representation of each Itemset so that the

Market Basket BI Table can juxtapose every occurrence of the Driver Object against every occurrence of the Correlation Object. To reverse the exploded representation of the Itemset, the Market Basket Analysis BI View retrieves the Driver Object in a sub-select that includes a GROUP BY clause. As a result, the DRIVER_QUANTITY_SUM for a given Driver Object is the total number of the Driver Objects in the Itemset.

DRIVER_DOLLARS_SUM

DRIVER_DOLLARS_SUM is an additive metric that presents the total monetary value of the Driver Objects in an Itemset. This value is calculated by summing the Dollar values from the Market Basket Table. The Market Basket Analysis BI View, however, operates against the Market Basket BI Table, which is an exploded representation of each Itemset so that the Market Basket BI Table can juxtapose every occurrence of the Driver Object against every occurrence of the Correlation Object. To reverse the exploded representation of the Itemset, the Market Basket Analysis BI View retrieves the Driver Object in a sub-select that includes a GROUP BY clause. As a result, the DRIVER_DOLLARS_SUM for a given Driver Object is the total monetary measure of the Driver Objects in the Itemset.

For any given data warehouse, dollars may not be a relevant measure of the Itemset. Frequently a monetary measure of the Itemset is included. A Market Basket Analysis effort may or may not include such a monetary measurement in the form of dollars or any other monetary denomination.

DRIVER_COUNT_SUM

DRIVER_COUNT_SUM is an additive metric that counts the number of Itemsets represented by a row of data returned by the Market Basket Analysis BI View. The "1 AS DRIVER_COUNT" statement in the Market Basket Query allows the Market Basket Analysis BI View to count the number of Itemsets by summing the DRIVER_COUNT. DRIVER_COUNT is included in the sub-select GROUP BY that reduces the exploded juxtaposed Driver Object from $n - 1$ rows to just one row. Once reduced to just one row, the sum of the DRIVER_COUNT values is also a count of the Itemsets.

CORR_QUANTITY_SUM

CORR_QUANTITY_SUM is an additive metric that presents the total number of Correlation Objects in an Itemset. This value is calculated by summing the Quantity values from the Market Basket BI Table. That summing operation occurs for the GROUP BY key of DRIVER_OBJECT_KEY and CORR_OBJECT_KEY. That compound key causes the sum of quantity of Correlation Objects to be calculated within the context of the Driver Object. That is to say, the CORR_QUANTITY_SUM for a given Correlation Object is the total number of the Correlation Objects in an Itemset and in the context of a Driver Object.

CORR_DOLLARS_SUM

CORR_DOLLARS_SUM is an additive metric that presents the total monetary measurement of Correlation Objects in an Itemset. This value is calculated by summing the Dollar values from the Market Basket BI Table. That summing operation occurs for the GROUP BY key of DRIVER_OBJECT_KEY and CORR_OBJECT_KEY. That compound key causes the sum of dollars of Correlation Objects to be calculated within the context of the Driver Object. That is to say, the CORR_DOLLARS_SUM for a given Correlation Object is the total monetary measurement of the Correlation Objects in an Itemset and in the context of a Driver Object.

For any given data warehouse, dollars may not be a relevant measure of the Itemset. Frequently a monetary measure of the Itemset is included. A Market Basket Analysis effort may or may not include such a monetary measurement in the form of dollars or any other monetary denomination.

CORR_COUNT_SUM

CORR_COUNT_SUM is an additive metric that counts the number of Itemsets represented by a row of data returned by the Market Basket Analysis BI View. The "1 AS CORR_COUNT" statement in the Market Basket Query allows the Market Basket Analysis BI View to count the number of Itemsets by summing the CORR_COUNT. As a result, the sum of the CORR_COUNT values is also a count of the Itemsets.

QUANTITY_RATIO

QUANTITY_RATIO is a nonadditive relative metric measurement of the penetration of the CORR_QUANTITY_SUM value relative to the DRIVER_QUANTITY_SUM value. This provides an indication of the number of Correlation Objects that occurred in an Itemset within the context of a Driver Object.

Although QUANTITY_RATIO is nonadditive, it can be recalculated by applying the CORR_QUANTITY_SUM/DRIVER_QUANTITY_SUM calculation.

DOLLARS_RATIO

DOLLARS_RATIO is a nonadditive relative metric measurement of the penetration of the CORR_DOLLARS_SUM value relative to the DRIVER_DOLLARS_SUM value. This provides an indication of the monetary value of Correlation Objects that occurred in an Itemset within the context of a Driver Object.

Although DOLLARS_RATIO is nonadditive, it can be recalculated by applying the CORR_DOLLARS_SUM/DRIVER_DOLLARS_SUM calculation.

COUNT_RATIO

COUNT_RATIO is a nonadditive relative metric measurement of the penetration of the CORR_COUNT_SUM value relative to the DRIVER_COUNT_SUM value. This provides an indication of the occurrences of Correlation Objects that occurred in an Itemset within the context of a Driver Object.

Although COUNT_RATIO is nonadditive, it can be recalculated by applying the CORR_COUNT_SUM/DRIVER_COUNT_SUM calculation.

Additional Group by Data Elements

In the SQL and data definitions provided above, the Itemset is identified by the ITEMSET_KEY. Noticeably absent is any reference to normal operations of a data warehouse, such as date, time, location, operator, agent, and so on. These references can all be included in the Market Basket Analysis application. The ITEMSET_KEY as used in the data in Table 5.4 is without any such references. The ITEMSET_KEY can, however, include any such references.

By adding Date, Time, and Location (as an example) to the ITEMSET_ KEY, which will cause the ITEMSET_KEY to be a compound key, the data in the Market Basket Analysis application can be stratified by Date, Time, and Location. The affinity between objects may be subject to numerous conditions. As mentioned earlier, the time of day, the day of the week, the location, and the Four P's of Marketing may have an effect on the objects and affinities discovered in the Market Basket BI Table. To allow the Market Basket Analysis application to separate "weekday" Itemsets from "weekend" Itemsets, and "promoted" Itemsets from "non-promoted" Itemsets, these and other attributes of the Itemset can be added to the Market Basket BI Table.

These attributes are attributes of the Itemset, not attributes of the objects in the Itemset. Because they are attributes of the Itemset, they need only be represented once in the Market Basket BI Table, as they clarify the Itemset and not the objects in the Itemset. These Itemset attributes allow the analyst to query the affinity between objects in the morning, the affinity between the objects in the evening, and the affinity between objects in Florida versus Georgia versus Alabama.

The Itemset attributes allow an analyst to stratify the Itemsets via the attributes that answer the *who*, *when*, *where*, and *how* questions. The *what* question has already been answered, as it is the objects in the Market Basket Table and the Market Basket BI Table. Itemset attributes do not within themselves contribute to the affinity between two objects. Instead, Itemset attributes are used to isolate groups of Itemsets to expose the pattern within that group of Itemsets. For example, by isolating the weekday morning data from the weekend data, the patterns within the weekday morning data are more visible as they are not obscured by the patterns of the weekend data. In that way, Itemset attributes allow the Market Basket Analysis BI View to isolate a group of Itemsets, and therefore the pattern in that group of Itemsets.

BEYOND THE MARKET BASKET ANALYSIS BI VIEW

A Market Basket Analysis application could deliver the application as described and be deemed a success with a positive ROI. The Market Basket Analysis team could congratulate each other on their achievement and look forward to future analysis and future actionable information. But, for those willing to go the extra mile, willing to do the extra-credit home-work, a Market Basket Analysis application can be expanded in at least two ways—Object Groups and Market Basket Reporting.

Object Groups

An enterprise may have a few groupings of objects such that even though the objects are individual and separate from each other, the group of those objects is perceived as a cohesive unit in the mind of the enterprise. In the context of an automotive repair shop, that group may be the combination of lubrication and oil, which in that industry is referred to as "lube and oil." If you took your car to an automotive repair shop and asked them to lube your car but not change the oil, they would wonder why someone would make such a strange request. The reverse is also true that a request to change the oil but not lubricate the car would be considered strange. So, while a "lube and oil" is made of lubricant that is not oil, and oil that is not lubricant, they are spoken in one breath and perceived to always occur in tandem.

For an enterprise with such a grouping of objects as "lube and oil," that group of objects can be incorporated as a single object. When analyzing the affinity between objects in the transactions of the enterprise, it is simultaneously redundant and confusing to include two objects that move in tandem only because they move in tandem. Instead, let them be one object. This will remove the redundancy and the 100% affinity, which could only serve to skew the affinity between the group of objects and other objects not in that group.

Market Basket Reporting in Batch

Finally, going all the way back to the example in Chapter 1 of the chair in the corner, the Market Basket BI SQL can be scheduled in batch to monitor the affinity between objects within the enterprise. During the analysis phase of the Market Basket Analysis application, you should expect to have found some object affinities that indicate the health of the enterprise. These would be Key Performance Indicators (KPIs). If you know that as long as Object A and Object B continue to have an affinity of approximately 75%, which indicates the enterprise is performing well, then you would want to monitor the affinity between Object A and Object B on a frequent and recurring basis. You would also want to automate that monitoring process so that it occurs even when you get busy and forget to run the query. You would then want that automated monitoring process to post an alert when the affinity between Object A and Object B falls below a threshold value, and possibly if that affinity rises above another threshold value. In that way, the Market Basket Analysis application can deliver a mechanism for monitoring the health of the enterprise by way of monitoring the interrelationships of the objects within the enterprise.

This is Market Basket Reporting via a batch schedule. The KPIs included in the Market Basket Reporting process should only be those KPIs that will require action when they send an alert. In other words, you don't want to monitor KPIs without an associated action. The goal of Market Basket Analysis is ROI via actionable information. Market Basket Reporting KPIs with an associated action are a clear and well-defined delivery of actionable information and, therefore, ROI.

6

Market Basket Architecture and Database Design

Market Basket Analysis has the connotation of a single database the size of China, a query engine the size of Mexico, and a result set the size of Rhode Island. This is definitely not true of this Market Basket Analysis solution design. On the contrary, this solution is designed to leverage the strengths, and avoid the weaknesses, of a Relational Database Management System (RDBMS) platform. To achieve both goals, this solution design incorporates the following elements:

- Market Basket Table—The one and only function of this table is to perform a recursive join. That recursive join is invoked during a batch ETL process. Therefore, the recursive join is never modified by analysts. As a result, once the Market Basket Table and the recursive SQL are optimized for each other, they remain optimized.
- Market Basket BI Table—The one and only function of this table is to perform the SUM and GROUP BY operations in an SQL statement. Because the Driver Object and Correlation Object are interchangeable, the Market Basket BI Table is actually a class, or group, of tables. All the Market Basket BI Tables for a single iteration of analysis share the same Data Definition Language (DDL) and are all queried in the same fashion. Therefore, once you know how to optimize one Market Basket BI Table, you know how to optimize all the Market Basket BI Tables.

It's really that simple. The Market Basket Table is basically a staging table for data on its way to a Market Basket BI Table. The Market Basket

BI Table is a datamart, in that the data in the Market Basket BI Table is a subset of the data in the data warehouse and the data is transformed to meet a specific requirement for a specific application. That application is, of course, the Market Basket Analysis application. But, before we look too closely at the tables, let's look first at the big picture, the architecture. The Market Basket set of applications includes two architectural branches— Analysis and Reporting.

Market Basket Analysis Architecture

The Analysis architectural branch, shown in Figure 6.1, begins with a data warehouse. The data from the data warehouse passes through a Market Basket Table and a Market Basket BI Table. Analysts query the Market Basket BI Table directly. All these steps occur at the direction of the analysts. These are not daily batch scheduled operations. Rather, the analysts choose which data will be analyzed and when the data will be refreshed to support that analysis.

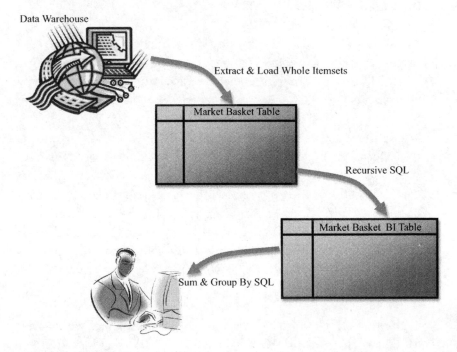

FIGURE 6.1
Market Basket Analysis architecture.

Data Warehouse

The data warehouse is the source system for the Market Basket Analysis application. The term *data warehouse* is used here to mean the collective set of data and data structures used for decision support, which may include tables that hold strategic long-range data as well as operational data store tables that hold tactical short-term data. Often, the most granular transactional data is found in an operational data store. An operational data store may be the only source of granular transactional data. If that is the case, then the term *data warehouse* can be considered to include the operational data store. If the operational data store is the only subset of the data warehouse that holds the detailed granular transactional data required by the Market Basket Analysis application, then the Market Basket Analysis application will extract its data only from the operational data store. If that is the case, then the data retention of an operational data store can be an issue, as typically data remains in an operational data store for only a few days.

If, however, the data warehouse (not including the operational data store) tables hold the granular transactional data required by a Market Basket Analysis application, then the Market Basket Analysis application can get its data from the granular transactional data within the data warehouse. If that is the case, then the data retention of the data in the data warehouse is much less of an issue than the data retention of the data in an operational data store. However, extracting large volumes of granular transactional data from a data warehouse can create contention for resources among data warehouse customers. For that reason, when extracting granular transactional data from a data warehouse the extract operation may need to be scheduled to occur during off-peak hours or in a performance partition that will not adversely affect data warehouse customers.

Market Basket Table

The general concept of the Market Basket Table is shown in Table 5.1. An Extract, Transform, and Load (ETL) application will truncate all rows from the Market Basket Table. Then, the ETL application will populate the Market Basket Table with data containing whole Itemsets. The Market Basket Table is a staging table. Data is loaded into the Market Basket Table so that data can be extracted from it. The value added by the Market Basket Table is the index strategy that will optimize the recursive

SQL, shown in Figure 5.2, which will extract data from the Market Basket Table.

Because the Market Basket Table is a staging table, never to be used by anything other than ETL applications, the data can be cycled through the Market Basket Table in manageable batches. The use of manageable batches of Market Basket data means the data volumes moving from the data warehouse to the Market Basket Table can be managed at a low enough volume to mitigate adverse effects on the data warehouse; furthermore, the same managed data volumes will help optimize the recursive SQL used to extract data from the Market Basket Table. Rather than recursively query all transactions for the entire enterprise, the ETL application that manages the data flow through the Market Basket Table can move data in and out of the Market Basket Table in managed subsets. Remember, the recursive SQL will recursively join all the rows in each Itemset individually, not all the rows throughout the enterprise. Therefore, the only minimum requirement for the recursive SQL to succeed is that each Itemset in the Market Basket Table be complete and lack no granular transaction rows. So, as long as the Itemsets in the Market Basket Table are complete, the recursive SQL can successfully deliver data into the Market Basket BI Table with one Itemset, one hundred Itemsets, or one million Itemsets.

Market Basket BI Table

The Market Basket BI Table is a class of tables that share the construction of a Market Basket BI Table. The general concept of a Market Basket BI Table is shown in Table 5.3. The SQL statement used to query a Market Basket BI Table, shown in Figure 5.7, uses a SUM and GROUP BY method. This query method simplifies the optimization of the Market Basket BI Tables. The intention of this Market Basket solution design is to isolate the recursive join operation from the affinity calculation operation. In that way, the Market Basket Analysis BI View is intended to perform one operation in one way, which presents the opportunity to optimize the Market Basket BI Table and the Market Basket Analysis BI View for each other.

A Market Basket BI Table can be retained for as long as an analyst needs to refer back to that table. The iterative and repetitive nature of Market Basket Analysis creates the need to compare observations, refine query conditions, and then compare again. For that reason an analyst may compare query results from multiple tables, viewing the result sets in a side-by-side fashion. This also invites the "junk drawer" syndrome. If the retention of Market Basket BI Tables is not managed, an analyst may consume all available space with Market Basket BI Tables that are no longer needed. For that reason, Market Basket analysts and the DBAs managing Market Basket database must work together to avoid the junk drawer syndrome.

Analysts

The final output of the Market Basket Analysis application is query results requested by, and delivered to, a Market Basket analyst. The analyst drives the applications that ultimately populate the Market Basket BI Table and consumes the data in the Market Basket Table. As such, the analyst is the initiator and consumer of the Market Basket data.

The temptation will be strong to allow others, who are not analysts, to view and then ultimately use the data in the Market Basket BI Table. Such use of the Market Basket BI Table and its data should be avoided at all costs. If non-analyst data warehouse customers require access to data in the Market Basket BI Table, then that is a requirement for a datamart specifically for that set of customers and separate from the Market Basket Analysis architecture. A successful Market Basket Analysis application will generate its own version of "the gravitational pull of data." When that happens, offer to provide the needed data in a datamart separate from the Market Basket Analysis architecture. If data warehouse customers are allowed to consume the data in the Market Basket Analysis architecture, they will eventually encumber the Market Basket Analysis application with their requirements for data and data retention so as to render the Market Basket Analysis unavailable for analysis.

Market Basket Reporting Architecture

The Reporting architectural branch, shown in Figure 6.2, also begins with a data warehouse. Again, the data passes through a Market Basket Table and a Market Basket BI Table. Then, any affinity that varies outside the threshold range is reported as an exception via an existing Exception Reporting method. The severity associated with the variance is directly related to the size of the variance. A small variance outside the threshold merits a lower severity; a large variance outside the threshold merits a higher severity.

A batch job schedule, rather than an analyst, initiates Market Basket Reporting. Market Basket Reporting focuses on the most recent set of data available in the data warehouse. If the ETL application that loads

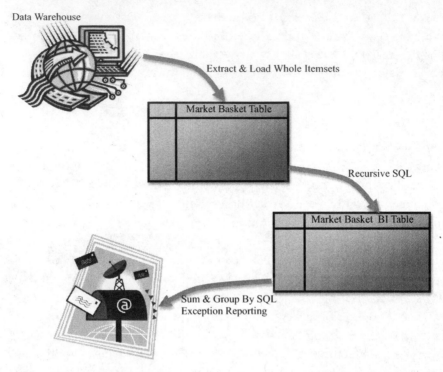

FIGURE 6.2
Market Basket Reporting architecture.

data into the data warehouse performs that load process in a batch schedule, then the Market Basket Reporting focuses on the most recent batch of data in the data warehouse. If, however, the ETL application that loads data into the data warehouse performs the load function in a continuous real-time data feed into the data warehouse, then the Market Basket Reporting can either leverage the control mechanism by which the real-time ETL is controlled or use its own control mechanism to verify that each Itemset has been included in the Market Basket Reporting one and only one time.

Data Warehouse

The Market Basket Reporting application uses only the most recent Itemsets. For that reason, if an operational data store holds the most recent data, then the operational data store is the sole source of data for the Market Basket Reporting application. In that case, the data warehouse is not needed so long as the operational data store continues to provide the most recent data. The most recent data may also be in the data warehouse, which would be redundant. However, even if the most recent data is in the data warehouse and the operational data store, the operational data store is still architecturally a better source of the most recent granular transactional data.

If an operational data store is not available or does not have the granular transactional data needed by the Market Basket Reporting application, then the data warehouse is the source of that data. Regularly scheduled batch jobs that extract data from the data warehouse should be scheduled and optimized to minimize the contention for resources. A data warehouse that is trying to prove its worth should minimize the opportunities to diminish its value and ROI by preventing the business users from using the data warehouse.

Market Basket Table

The Market Basket Table in a Market Basket Reporting application functions identically to the Market Basket Table in the Market Basket Analysis application. Physically, the two tables should be two separate tables. It would be adverse to the reporting and analysis applications if they were to simultaneously truncate and load the same table. The reporting application, therefore, should have its own Market Basket Table that is not manipulated by an analysis application.

Market Basket BI Table

The Market Basket BI Table in a Market Basket Reporting application will be a narrower table than the Market Basket BI Table in a Market Basket Analysis application because the reporting application will provide data to a predefined set of SQL statement(s). Therefore, the reporting application does not need to support the possible permutations of data that are needed to support the analysis application. So, all the Itemset attributes that are used to stratify Market Basket BI Table are not included in the reporting version of the Market Basket BI Table. Any such stratification (e.g., Itemsets that occurred in Georgia, Itemsets that occurred during the weekend, Itemsets that occurred online) is achieved by the conditions programmed into the ETL application that loads the Market Basket BI Table. The one exception to the removal of the Itemset attributes is that when a single Market Basket BI Table is used for multiple exception reports. In that case, a single Market Basket BI Table can be leveraged for two or more exception reports.

Market Basket KPI Exception Reporting

The Market Basket KPI Exception Reporting application uses a SUM and GROUP BY query, which was defined as a KPI during Market Basket Analysis. During analysis, an analyst discovered an affinity that confirms the current state of the enterprise or predicts a future state of the enterprise. That affinity was defined as a query, for example:

- What is the affinity between motor oil and oil filters?
- What is the affinity between hamburger meat and hamburger buns?
- What is the affinity between steak and dessert?

Each of these queries will deliver an affinity. If that affinity falls below a threshold value, that is an indication that the enterprise needs attention in that area. For example:

- What is the affinity between motor oil and oil filters?
  - Good—between 50% and 75%
  - Bad—between 40% and 50%
  - Red Alert—below 40%
- What is the affinity between hamburger meat and hamburger buns?
  - Good—between 70% and 95%
  - Bad—between 50% and 70%
  - Red Alert—below 50%
- What is the affinity between steak and dessert?
  - Good—between 80% and 95%
  - Bad—between 70% and 80%
  - Red Alert—below 70%

The exception reporting method leveraged by the Market Basket KPI Exception Reporting application can be the standard method used by the data warehouse. There is no need to invent a new wheel for exception reporting if one already exists. If, however, the data warehouse does not already have an exception reporting method, then the creation of an exception reporting method should be a prerequisite for the implementation of a Market Basket KPI Exception Reporting application.

MARKET BASKET DATA DEFINITION LANGUAGE (DDL)

The intended audience for this section is the database administrator (DBA) who will create the database and tables used by the Market Basket applications. This section is not intended in any way to be a tutorial for the creation of relational tables. Rather, this section is intended to leverage the knowledge and skill of the DBA who will create the Market Basket tables. By referencing the SQL that will use these Market Basket tables and the suggested optimizations, a DBA can then choose the DDL and index strategy that will most efficiently deliver the Market Basket data.

So, if you are that DBA, and you disagree with the suggested optimizations because you know of a superior alternative, then please implement that superior alternative that will optimize the Market Basket applications. Regardless, please consider the Market Basket queries and the suggested index strategies as you choose an optimization method for the Market Basket application. The pitfalls of any solution design expressed in the context of a platform and technology is that the solution design will not be compliant with the standards observed in your shop, or that you will read this book after the suggested method has become obsolete. If either is the case, then please consider the intended query performance and implement a solution design that you know will deliver an optimized performance and simultaneously adhere to your shop standards.

Construction of the Market Basket Table

The purpose of the Market Basket Table is to facilitate the recursive query in Figure 5.6. That is the only expectation of the Market Basket Table. The equality statement in the recursive join is A.ITEMSET_KEY = B.ITEMSET_KEY. The general concept for optimizing the recursive query is to co-locate all rows in one data block in such a way that the RDBMS knows the rows are all co-located in the same data block. When all rows sharing the same ITEMSET_KEY key are located in the same data block, and the RDBMS knows they are in the same data block, the RDBMS knows that it does not have to move the rows during the join operation, which reduces the I/O to a minimum. In that way, the recursive join is optimized by the reduction of the required I/O.

The suggestions listed below, because they are specific to a platform, will probably become obsolete in a few years from the time of this writing. The purpose of the suggestions is to provide tangible examples of co-located ITEMSET_KEY values. Even if the suggestions have become obsolete, the intention is to communicate the optimization of the recursive join by co-locating all Market Basket Table rows by their ITEMSET_KEYs.

Teradata

All rows are assigned a data block based on the hash value of the Primary Index of a table. For the Market Basket Table, define the column ITEMSET_KEY as the Primary Index. Doing so will cause all rows with the same ITEMSET_KEY value to be located in one hash location. The recursive join will explain as a ROW HASH MATCH SCAN, which will mean that the RDBMS knows the rows are all in the same hash location and do not need to move during the join process. As a result, the recursive join will not redistribute any rows. Rather, it will leave them in place.

Oracle

Oracle uses a Clustered Index to assign rows to data blocks. That assignment is based on the value of the Cluster Key. By defining the ITEMSET_KEY as the Cluster Key, all the rows in a Market Basket Table with the same ITEMSET_KEY value will have the same Cluster Key and will reside in the same data block because the Clustered Index places them there.

A Clustered Index can be used to locate rows from two tables in the same data block. Even though the Market Basket application has only one Market Basket Table, the recursive join treats the one Market Basket Table as two tables that coincidentally happen to be completely identical to each other. The assignment of the join column as the Cluster Key optimizes the join between those two table aliases because the rows that will join to each other are in the same cluster, and the RDBMS knows they are in the same cluster.

DB2

The DB2 RDBMS includes two distinctly different platforms. DB2 for OS/390 operates on a mainframe. DB2 UDB operates on Linux, Unix, and Windows. Both versions of DB2 include a clustered index feature, which physically locates all rows in the same page space by the clustered index key. By defining the ITEMSET_KEY as the clustered index key,

DB2 will place the rows of the Market Basket Table in the sequence of the ITEMSET_KEY and locate all rows with the same ITEMSET_KEY value in the same page space. The two versions of DB2 have slight differences in their use of the clustered index.

DB2 for OS/390 will by default use the first defined index as the clustering index. The rows in a DB2 for OS/390 table will be stored in the sequence of the clustered key, which will have the beneficial by-product of locating all the rows of an Itemset in the same page space. DB2 UDB does not by default use the first defined index as a clustering index. Instead, DB2 UDB requires the explicit definition of a clustering index. Once a clustering index has been defined in DB2 UDB, rows will be placed in a page space according to the clustered index key.

The purpose of a clustered index in both versions of DB2 is the reduction of page I/O by placing rows that will join with each other near each other. DB2 includes the option to turn off clustering. However, as long as clustering is turned on and the ITEMSET_KEY has been defined as the clustered index key, a clustered index will help optimize the recursive join of the Market Basket Query.

SQL Server

SQL Server also offers a clustered index that causes the RDBMS to store the rows of a table in the order of the clustered index key. A clustered index performs best with a minimal number of columns included in the clustered index key. For that reason, a single ITEMSET_KEY column provides an optimal clustered index key. A primary key constraint creates a clustered index if a table does not already have a clustered index. A Market Basket Table in SQL Server, therefore, could be optimized for the recursive join of the Market Basket Query by defining the ITEMSET_KEY as the primary key such that the RDBMS defines the ITEMSET_KEY primary key as a clustered index. This use of a clustered index will, like Oracle and DB2, have the benefit of reducing I/O during the recursive join in the Market Basket Query.

Product Join

The recursive join in the Market Basket Query produces a product join, which creates an explosion of data. As each row of the Market Basket Table joins to every other row of the Market Basket Table, the number of rows is multiplied by a factor of $n^*(n - 1)$, where n = the number of rows. That is by definition a product join, otherwise known as a Cartesian join. While the optimization suggestions mentioned above will avoid significant I/O, the product join will incur significant CPU cycles. For that reason, data is loaded into the Market Basket Table in manageable batches, which will be discussed in Chapter 7. This will prevent the recursive join of the Market Basket Table from overwhelming the RDBMS.

Construction of the Market Basket BI Table

The Market Basket BI Table is also a class of Market Basket tables. A Market Basket application may include multiple Market Basket BI Tables. A Market Basket BI Table involved in the same analysis effort should be based on the same DDL so the result set of the Market Basket Analysis BI View will return comparable data. Multiple Market Basket BI Tables allow an analyst to engage in iterative analysis without re-creating a Market Basket BI Table between every iteration of analysis.

The purpose of the Market Basket BI Table is to facilitate the SUM and GROUP BY operations in the query in Figure 5.7. Unfortunately, the query in Figure 5.7 uses more than one GROUP BY statement. The Market Basket Analysis BI View has two GROUP BY statements that apply directly to the Market Basket BI Table. The first GROUP BY, shown in Figure 6.3, is used to build the Driver half of the Itemsets. The second GROUP BY, shown in Figure 6.4, is used to build the Correlation half of the Itemsets.

The approach to optimize the GROUP BY statements in Figure 6.3 and Figure 6.4 is a combination of a primary index and a secondary index, which are available in all RDBMS platforms. One approach is to apply a primary index to the Driver Group By in Figure 6.3, and a secondary index to the Correlation Group By in Figure 6.4. The other approach is to apply a primary index to the Correlation Group By in Figure 6.4, and a secondary index to the Driver Group By in Figure 6.3. The index method chosen for a Market Basket BI Table can be based on either approach— primary Driver/secondary Correlation or primary Correlation/secondary driver. The decision to use one approach rather than the other is based only on the performance delivered by the index method. The SUM and GROUP BY operations have always been the bread and butter of relational tables. The optimization of a SUM and GROUP BY operation, therefore, should be rather simple.

```
(SELECT
DRIVER_OBJECT_KEY
,SUM(DRIVER_QUANTITY) AS DRIVER_QUANTITY_SUM
,SUM(DRIVER_DOLLARS) AS DRIVER_DOLLARS_SUM
,SUM(DRIVER_COUNT) AS DRIVER_COUNT_SUM
FROM(SELECT
ITEMSET_KEY
,DRIVER_OBJECT_KEY
,DRIVER_QUANTITY
,DRIVER_DOLLARS
,DRIVER_COUNT
FROM MARKET_BASKET_BI_TABLE
GROUP BY
ITEMSET_KEY
,DRIVER_OBJECT_KEY
,DRIVER_QUANTITY
,DRIVER_DOLLARS
,DRIVER_COUNT)
GROUP BY
DRIVER_OBJECT_KEY)DRIVER
```

FIGURE 6.3
Driver Group By.

```
(SELECT
DRIVER_OBJECT_KEY
,CORR_OBJECT_KEY
,SUM(CORR_QUANTITY) AS CORR_QUANTITY_SUM
,SUM(CORR_DOLLARS) AS CORR_DOLLARS_SUM
,SUM(CORR_COUNT) AS CORR_COUNT_SUM
FROM MARKET_BASKET_BI_TABLE
GROUP BY
DRIVER_OBJECT_KEY
,CORR_OBJECT_KEY)CORR
```

FIGURE 6.4
Correlation Group By.

DATAMART ARCHITECTURE

The datamart architecture may seem unusual. If you were expecting an enormous table with every permutation of Market Basket data conceivable, then the datamart architecture may seem surprising as well as unusual. However, the datamart architecture using a class of Market Basket Tables and a class of Market Basket BI Tables leverages the strengths of the RDBMS platforms while mitigating the performance bottlenecks of the RDBMS platforms. The iterative analytic approach removes the need to query all the data in a single query. The staging table method removes the need to simultaneously perform the recursive join and calculate the affinity. The clear delineations of the Market Basket tables and the ETL processes that populate them allow each ETL step to perform one function at a time, and each table to support one BI function at a time.

7

ETL into a Market Basket Datamart

The purpose of the Market Basket Extract, Transform, and Load (ETL) application is specifically to populate a Market Basket BI Table. If a Market Basket application includes the Analysis branch shown in Figure 6.1, then an ETL application populates data in a set of Market Basket tables that are dedicated to the Analysis branch. If a Market Basket application includes the Reporting branch shown in Figure 6.2, then an ETL application populates data in a set of Market Basket tables that are dedicated to the Reporting branch. For every set of Market Basket Analysis tables, a set of ETL applications populates those tables. For every set of Market Basket Reporting tables, a separate set of ETL applications populates those tables as well. The number of Market Basket ETL applications equals the number of sets of Market Basket tables.

REQUIREMENT: POPULATE THE MARKET BASKET BI TABLE

The first requirement of the Market Basket ETL is to extract data from the data warehouse and load that data in the Market Basket BI Table. This requirement may sound rather simple, but it is not. Although it may seem that this requirement can be met by a SELECT statement that writes data to an extract file, and then an INSERT statement that loads the data in the extract file, an ETL application is not quite that simple. To avoid "garbage out," an ETL application must avoid "garbage in." To avoid "garbage in," an ETL application must include safeguards to protect the data, and therefore the Market Basket application that will use the data.

Singularity

Each Itemset must be represented once, and only once. This is a basic requirement of every ETL application. The initial extract application of an ETL application must be able to recognize when it has, and has not, encountered a set of data before. Data coming from an OLTP system can be rather tricky that way. Fortunately, however, a data warehouse presents a much more stable and controlled data source. Regardless, extracting data from a data warehouse is not time to relax on this, the most basic of ETL requirements. The Market Basket ETL application that extracts data from the data warehouse must be able to control the data such that each set of data and each row of data are allowed to pass through to the Market Basket Table only once.

Completeness

Each Itemset must be complete. This is another basic requirement of every ETL application. A set of data must be complete such that a set of data is a complete set of data, not a partial set of data. The goal of this requirement is to meet the expectation of the analysts. The expectation of analysts is a subtle, yet not quite so subtle, requirement. Analysts have the expectation that the data in an Itemset is, unless otherwise posted, a full complement of the data in that Itemset.

- Date—If a set of data represents all the Itemsets that happened on a specific date, then analysts assume that date is fully represented within that set of Itemsets. All rows of data associated with a date are presented with that date. All rows of data not associated with a date are not presented with that date. Therefore, if an analyst is looking for an Itemset, and does not see that Itemset on a specific date, the analyst does not see it on that date because it did not occur on that date. An analyst can operate with this assumption because the data is complete for that date.
- Objects—The set of objects in an Itemset is all the objects that occurred in that Itemset. If an object is not listed within an Itemset, it is not there because it did not occur within that Itemset. Therefore, if an analyst is looking for an object, and does not see it within an Itemset, the analyst does not see it there because it did not occur within that Itemset. An analyst can operate with this assumption because the data is complete for that Itemset.

An analyst cannot analyze data that is not there. Also, analysts tend to get rather upset when they publish conclusions based on data and then need to revise those conclusions because apparent gaps in that data have been filled in by additional data that led to different conclusions. That sort of behavior does not inspire confidence in a data warehouse or a Market Basket application. To that end, it would be better to delay releasing a set of data in the Market Basket application until that data is complete than to publish an incomplete set of data.

Yes, it is technically feasible to provide metadata that would tell the Market Basket analysts which data is incomplete and what exactly about that data is incomplete. It is also technically feasible to design and deliver a user interface for analysis that would leverage such metadata. That would be an advanced use of metadata for the Completeness requirement. If your data warehouse has such an advanced use of metadata, then you most probably did not continue reading this section on the Completeness requirement down to this paragraph. That being the case, you should accept the "all or nothing" form of the Completeness requirement, such that every set of data in your Market Basket application is complete without any gaps.

Identity

Each group of data must be uniquely identifiable. Each Itemset must be uniquely identifiable within a group of data. Each row of data must be uniquely identifiable within an Itemset.

No, the analysts will not perform any analysis on the unique identifiers of the groups, Itemsets, or rows of data. To that end, the analysts should never be aware of the unique identifiers of the groups, Itemsets, or rows of data. The audience of this requirement is the ETL application, not the analysts.

After a Market Basket application gets busy, the Market Basket ETL application will have multiple iterations of ETL occurring simultaneously. So, the ETL application cannot assume one and only one iteration of ETL will occur at a moment in time. In that way, an ETL can become a victim of its own success. The answer to that problem is control. An ETL application must be able to control each phase of each iteration of ETL individually, and separately from all the other phases and iterations of ETL. The key to such a level of control is the ability to uniquely identify each and every group of data, Itemset, and row.

This requirement does not mean that the ETL application must maintain a mirror image of the data for every unique identifier. That would mean a mirror image for every row, another mirror image for every Itemset, and another mirror image for every group. This requirement is not about maintaining mirror images of data. Rather, this requirement is about the ability to know what the ETL has done, is doing, and has yet to do. To maintain that level of control, an ETL application needs *handles* or *name tags* for the groupings of data. That way, an ETL application can maintain a log of groups of data. By looking in a group of data the ETL application can see all the unique identifiers of the Itemsets, and if necessary, all the unique identifiers of the rows.

That log of ETL activity will eventually become very important in the defense of the ETL application. The day will soon come when an analyst will need to know what data was in the Market Basket application and what data had not yet arrived in the Market Basket application as of a moment in time. That is when the log of ETL activity will become very, very handy. That is also when the ability to tie every row of every Itemset of every group of data back to an ETL activity at a moment in time will become very, very necessary.

Metadata

Metadata comes in two forms: Static Metadata and Dynamic Metadata. Static Metadata is the descriptions and definitions of the structures of the data warehouse and the processes of the ETL application. Static Metadata answers the "What is that?" questions of a data warehouse. Dynamic Metadata is the log of the activities of the ETL application as it populates the data warehouse. Dynamic Metadata answers the "What happened?" questions of a data warehouse.

This is true for all ETL applications, including those that populate a data warehouse and those that populate a Market Basket application. For that reason, the ETL application that populates the data warehouse from which the Market Basket application gets its data may already have established Metadata structures (i.e., log tables) and processes (i.e., logging methods). If that is the case, then the already established ETL structures and processes that are used by the ETL application that populates the data warehouse should also be used by the ETL application that populates the Market Basket application.

If, however, a data warehouse ETL application does not already have Metadata structures and processes already created and operating within the data warehouse ETL, the Market Basket ETL application will have to create those structures and processes for itself. This would actually be a reasonable cause to pause the creation of a Market Basket ETL application until the construction of the data warehouse ETL Metadata structures and processes is complete. The level of confidence in the completeness and identity of the data within the Market Basket ETL application is in large part based on the completeness and identity of the data in the data warehouse ETL. If the data warehouse ETL is not able to guarantee the completeness and identity of its data, then the Market Basket ETL application will most probably not be able to guarantee the completeness and identity of the data it delivers to the Market Basket application.

Data Quality

Data quality is assessed by one of two methods: looking for something that should be there, or looking for something that should not be there. The "looking for something that should be there" method programmatically calculates the interrelationships within the data (e.g., Summed detail rows should equal header rows, units multiplied by unit price should equal total price) and posts an alert when the expected condition has not occurred. The "looking for something that should not be there" method programmatically looks for data that is obviously wrong (e.g., negative unit price, null values, alpha characters in a numeric field) and posts an alert when the unexpected condition has occurred. As the data was extracted from the original source, transformed in the ETL application, and then loaded into the data warehouse, that data should have gone through a data quality assessment.

If the data did indeed go through a data quality assessment on its way to the data warehouse, then the guarantees provided by those data quality assessments extend to the data in the data warehouse and now to the data coming from the data warehouse to the Market Basket application. Even if that is true, the Market Basket ETL application may need to include its own data quality assessments. The analysis of the data in the Market Basket application may expose, or assume, data behaviors or data interrelationships that are not already guaranteed by the data warehouse ETL. If that is the case, then the Market Basket ETL application will need to assess the data from the data warehouse in the Market Basket ETL application.

If the data did not go through a data quality assessment on its way into the data warehouse, then the Market Basket ETL must provide all the guarantees for all the data that comes from the data warehouse to the Market Basket application. Either way, the data quality methods are the same. The only difference is the inclusion of specific data quality assessments, which will lead to specific data quality guarantees.

If the data warehouse ETL does not already assess the quality of the data on its way to the data warehouse, that would be another reasonable cause to pause the creation of the Market Basket ETL until the data warehouse ETL has included data quality assessments in its processes. This may seem rather picky, but it is not. The time and energy expended in guaranteeing the data quality within the data warehouse should be directly associated with the data warehouse and not the Market Basket application. If that time and energy expenditure to create data quality assessments in the data warehouse is associated with the Market Basket application, it will diminish the perceived ROI and the Market Basket application and increase the perceived responsibilities of the Market Basket ETL. In that situation, the Market Basket ETL will be perceived to be the consumer and owner of the data warehouse ETL. While that may be true insofar as the human team members for the data warehouse and the Market Basket ETL may indeed be the same persons, in terms of management's perception of budgets, roles, and responsibilities, the Market Basket application can only be best served by incurring only those expenses directly associated with the Market Basket application and owning only those responsibilities directly achieved by the Market Basket ETL.

MARKET BASKET ETL DESIGN

ETL is often thought to be an application, or set of applications, that retrieves data from an operational source system, conforms it to the design of a data warehouse, and then loads that conformed data into the data warehouse. So, it may seem strange to think of ETL as a set of applications that pull data from a data warehouse, conform that data to the design of a Market Basket application (or any other datamart), and then load that data into the Market Basket application (or, again, any other datamart). But, in the world of data warehousing, that is exactly what happens. ETL is a generalized name given to applications that move data in a controlled and intelligent fashion from a source platform to a destination platform.

Typically, ETL pulls data from a data warehouse and loads that data into a separate datamart for one of two primary reasons. The first reason is the separation of resource consumption. Architecturally, a data warehouse is a large data store with many customers. If a specific group of customers or application requires query response times and access patterns that will contend with the "large data store" design of a data warehouse and/or the other customers, a datamart allows that group or application to have clear and unchallenged access to the data they require. The second reason is the separation of structure designs. If a specific group or application requires that the data be provided in a structural design that is not conducive to the other customers of the data warehouse (and, yes, the Market Basket BI Table is not conducive to the other customers of a data warehouse), a datamart allows that group or application to have data in the structural design they require.

In the context of a Market Basket application, the Market Basket BI Table is a datamart that allows the Market Basket analysts to have their data in a form that is conducive to Market Basket Analysis. The Market Basket ETL application pulls data from the data warehouse, conforms it to the design of the Market Basket BI Table, and then loads that data into the Market Basket BI Table. Data in the Market Basket BI Table is then available for analysis. The Market Basket ETL application is, therefore, a datamart specifically designed for the purpose of Market Basket Analysis, which is populated by the Market Basket ETL application.

Unless a value-adding, ROI-generating requirement compels the use of real-time ETL, typically ETL applications are batch applications. Even then, real-time ETL is used only for tactical data that is sensitive to the immediate delivery of data from a source system. Market Basket analysts are looking at the data strategically, not tactically. The search for broad patterns over long periods of time is by definition strategic in nature. For that reason, Market Basket ETL is a batch ETL application. So, the first design decision of a Market Basket ETL application is that Market Basket ETL is a batch, not a real-time, application.

Step 1: Extract from a Fact Table and Load to a Market Basket Table

The source data for a Market Basket application is a Fact table in a data warehouse. That Fact table may contain sales transactions at a retail store, dinner receipts from a restaurant, work orders from a service provider, or click streams from an online retailer. Because the source table is a Fact table from the data warehouse, the Market Basket application can trust the quality of the data in that Fact table. If the quality of the data in the Fact table is not trustworthy, then the quality of the data in the data warehouse should be addressed before the Market Basket Analysis can begin.

A very small sample Fact table is shown in Table 7.1. The data in Table 7.1 will be the source of the sample tables in the remainder of this chapter.

The first operation of the Market Basket ETL application is the extract from the Fact table and load into the Market Basket Table. Figure 7.1 shows this as one operation. A mature ETL application will assess the quality of the data as it passes by. While the Market Basket ETL application has some level of trust in the source Fact table, data quality assessments still provide some confidence that the Market Basket ETL application has maintained

TABLE 7.1

Fact Table

Temset_key	Object_key	Quantity	Dollars
1	15	1	$15.31
2	16	1	$12.21
2	16	1	$12.21
2	43	1	$14.32
2	57	1	$9.09
2	57	1	$9.09
2	64	1	$12.37
3	15	1	$15.31
3	15	1	$15.31
3	16	1	$12.21
3	64	1	$12.37
3	78	1	$13.44
3	78	1	$13.44
3	78	1	$13.44
3	78	1	$13.44
3	98	1	$2.45
4	43	1	$14.32
4	43	1	$14.32
4	43	1	$14.32
4	57	1	$9.09
4	78	1	$13.44
4	87	1	$16.87
4	98	1	$2.45

```
DELETE FROM
MARKET_BASKET_TABLE
;
INSERT INTO MARKET_BASKET_TABLE
(ITEMSET_KEY
,OBJECT_KEY
,QUANTITY
,DOLLARS)
SELECT
ITEMSET_KEY
,OBJECT_KEY
,SUM(QUANTITY) AS QUANTITY_SUM
,SUM(DOLLARS) AS DOLLARS_SUM
FROM FACT_TABLE
GROUP BY
ITEMSET_KEY
,OBJECT_KEY
;
```

FIGURE 7.1
Load Market Basket Table.

the quality and integrity of the data as it passes through the Market Basket ETL application. Chapters 8 and 9 of *Building and Maintaining a Data Warehouse* explain methods by which metadata and data quality work together to warranty data as it passes through an ETL application.

At the end of this initial step, the Market Basket Table will contain a set of rows for every Itemset. Each Itemset will be uniquely identified by its Itemset_Key. The Itemset_Key in Table 7.2 is a single sequential numeric value. This numeric key structure may not be true in your data warehouse and your Market Basket application.

The Itemset_Key is defined by its role and purpose, not by its structure. An Itemset_Key must uniquely identify each and every individual transaction such that each and every transaction has one and only one Itemset_Key, and each and every Itemset_Key has one and only one transaction. The Itemset_Key can never repeat for another transaction. The Itemset_Key can include, and usually is, a compound key including a date. The inclusion of a date in the Itemset_Key means the Itemset_Key, sans the date portion, must be unique only within a twenty-four-hour period, rather than all of eternity. Twenty-four hours is a much more manageable span of time. So, frequently the date is included in the Itemset_Key. As explained in Chapter 5, date and time are often included in the Itemset_Key as they allow the analyst to stratify the data in a Market Basket Analysis application.

TABLE 7.2

Market Basket Table

Itemset_key	Object_key	Quantity	Dollars
1	0	0	$0.00
1	15	1	$15.31
2	16	2	$24.42
2	43	1	$14.32
2	57	2	$18.18
2	64	1	$12.37
3	15	2	$30.62
3	16	1	$12.21
3	64	1	$12.37
3	78	4	$53.76
3	98	1	$2.45
4	43	3	$42.96
4	57	1	$9.09
4	78	1	$13.44
4	87	1	$16.87
4	98	1	$2.45

Two transformations to the data in an Itemset occur in this step. The first step is for the case of the Single Object Itemset. If an Itemset includes only one object, this step will add a "mirror" row of data for the same Itemset_Key, but with zero in the Object_Key and numeric metric columns (i.e., Quantity and Dollars). The reason for this addition to the data extracted from the Fact table is that in the recursive join, which will happen in the next step, every Itemset must have a second row with which it can join. In the case of a Single Object Itemset, that second row must be manufactured by the Market Basket ETL application.

The second transformation is the summation of multiple Fact table rows into one row per object. A single object may exist in many rows of data in a Fact table. But, for the purposes of Market Basket Analysis, the presence of that object in an Itemset is binary, that is, the object is either in the Itemset or not in the Itemset. So the first operation includes a SUM and GROUP BY statement to consolidate multiple rows of data for a single object into one row of data for a single object. This operation also allows the recursive join in the next step to trust that an object will not be able to join to itself. If, for a single object, there is no second row, then that object will not be able to join to itself.

Step 2: Recursively Join the Market Basket Table and Load a Market Basket BI Table

The second step joins the Market Basket Table to itself by referencing the Market Basket Table twice. The first reference to the Market Basket Table has the alias *A*. The second reference to the Market Basket Table has the alias *B*. In the RDBMS platform this has the effect of operating on the same Market Basket Table as though it were two separate tables. Chapter 6 explained a database design that will optimize this recursive join.

Figure 7.2 shows this recursive join and load into the Market Basket BI Table as a single operation. A Market Basket ETL application may perform this operation in one step, or it may perform it as a two-step operation. The important aspects of the SQL in Figure 7.2 are the recursive join and the nonequality.

```
DELETE FROM MARKET_BASKET_BI_TABLE
;
INSERT INTO MARKET_BASKET_BI_TABLE
( ITEMSET_KEY
, DRIVER_OBJECT_KEY
, DRIVER_QUANTITY
, DRIVER_DOLLARS
, DRIVER_COUNT
, CORR_OBJECT_KEY
, CORR_QUANTITY
, CORR_DOLLARS
, CORR_COUNT)
SELECT
A.ITEMSET_KEY
, A.OBJECT_KEY AS DRIVER_OBJECT_KEY
, A.QUANTITY AS DRIVER_QUANTITY
, A.DOLLARS AS DRIVER_DOLLARS
, 1 AS DRIVER_COUNT
, B.OBJECT_KEY AS CORR_OBJECT_KEY
, B.QUANTITY AS CORR_QUANTITY
, B.DOLLARS AS CORR_DOLLARS
, 1 AS CORR_COUNT
FROM MARKET_BASKET_TABLE A
INNER JOIN MARKET_BASKET_TABLE B
ON A.ITEMSET_KEY = B.ITEMSET_KEY
WHERE A.OBJECT_KEY <> B.OBJECT_KEY
AND A.OBJECT_KEY <> 0
;
```

FIGURE 7.2
Load Market Basket BI Table.

The recursive join juxtaposes all the objects in an Itemset against all the other objects in an Itemset. This is the crux of the Market Basket Analysis application as it provides the first answer to the question in the Market Basket Scope Statement. The recursive join juxtaposes the Driver and Correlation Objects in a single row of data for the first time.

The inequality at the bottom of Figure 7.2 (A.OBJECT_KEY <> B.OBJECT_KEY) prevents an object in the Itemset from joining to itself. Without that inequality, all objects in an Itemset would have one row wherein that object is both the Driver Object and the Correlation Object. However, with that inequality in place, an object can be only the Driver Object or the Correlation Object, never both.

The other inequality at the bottom of Figure 7.2 (A.OBJECT_KEY <> 0) prevents the zero-filled row that was manufactured for the case of the Single Object Itemset from appearing as a Driver Object. Table 7.3 shows the effect of this inequality. The first two rows of Table 7.3 show the Single Object Itemset as it would be without the inequality. In one row, the Object_Key 15 is the Driver Object and Object_Key 0 is the Correlation Object. In the other row, the Object_Key 0 is the Driver Object and Object_Key 15 is the Correlation Object. The meaning of the zero-filled row for the Single Object Itemset is to indicate that nothing happened. When a customer purchases one item, what else did that customer purchase? Nothing. So, rather than allow a zero-filled row to be a Driver Object, the inequality excludes rows wherein the Driver_Object_Key = 0.

The Market Basket Table was a staging table. Reading the data from the Market Basket Table, the SQL in Figure 7.2 performs the recursive join, prevents objects from being both the Driver Object and the Correlation Object, and prevents the zero-filled object from being a Driver Object as it then loads the data into the Market Basket BI Table. The output of this SQL and the rows in the Market Basket BI Table are shown in Table 7.4.

The DRIVER_COUNT and CORR_COUNT output fields facilitate a count of the distinct objects in an Itemset. These two fields are manufactured in the SQL by the statements "1 AS DRIVER_COUNT" and "1 AS CORR_COUNT." The manufacture of these fields could be delayed until the next step. However, understanding and validating the data in the Market Basket tables is confusing enough on its own. The analysts in a Market Basket Analysis effort are often better served by the presence of these COUNT fields in the Market Basket BI Table than by assuming their presence in the Market Basket BI View.

TABLE 7.3

Single Object Itemset

Itemset Key	Driver Object Key	Driver Quantity	Driver Dollars	Driver Count	Corr Object Key	Corr Quantity	Corr Dollars	Corr Count
1	15	1	$15.31	1	0	0	$0.00	1
1	0	0	$0.00	1	15	1	$15.31	1

Itemset Key	Driver Object Key	Driver Quantity	Driver Dollars	Driver Count	Corr Object Key	Corr Quantity	Corr Dollars	Corr Count
1	15	1	$15.31	1	0	0	$0.00	1

TABLE 7.4

Market Basket BI Table

Itemset Key	Driver Object Key	Driver Quantity	Driver Dollars	Driver Count	Corr Object Key	Corr Quantity	Corr Dollars	Corr Count
1	15	1	$15.31	1	0	0	$0.00	1
2	16	2	$24.42	1	43	1	$14.32	1
2	16	2	$24.42	1	57	2	$18.18	1
2	16	2	$24.42	1	64	1	$12.37	1
2	43	1	$14.32	1	16	2	$24.42	1
2	43	1	$14.32	1	57	2	$18.18	1
2	43	1	$14.32	1	64	1	$12.37	1
2	57	2	$18.18	1	16	2	$24.42	1
2	57	2	$18.18	1	43	1	$14.32	1
2	57	2	$18.18	1	64	1	$12.37	1
2	64	1	$12.37	1	16	2	$24.42	1
2	64	1	$12.37	1	43	1	$14.32	1
2	64	1	$12.37	1	57	2	$18.18	1
3	15	2	$30.62	1	16	1	$12.21	1
3	15	2	$30.62	1	64	1	$12.37	1
3	15	2	$30.62	1	78	4	$53.76	1
3	15	2	$30.62	1	98	1	$2.45	1
3	16	1	$12.21	1	15	2	$30.62	1
3	16	1	$12.21	1	64	1	$12.37	1
3	16	1	$12.21	1	78	4	$53.76	1
3	16	1	$12.21	1	98	1	$2.45	1
3	64	1	$12.37	1	15	2	$30.62	1
3	64	1	$12.37	1	16	1	$12.21	1
3	64	1	$12.37	1	78	4	$53.76	1
3	64	1	$12.37	1	98	1	$2.45	1
3	78	4	$53.76	1	15	2	$30.62	1
3	78	4	$53.76	1	16	1	$12.21	1
3	78	4	$53.76	1	64	1	$12.37	1
3	78	4	$53.76	1	98	1	$2.45	1
3	98	1	$2.45	1	15	2	$30.62	1
3	98	1	$2.45	1	16	1	$12.21	1
3	98	1	$2.45	1	64	1	$12.37	1
3	98	1	$2.45	1	78	4	$53.76	1
4	43	3	$42.96	1	57	1	$9.09	1
4	43	3	$42.96	1	78	1	$13.44	1
4	43	3	$42.96	1	87	1	$16.87	1

(*Continued*)

TABLE 7.4 (CONTINUED)

Market Basket BI Table

Itemset Key	Driver Object Key	Driver Quantity	Driver Dollars	Driver Count	Corr Object Key	Corr Quantity	Corr Dollars	Corr Count
4	43	3	$42.96	1	98	1	$2.45	1
4	57	1	$9.09	1	43	3	$42.96	1
4	57	1	$9.09	1	78	1	$13.44	1
4	57	1	$9.09	1	87	1	$16.87	1
4	57	1	$9.09	1	98	1	$2.45	1
4	78	1	$13.44	1	43	3	$42.96	1
4	78	1	$13.44	1	57	1	$9.09	1
4	78	1	$13.44	1	87	1	$16.87	1
4	78	1	$13.44	1	98	1	$2.45	1
4	87	1	$16.87	1	43	3	$42.96	1
4	87	1	$16.87	1	57	1	$9.09	1
4	87	1	$16.87	1	78	1	$13.44	1
4	87	1	$16.87	1	98	1	$2.45	1
4	98	1	$2.45	1	43	3	$42.96	1
4	98	1	$2.45	1	57	1	$9.09	1
4	98	1	$2.45	1	78	1	$13.44	1
4	98	1	$2.45	1	87	1	$16.87	1

The Market Basket BI Table is the first table that may be customer-facing toward an analyst. As the Market Basket BI Table juxtaposes the Driver Object and Correlation Object with all the metric measurements included, it can be the terminus for an iteration of analysis.

Step 3: Arithmetic Juxtaposition of Driver Objects and Correlation Objects

The Market Basket BI View, shown in Figure 7.3, arithmetically removes the Itemset from the juxtaposition of the Driver Object and Correlation Object. The additive metrics in the Market Basket Table (i.e., Quantity and Dollars) are both present in the Market Basket BI View as summations of the Quantity and Dollar fields. The Market Basket Analysis BI View also calculates ratios based on the summed additive metrics. The ratios provide a relative frame of reference that enhances the inferences that can be gleaned from the Market Basket Analysis.

```
SELECT
DRIVER.DRIVER_OBJECT_KEY
, CORR.CORR_OBJECT_KEY
, DRIVER.DRIVER_QUANTITY_SUM
, DRIVER.DRIVER_DOLLARS_SUM
, DRIVER.DRIVER_COUNT_SUM
, CORR.CORR_QUANTITY_SUM
, CORR.CORR_DOLLARS_SUM
, CORR.CORR_COUNT_SUM
, CORR.CORR_QUANTITY_SUM/DRIVER.DRIVER_QUANTITY_SUM AS
QUANTITY_RATIO
, CORR.CORR_DOLLARS_SUM/DRIVER.DRIVER_DOLLARS_SUM AS DOLLARS_RATIO
, CORR.CORR_COUNT_SUM/DRIVER.DRIVER_COUNT_SUM AS COUNT_RATIO
FROM
(SELECT
DRIVER_OBJECT_KEY
,SUM(DRIVER_QUANTITY) AS DRIVER_QUANTITY_SUM
,SUM(DRIVER_DOLLARS) AS DRIVER_DOLLARS_SUM
,SUM(DRIVER_COUNT) AS DRIVER_COUNT_SUM
FROM(SELECT
ITEMSET_KEY
,DRIVER_OBJECT_KEY
,DRIVER_QUANTITY
,DRIVER_DOLLARS
,DRIVER_COUNT
FROM MARKET_BASKET_BI_TABLE
GROUP BY
ITEMSET_KEY
,DRIVER_OBJECT_KEY
,DRIVER_QUANTITY
,DRIVER_DOLLARS
,DRIVER_COUNT)
GROUP BY
DRIVER_OBJECT_KEY)DRIVER
INNER JOIN
(SELECT
DRIVER_OBJECT_KEY
,CORR_OBJECT_KEY
,SUM(CORR_QUANTITY) AS CORR_QUANTITY_SUM
,SUM(CORR_DOLLARS) AS CORR_DOLLARS_SUM
,SUM(CORR_COUNT) AS CORR_COUNT_SUM
FROM MARKET_BASKET_BI_TABLE
GROUP BY
DRIVER_OBJECT_KEY
,CORR_OBJECT_KEY)CORR
ON DRIVER.DRIVER_OBJECT_KEY = CORR.DRIVER_OBJECT_KEY
ORDER BY
DRIVER.DRIVER_OBJECT_KEY
```

FIGURE 7.3
Market Basket Analysis BI View.

The output from the Market Basket Analysis BI View, shown in Table 7.5, includes the additive and relative data columns. If a Market Basket Analysis effort is early in its life cycle, it will perform more of an analytics function than a reporting function. If that is the case, then the Market Basket Analysis BI View may persist as only a view. If, however, the Market Basket Analysis effort is in its maturity, then the stable

TABLE 7.5

Market Basket Analysis BI View

Driver Object Key	Corr Object Key	Driver Quantity Sum	Driver Dollars Sum	Driver Count Sum	Corr Quantitym Sum	Corr Dollars Sum	Corr Count Sum	Quantity Ratio	Dollars Ratio	Count Ratio
15	0	3	$45.93	2	0	$0.00	1	0.0000%	0.0000%	50.0000%
15	16	3	$45.93	2	1	$12.21	1	33.3333%	26.5839%	50.0000%
15	64	3	$45.93	2	1	$12.37	1	33.3333%	26.9323%	50.0000%
15	78	3	$45.93	2	4	$53.76	1	133.3333%	117.0477%	50.0000%
15	98	3	$45.93	2	1	$2.45	1	33.3333%	5.3342%	50.0000%
16	15	3	$36.63	2	2	$30.62	1	66.6667%	83.5927%	50.0000%
16	43	3	$36.63	2	1	$14.32	1	33.3333%	39.0936%	50.0000%
16	57	3	$36.63	2	2	$18.18	1	66.6667%	49.6314%	50.0000%
16	64	3	$36.63	2	2	$24.74	2	66.6667%	67.5403%	100.0000%
16	78	3	$36.63	2	4	$53.76	1	133.3333%	146.7649%	50.0000%
16	98	3	$36.63	2	1	$2.45	1	33.3333%	6.6885%	50.0000%
43	16	4	$57.28	2	2	$24.42	1	50.0000%	42.6327%	50.0000%
43	57	4	$57.28	2	3	$27.27	2	75.0000%	47.6082%	100.0000%
43	64	4	$57.28	2	1	$12.37	1	25.0000%	21.5957%	50.0000%
43	78	4	$57.28	2	1	$13.44	1	25.0000%	23.4637%	50.0000%
43	87	4	$57.28	2	1	$16.87	1	25.0000%	29.4518%	50.0000%
43	98	4	$57.28	2	1	$2.45	1	25.0000%	4.2772%	50.0000%
57	16	3	$27.27	2	2	$24.42	1	66.6667%	89.5490%	50.0000%
57	43	3	$27.27	2	4	$57.28	2	133.3333%	210.0477%	100.0000%

(*Continued*)

TABLE 7.5 (CONTINUED)
Market Basket Analysis BI View

Driver Object Key	Corr Object Key	Driver Quantity Sum	Driver Dollars Sum	Driver Count Sum	Corr Quantitym Sum	Corr Dollars Sum	Corr Count Sum	Quantity Ratio	Dollars Ratio	Count Ratio
57	64	3	$27.27	2	1	$12.37	1	33.3333%	45.3612%	50.0000%
57	78	3	$27.27	2	1	$13.44	1	33.3333%	49.2849%	50.0000%
57	87	3	$27.27	2	1	$16.87	1	33.3333%	61.8629%	50.0000%
57	98	3	$27.27	2	1	$2.45	1	33.3333%	8.9842%	50.0000%
64	15	1	$12.37	1	2	$30.62	1	200.0000%	247.5344%	100.0000%
64	16	1	$12.37	1	3	$36.63	2	300.0000%	296.1196%	200.0000%
64	43	1	$12.37	1	1	$14.32	1	100.0000%	115.7639%	100.0000%
64	57	1	$12.37	1	2	$18.18	1	200.0000%	146.9685%	100.0000%
64	78	1	$12.37	1	4	$53.76	1	400.0000%	434.5998%	100.0000%
64	98	1	$12.37	1	1	$2.45	1	100.0000%	19.8060%	100.0000%
78	15	5	$67.20	2	2	$30.62	1	40.0000%	45.5655%	50.0000%
78	16	5	$67.20	2	1	$12.21	1	20.0000%	18.1696%	50.0000%
78	43	5	$67.20	2	3	$42.96	1	60.0000%	63.9286%	50.0000%
78	57	5	$67.20	2	1	$9.09	1	20.0000%	13.5268%	50.0000%
78	64	5	$67.20	2	1	$12.37	1	20.0000%	18.4077%	50.0000%
78	87	5	$67.20	2	1	$16.87	1	20.0000%	25.1042%	50.0000%
78	98	5	$67.20	2	2	$4.90	2	40.0000%	7.2917%	100.0000%
87	43	1	$16.87	1	3	$42.96	1	300.0000%	254.6532%	100.0000%
87	57	1	$16.87	1	1	$9.09	1	100.0000%	53.8826%	100.0000%
87	78	1	$16.87	1	1	$13.44	1	100.0000%	79.6680%	100.0000%

87	98	1	$16.87	1	1	$2.45	1	100.0000%	14.5228%	100.0000%
98	15	1	$2.45	1	2	$30.62	1	200.0000%	1249.7959%	100.0000%
98	16	1	$2.45	1	1	$12.21	1	100.0000%	498.3673%	100.0000%
98	43	1	$2.45	1	3	$42.96	1	300.0000%	1753.4694%	100.0000%
98	57	1	$2.45	1	1	$9.09	1	100.0000%	371.0204%	100.0000%
98	64	1	$2.45	1	1	$12.37	1	100.0000%	504.8980%	100.0000%
98	78	1	$2.45	1	5	$67.20	2	500.0000%	2742.8571%	200.0000%
98	87	1	$2.45	1	1	$16.87	1	100.0000%	688.5714%	100.0000%

and repeated Market Basket Reporting functions have begun. If that is the case, then the SQL in the Market Basket Analysis BI View should be performed as a final step in an ETL application that culminates in a Market Basket Analysis BI report. That would mean the Market Basket Analysis BI View is a table that can be referenced by the Market Basket Reporting application and the business analysts who receive reports from that application, which would mean the table created from the Market Basket Analysis BI View is the terminus of the Market Basket Analysis, rather than the Market Basket BI Table in Step 2.

Step 4: Load a Market Basket BI Table Using a Correlation Hierarchy

The Market Basket Analysis BI View is very powerful in that it provides cumulative and relative information about the correlations between objects in the Itemsets of an enterprise. That information, powerful as it may be, is limited in that it only considers objects that are hierarchical peers. An object is probably a member of hierarchical groupings (e.g., departments, regions, distribution channels). A successful Market Basket Analysis effort will soon lead to an analysis of the correlations between an object and hierarchies above that object. A retail clothing store might analyze the correlations between each individual shirt and the hierarchical group called "pants." An automotive parts retailer might analyze the correlations between each individual brand of motor oil and the hierarchical group called "miscellaneous" (i.e., those little knickknacks at the front of the store). For that form of Market Basket Analysis, the objects must be juxtaposed with their hierarchical grouping.

To facilitate this discussion the hierarchical table in Table 7.6 will provide the hierarchies. The hierarchies in Table 7.6 can mean anything. The names of the hierarchies are not important. The presence and groupings of the hierarchies constitute the relevance of Table 7.6.

The Market Basket data already exists in its juxtaposed form in the Market Basket BI Table. This step will leverage the presence of the juxtaposed data in the Market Basket BI Table. The SQL in Figure 7.4 loads a new Market Basket table called MARKET_BASKET_BI_TABLE_CORR_HIERARCHY. This reflects an architectural decision to segregate separate sets of Market Basket data into separate tables, rather than by a type code in a single table. By the time a Market Basket Analysis effort reaches maturity,

TABLE 7.6

Hierarchy Dimension

Object_key	Hierarchy_key
78	1124
98	1124
16	6543
43	6543
64	6543
15	9792
57	9792
87	9792
0	0

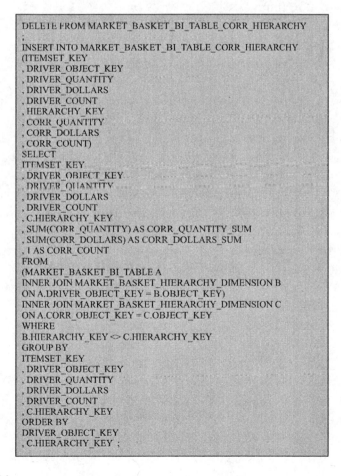

```
DELETE FROM MARKET_BASKET_BI_TABLE_CORR_HIERARCHY
;
INSERT INTO MARKET_BASKET_BI_TABLE_CORR_HIERARCHY
(ITEMSET_KEY
, DRIVER_OBJECT_KEY
, DRIVER_QUANTITY
, DRIVER_DOLLARS
, DRIVER_COUNT
, HIERARCHY_KEY
, CORR_QUANTITY
, CORR_DOLLARS
, CORR_COUNT)
SELECT
ITEMSET_KEY
, DRIVER_OBJECT_KEY
, DRIVER_QUANTITY
, DRIVER_DOLLARS
, DRIVER_COUNT
, C.HIERARCHY_KEY
, SUM(CORR_QUANTITY) AS CORR_QUANTITY_SUM
, SUM(CORR_DOLLARS) AS CORR_DOLLARS_SUM
, 1 AS CORR_COUNT
FROM
(MARKET_BASKET_BI_TABLE A
INNER JOIN MARKET_BASKET_HIERARCHY_DIMENSION B
ON A.DRIVER_OBJECT_KEY = B.OBJECT_KEY)
INNER JOIN MARKET_BASKET_HIERARCHY_DIMENSION C
ON A.CORR_OBJECT_KEY = C.OBJECT_KEY
WHERE
B.HIERARCHY_KEY <> C.HIERARCHY_KEY
GROUP BY
ITEMSET_KEY
, DRIVER_OBJECT_KEY
, DRIVER_QUANTITY
, DRIVER_DOLLARS
, DRIVER_COUNT
, C.HIERARCHY_KEY
ORDER BY
DRIVER_OBJECT_KEY
, C.HIERARCHY_KEY ;
```

FIGURE 7.4

Load Market Basket BI Table with correlation hierarchy.

you'll have quite a few efforts and even more tables present at any one time. So, a method for keeping them organized should be chosen earlier rather than later.

The SQL in Figure 7.4 performs three primary functions as it extracts data from the Market Basket BI Table and loads it into the MARKET_ BASKET_BI_TABLE_CORR_HIERARCHY table. First, the "1 AS CORR_COUNT" statement resets the counter that will be used to count the number of occurrences of each hierarchical group within each Itemset. When combining objects into their hierarchical groups this counter is not additive. So, it is reset back to one, meaning the hierarchical group appeared once in an Itemset. This is true even if a hierarchical group was represented by two hundred objects. In the binary sense, a hierarchical was in, or not in, an Itemset.

The second primary function of the SQL in Figure 7.4 is that it joins the Driver Object to the hierarchy and then joins the Correlation Object to the hierarchy as a separate alias. The use of a separate alias for the hierarchy join causes the RDBMS platform to handle the two joins and join table independently of each other, even though they are the same tables.

The third primary function of the SQL in Figure 7.4 is that it excludes those rows that join to the same hierarchical group for both the Driver Object and the Correlation Object. This has the effect of preventing a Driver Object from correlating to its own hierarchical group, which is conceptually the same as preventing an object from correlating with itself. The output of this is shown in Table 7.7.

The Market Basket Analysis BI View shown in Figure 7.5 is very similar to that in Figure 7.3. The difference is that the Correlation Object in Figure 7.5 has the name Hierarchy_Key, not CORR_OBJECT_KEY. Again, this reflects the need to organize the tables in a Market Basket Analysis application, by using column names that reflect the nature of the data in them. But, in general, the SQL in Figure 7.5 operates in a fashion similar to the SQL in Figure 7.3.

The output of the SQL in Figure 7.5 is shown in Table 7.8. The data in Table 7.8 can be presented in the form of a view or a physical table. The criteria for that decision are the same as the criteria for the decision to present the Market Basket Analysis BI View as a view or a physical table. A Market Basket Analysis effort that is still in the analysis, and not the reporting, phase would benefit from the use of a view and avoidance of the overhead of another table. A Market Basket Analysis effort that is in

TABLE 7.7

Market Basket BI Table with Correlation Hierarchy

Itemset Key	Driver Object Key	Driver Quantity	Driver Dollars	Driver Count	Hierarchy Key	Corr Quantity	Corr Dollars	Corr Count
1	15	1	$15.31	1	0	0	$0.00	1
2	16	2	$24.42	1	9792	2	$18.18	1
2	43	1	$14.32	1	9792	2	$18.18	1
2	57	2	$18.18	1	6543	4	$51.11	1
2	64	1	$12.37	1	9792	2	$18.18	1
3	15	2	$30.62	1	1124	5	$56.21	1
3	15	2	$30.62	1	6543	2	$24.58	1
3	16	1	$12.21	1	1124	5	$56.21	1
3	16	1	$12.21	1	9792	2	$30.62	1
3	64	1	$12.37	1	1124	5	$56.21	1
3	64	1	$12.37	1	9792	2	$30.62	1
3	78	4	$53.76	1	6543	2	$24.58	1
3	78	4	$53.76	1	9792	2	$30.62	1
3	98	1	$2.45	1	6543	2	$24.58	1
3	98	1	$2.45	1	9792	2	$30.62	1
4	43	3	$42.96	1	1124	2	$15.89	1
4	43	3	$42.96	1	9792	2	$25.96	1
4	57	1	$9.09	1	1124	2	$15.89	1
4	57	1	$9.09	1	6543	3	$42.96	1
4	78	1	$13.44	1	6543	3	$42.96	1
4	78	1	$13.44	1	9792	2	$25.96	1
4	87	1	$16.87	1	1124	2	$15.89	1
4	87	1	$16.87	1	6543	3	$42.96	1
4	98	1	$2.45	1	6543	3	$42.96	1
4	98	1	$2.45	1	9792	2	$25.96	1

the reporting phase would benefit from the use of a physical table, which would be a datamart.

Step 5: Load a Market Basket BI Table Using a Driver Hierarchy

If a Market Basket Analysis effort can consider the correlations from objects leading to hierarchical groups, then that same Market Basket Analysis effort can also consider the correlations from hierarchical groups leading to objects. Using again the hierarchical groups in Table 7.6, the SQL in Figure 7.6 extracts data from the Market Basket

```
SELECT
DRIVER.DRIVER_OBJECT_KEY
, CORR.HIERARCHY_KEY
, DRIVER.DRIVER_QUANTITY_SUM
, DRIVER.DRIVER_DOLLARS_SUM
, DRIVER.DRIVER_COUNT_SUM
, CORR.CORR_QUANTITY_SUM
, CORR.CORR_DOLLARS_SUM
, CORR.CORR_COUNT_SUM
, CORR.CORR_QUANTITY_SUM/DRIVER.DRIVER_QUANTITY_SUM AS QUANTITY_RATIO
, CORR.CORR_DOLLARS_SUM/DRIVER.DRIVER_DOLLARS_SUM AS DOLLARS_RATIO
, CORR.CORR_COUNT_SUM/DRIVER.DRIVER_COUNT_SUM AS COUNT_RATIO
FROM
(SELECT
DRIVER_OBJECT_KEY
,SUM(DRIVER_QUANTITY) AS DRIVER_QUANTITY_SUM
,SUM(DRIVER_DOLLARS) AS DRIVER_DOLLARS_SUM
,SUM(DRIVER_COUNT) AS DRIVER_COUNT_SUM
FROM(SELECT
ITEMSET_KEY
,DRIVER_OBJECT_KEY
,DRIVER_QUANTITY
,DRIVER_DOLLARS
,DRIVER_COUNT
FROM MARKET_BASKET_BI_TABLE_CORR_HIERARCHY
GROUP BY
ITEMSET_KEY
,DRIVER_OBJECT_KEY
,DRIVER_QUANTITY
,DRIVER_DOLLARS
,DRIVER_COUNT)
GROUP BY
DRIVER_OBJECT_KEY)DRIVER
INNER JOIN
(SELECT
DRIVER_OBJECT_KEY
,HIERARCHY_KEY
,SUM(CORR_QUANTITY) AS CORR_QUANTITY_SUM
,SUM(CORR_DOLLARS) AS CORR_DOLLARS_SUM
,SUM(CORR_COUNT) AS CORR_COUNT_SUM
FROM MARKET_BASKET_BI_TABLE_CORR_HIERARCHY
GROUP BY
DRIVER_OBJECT_KEY
,HIERARCHY_KEY)CORR
ON DRIVER.DRIVER_OBJECT_KEY = CORR.DRIVER_OBJECT_KEY
ORDER BY
DRIVER.DRIVER_OBJECT_KEY
, CORR.HIERARCHY_KEY
```

FIGURE 7.5
Market Basket Analysis BI View with correlation hierarchy.

BI Table and loads the MARKET_BASKET_BI_TABLE_DRIVER_HIERARCHY table.

The SQL in Figure 7.6 performs three primary functions as it extracts data from the Market Basket BI Table and loads it into the MARKET_BASKET_BI_TABLE_DRIVER_HIERARCHY table. First, the "1 AS DRIVER_COUNT" statement resets the counter that will be used to count the number of occurrences of each hierarchical group within each Itemset. When combining objects into their hierarchical groups this

TABLE 7.8

Market Basket Analysis BI View with Correlation Hierarchy

Driver Object Key	Hierarchy Key	Driver Quantity Sum	Driver Dollars Sum	Driver Count Sum	Corr Quantity Sum	Corr Dollars Sum	Corr Count Sum	Quantity Ratio	Dollars Ratio	Count Ratio
15	0	3	$45.93	2	0	$0.00	1	0.0000%	0.0000%	50.0000%
15	1124	3	$45.93	2	5	$56.21	1	166.6667%	122.3819%	50.0000%
15	6543	3	$45.93	2	2	$24.58	1	66.6667%	53.5162%	50.0000%
16	1124	3	$36.63	2	5	$56.21	1	166.6667%	153.4535%	50.0000%
16	9792	3	$36.63	2	4	$48.80	2	133.3333%	133.2241%	100.0000%
43	1124	4	$57.28	2	2	$15.89	1	50.0000%	27.7409%	50.0000%
43	9792	4	$57.28	2	4	$44.14	2	100.0000%	77.0601%	100.0000%
57	1124	3	$27.27	2	2	$15.89	1	66.6667%	58.2692%	50.0000%
57	6543	3	$27.27	2	7	$94.07	2	233.3333%	344.9578%	100.0000%
64	1124	2	$24.74	2	5	$56.21	1	250.0000%	227.2029%	50.0000%
64	9792	2	$24.74	2	4	$48.80	2	200.0000%	197.2514%	100.0000%
78	6543	5	$67.20	2	5	$67.54	2	100.0000%	100.5060%	100.0000%
78	9792	5	$67.20	2	4	$56.58	2	80.0000%	84.1964%	100.0000%
87	1124	1	$16.87	1	2	$15.89	1	200.0000%	94.1909%	100.0000%
87	6543	1	$16.87	1	3	$42.96	1	300.0000%	254.6532%	100.0000%
98	6543	2	$4.90	2	5	$67.54	2	250.0000%	1378.3673%	100.0000%
98	9792	2	$4.90	2	4	$56.58	2	200.0000%	1154.6939%	100.0000%

```
DELETE FROM MARKET_BASKET_BI_TABLE_DRIVER_HIERARCHY
;
INSERT INTO MARKET_BASKET_BI_TABLE_DRIVER_HIERARCHY
(ITEMSET_KEY
,HIERARCHY_KEY
,DRIVER_QUANTITY
,DRIVER_DOLLARS
,DRIVER_COUNT
,CORR_OBJECT_KEY
,CORR_QUANTITY
,CORR_DOLLARS
,CORR_COUNT)
SELECT
ITEMSET_KEY
, B.HIERARCHY_KEY
, SUM(DRIVER_QUANTITY) AS DRIVER_QUANTITY_SUM
, SUM(DRIVER_DOLLARS) AS DRIVER_DOLLARS_SUM
, 1 AS DRIVER_COUNT
, CORR_OBJECT_KEY
, CORR_QUANTITY
, CORR_DOLLARS
, CORR_COUNT
FROM
MARKET_BASKET_BI_TABLE A
INNER JOIN MARKET_BASKET_HIERARCHY_DIMENSION B
ON A.DRIVER_OBJECT_KEY = B.OBJECT_KEY
INNER JOIN MARKET_BASKET_HIERARCHY_DIMENSION C
ON A.CORR_OBJECT_KEY = C.OBJECT_KEY
WHERE
B.HIERARCHY_KEY <> C.HIERARCHY_KEY
GROUP BY
ITEMSET_KEY
, B.HIERARCHY_KEY
, CORR_OBJECT_KEY
, CORR_QUANTITY
, CORR_DOLLARS
, CORR_COUNT
ORDER BY
ITEMSET_KEY
, B.HIERARCHY_KEY
, CORR_OBJECT_KEY
```

FIGURE 7.6
Load Market Basket BI Table with driver hierarchy.

counter is not additive. So, it is reset back to one, meaning the hierarchical group appeared once in an Itemset. This is true even if a hierarchical group was represented by two hundred objects. In the binary sense, a hierarchical was in, or not in, an Itemset.

The second primary function of the SQL in Figure 7.6 is that it joins the Driver Object to the hierarchy and then joins the Correlation

TABLE 7.9

Market Basket BI Table with Driver Hierarchy

Itemset Key	Hierarchy Key	Driver Quantity	Driver Dollars	Driver Count	Corr Objectkey	Corr Quantity	Corr Dollars	Corr Count
1	9792	1	$15.31	1	0	0	$0.00	1
2	6543	4	$51.11	1	57	2	$18.18	1
2	9792	2	$18.18	1	16	2	$24.42	1
2	9792	2	$18.18	1	43	1	$14.32	1
2	9792	2	$18.18	1	64	1	$12.37	1
3	1124	5	$56.21	1	15	2	$30.62	1
3	1124	5	$56.21	1	16	1	$12.21	1
3	1124	5	$56.21	1	64	1	$12.37	1
3	6543	2	$24.58	1	15	2	$30.62	1
3	6543	2	$24.58	1	78	4	$53.76	1
3	6543	2	$24.58	1	98	1	$2.45	1
3	9792	2	$30.62	1	16	1	$12.21	1
3	9792	2	$30.62	1	64	1	$12.37	1
3	9792	2	$30.62	1	78	4	$53.76	1
3	9792	2	$30.62	1	98	1	$2.45	1
4	1124	2	$15.89	1	43	3	$42.96	1
4	1124	2	$15.89	1	57	1	$9.09	1
4	1124	2	$15.89	1	87	1	$16.87	1
4	6543	3	$42.96	1	57	1	$9.09	1
4	6543	3	$42.96	1	78	1	$13.44	1
4	6543	3	$42.96	1	87	1	$16.87	1
4	6543	3	$42.96	1	98	1	$2.45	1
4	9792	2	$25.96	1	43	3	$42.96	1
4	9792	2	$25.96	1	78	1	$13.44	1
4	9792	2	$25.96	1	98	1	$2.45	1

Object to the hierarchy as a separate alias. The use of a separate alias for the hierarchy join causes the RDBMS platform to handle the two joins and join table independently of each other, even though they are the same tables.

The third primary function of the SQL in Figure 7.6 is that it excludes those rows that join to the same hierarchical group for both the Driver Object and the Correlation Object. This has the effect of preventing a hierarchical group from correlating to its own objects, which is conceptually the same as preventing an object from correlating with itself. The output of this is shown in Table 7.9.

```
SELECT
DRIVER.HIERARCHY_KEY
, CORR.CORR_OBJECT_KEY
, DRIVER.DRIVER_QUANTITY_SUM
, DRIVER.DRIVER_DOLLARS_SUM
, DRIVER.DRIVER_COUNT_SUM
, CORR.CORR_QUANTITY_SUM
, CORR.CORR_DOLLARS_SUM
, CORR.CORR_COUNT_SUM
, CORR.CORR_QUANTITY_SUM/DRIVER.DRIVER_QUANTITY_SUM AS QUANTITY_RATIO
, CORR.CORR_DOLLARS_SUM/DRIVER.DRIVER_DOLLARS_SUM AS DOLLARS_RATIO
, CORR.CORR_COUNT_SUM/DRIVER.DRIVER_COUNT_SUM AS COUNT_RATIO
FROM
(SELECT
HIERARCHY_KEY
,SUM(DRIVER_QUANTITY) AS DRIVER_QUANTITY_SUM
,SUM(DRIVER_DOLLARS) AS DRIVER_DOLLARS_SUM
,SUM(DRIVER_COUNT) AS DRIVER_COUNT_SUM
FROM(SELECT
ITEMSET_KEY
,HIERARCHY_KEY
,DRIVER_QUANTITY
,DRIVER_DOLLARS
,DRIVER_COUNT
FROM MARKET_BASKET_BI_TABLE_DRIVER_HIERARCHY
GROUP BY
ITEMSET_KEY
,HIERARCHY_KEY
,DRIVER_QUANTITY
,DRIVER_DOLLARS
,DRIVER_COUNT)
GROUP BY
HIERARCHY_KEY)DRIVER
INNER JOIN
(SELECT
HIERARCHY_KEY
,CORR_OBJECT_KEY
,SUM(CORR_QUANTITY) AS CORR_QUANTITY_SUM
,SUM(CORR_DOLLARS) AS CORR_DOLLARS_SUM
,SUM(CORR_COUNT) AS CORR_COUNT_SUM
FROM MARKET_BASKET_BI_TABLE_DRIVER_HIERARCHY
GROUP BY
HIERARCHY_KEY
,CORR_OBJECT_KEY)CORR
ON DRIVER.HIERARCHY_KEY = CORR.HIERARCHY_KEY
ORDER BY
DRIVER.HIERARCHY_KEY
, CORR.CORR_OBJECT_KEY
```

FIGURE 7.7

Market Basket Analysis BI View with driver hierarchy.

The Market Basket Analysis BI View shown in Figure 7.7 is very similar to that in Figure 7.3 and Figure 7.5. The difference is that the Driver Object in Figure 7.7 has the name Hierarchy_Key, not DRIVER_OBJECT_KEY. Again, this reflects the need to organize the tables in a Market Basket Analysis application, by using column names that reflect the nature of the

TABLE 7.10

Market Basket Analysis BI View with Driver Hierarchy

Hierarchy Key	Corr Object Key	Driver Quantity Sum	Driver Dollars Sum	Driver Count Sum	Corr Quantity Sum	Corr Dollars Sum	Corr Count Sum	Quantity Ratio	Dollars Ratio	Count Ratio
1124	15	7	$72.10	2	2	$30.62	1	28.5714%	42.4688%	50.0000%
1124	16	7	$72.10	2	1	$12.21	1	14.2857%	16.9348%	50.0000%
1124	43	7	$72.10	2	3	$42.96	1	42.8571%	59.5839%	50.0000%
1124	57	7	$72.10	2	1	$9.09	1	14.2857%	12.6075%	50.0000%
1124	64	7	$72.10	2	1	$12.37	1	14.2857%	17.1567%	50.0000%
1124	87	7	$72.10	2	1	$16.87	1	14.2857%	23.3981%	50.0000%
6543	15	9	$118.65	3	2	$30.62	1	22.2222%	25.8070%	33.3333%
6543	57	9	$118.65	3	3	$27.27	2	33.3333%	22.9836%	66.6667%
6543	78	9	$118.65	3	5	$67.20	2	55.5556%	56.6372%	66.6667%
6543	87	9	$118.65	3	1	$16.87	1	11.1111%	14.2183%	33.3333%
6543	98	9	$118.65	3	2	$4.90	2	22.2222%	4.1298%	66.6667%
9792	0	7	$90.07	4	0	$0.00	1	0.0000%	0.0000%	25.0000%
9792	16	7	$90.07	4	3	$36.63	2	42.8571%	40.6684%	50.0000%
9792	43	7	$90.07	4	4	$57.28	2	57.1429%	63.5950%	50.0000%
9792	64	7	$90.07	4	2	$24.74	2	28.5714%	27.4675%	50.0000%
9792	78	7	$90.07	4	5	$67.20	2	71.4286%	74.6086%	50.0000%
9792	98	7	$90.07	4	2	$4.90	2	28.5714%	5.4402%	50.0000%

```
DELETE FROM MARKET_BASKET_TABLE
;
INSERT INTO MARKET_BASKET_TABLE
(ITEMSET_KEY
,OBJECT_KEY
,QUANTITY
,DOLLARS)
SELECT
ITEMSET_KEY
,B.HIERARCHY_KEY
,SUM(QUANTITY) AS QUANTITY_SUM
,SUM(DOLLARS) AS DOLLARS_SUM
FROM FACT_TABLE A
INNER JOIN
MARKET_BASKET_HIERARCHY_DIMENSION B
ON A.OBJECT_KEY = B.OBJECT_KEY
GROUP BY
ITEMSET_KEY
,B.HIERARCHY_KEY
;
```

FIGURE 7.8
Load Market Basket Table with hierarchies.

data in them. But, in general, the SQL in Figure 7.7 operates in a fashion similar to the SQL in Figure 7.3 and Figure 7.5.

The output of the SQL in Figure 7.7 is shown in Table 7.10. The data in Table 7.10 can be presented in the form of a view or a physical table for the same criteria as discussed previously.

Step 6: Load a Market Basket BI Table Using the Same Hierarchy as Driver and Correlation

If a Market Basket Analysis effort can consider the correlations from objects leading to hierarchical groups, and hierarchical groups leading to objects, then that same Market Basket Analysis effort can also consider the correlations from hierarchical groups leading to hierarchical groups. It was inevitable. Using again the hierarchical groups in Table 7.6, the SQL in Figure 7.8 extracts data from the original Fact table and loads the MARKET_BASKET_TABLE.

This method works because the Driver Object and Correlation Object are hierarchical peers. Contrary to the method of organizing data into separate tables, this method shows that Market Basket Analysis methods apply to all hierarchies of objects when the Driver and Correlation Objects are hierarchical peers. When they are peers, no additional SQL is required

TABLE 7.11

Market Basket Table with Hierarchies

Itemset_key	Object_key	Quantity	Dollars
1	0	0	$0.00
1	9792	1	$15.31
2	6543	4	$51.11
2	9792	2	$18.18
3	1124	5	$56.21
3	6543	2	$24.58
3	9792	2	$30.62
4	1124	2	$15.89
4	6543	3	$42.96
4	9792	2	$25.96

TABLE 7.12

Market Basket BI Table with Hierarchies

Itemset Key	Driver Object Key	Driver Quantity	Driver Dollars	Driver Count	Corr Object Key	Corr Quantity	Corr Dollars	Corr Count
1	9792	1	$15.31	1	0	0	$0.00	1
2	6543	4	$51.11	1	9792	2	$18.18	1
2	9792	2	$18.18	1	6543	4	$51.11	1
3	1124	5	$56.21	1	6543	2	$24.58	1
3	1124	5	$56.21	1	9792	2	$30.62	1
3	6543	2	$24.58	1	1124	5	$56.21	1
3	6543	2	$24.58	1	9792	2	$30.62	1
3	9792	2	$30.62	1	1124	5	$56.21	1
3	9792	2	$30.62	1	6543	2	$24.58	1
4	1124	2	$15.89	1	6543	3	$42.96	1
4	1124	2	$15.89	1	9792	2	$25.96	1
4	6543	3	$42.96	1	1124	2	$15.89	1
4	6543	3	$42.96	1	9792	2	$25.96	1
4	9792	2	$25.96	1	1124	2	$15.89	1
4	9792	2	$25.96	1	6543	3	$42.96	1

to avoid self-identifying correlations obscured by an object and its hierarchical group.

The Market Basket Table, loaded with objects represented by their hierarchical groups, is shown in Table 7.11. The number of rows decreases as the objects are abstracted up their hierarchies.

TABLE 7.13

Market Basket Analysis BI View with Hierarchies

Driver Object Key	Corr Object Key	Driver Quantity Sum	Driver Dollars Sum	Driver Count Sum	Corr Quantity Sum	Corr Dollars Sum	Corr Count Sum	Quantity Ratio	Dollars Ratio	Count Ratio
1124	6543	7	$72.10	2	5	$67.54	2	71.4286%	93.6755%	100.0000%
1124	9792	7	$72.10	2	4	$56.58	2	57.1429%	78.4743%	100.0000%
6543	1124	9	$118.65	3	7	$72.10	2	77.7778%	60.7670%	66.6667%
6543	9792	9	$118.65	3	6	$74.76	3	66.6667%	63.0088%	100.0000%
9792	0	7	$90.07	4	0	$0.00	1	0.0000%	0.0000%	25.0000%
9792	1124	7	$90.07	4	7	$72.10	2	100.0000%	80.0489%	50.0000%
9792	6543	7	$90.07	4	9	$118.65	3	128.5714%	131.7309%	75.0000%

The SQL in Figure 7.2 reads the Market Basket Table and loads the Market Basket BI Table. The output, shown in Table 7.12, is very similar to the output shown in Table 7.4. The difference is that the Object_Keys in Table 7.4 refer to objects while the Object_Keys in Table 7.12 refer to hierarchical groups of objects.

The output of the Market Basket BI View is shown in Table 7.13. This output is similar to the output shown in Table 7.5. The difference is that the Object_Keys in Table 7.5 refer to objects while the Object_Keys in Table 7.13 refer to hierarchical groups of objects.

Again, this shows that Market Basket Analysis methods apply to all hierarchies of objects when the Driver and Correlation Objects are hierarchical peers. These steps show how to perform Market Basket Analysis in three frames of reference:

- Peer leading to Peer
- Peer leading to Hierarchy
- Hierarchy leading to Peer

These methods are important to a single Market Basket Analysis effort because all three will occur, yet they are not completely cumulative from one to the other. They also repeat at the point of Peer leading to Peer. The analytic phase of a Market Basket Analysis effort will follow this cycle up through the hierarchies of objects and then back down a different hierarchy of the same objects. So, a Market Basket ETL application must be able to traverse these levels of Market Basket Analysis through the hierarchical groupings of objects.

8

What Is Time Variance?

This discussion of Time Variance in a data warehouse assumes a shared understanding of data warehousing. If you are unsure of the meaning and application of such terms as *transaction table, fact table, dimension table,* or *entity,* then please have a copy of *Building and Maintaining a Data Warehouse* handy. These terms and the methods by which we use them are explained in *Building and Maintaining a Data Warehouse.* So, rather than try to surmise the meaning and application of data warehouse jargon, please be ready to reference *Building and Maintaining a Data Warehouse,* which is a book on the basics of data warehousing.

Time Variance. This is one of those phrases penned by IT people, for IT people. It's a bit of shorthand. The phrase *Time Variance* is full of meaning. Rather than spend ten minutes to define Time Variance every time we discuss one of the concepts of time in a data warehouse, we simply use the phrase *Time Variance.* Before we define a solution that delivers Time Variance in a data warehouse, we need to have a common understanding of time—time in a data warehouse and time in Time Variance. First, we start with the ubiquitous invisible object in every Itemset—time.

TIME

Walk into any jewelry store, up to the wristwatch display case, and you'll see it. It's on the face of every wristwatch. They calculate time in different ways. Some of them calculate time gears, some with quartz, and some with a computer chip. They display time in different ways. Some display time digitally. Some use two hands in an analog display. Some display twelve hours, twenty-four hours, the date and weekday. Some even display the phase of the moon. So, are they all correct? Maybe. Are any of them wrong? Yes, if only by mere seconds. If all that isn't confusing enough, all those wristwatches display times that are close, but not all equal. They all have the time, right? No, of course not. Time is an abstract concept with concrete consequences. There is no way to "have" time. Regardless, we all monitor, record, predict, calculate, and live by time in our daily lives. So, even though we can't hold it, we display it; even though we don't know it exactly, we control our lives by it. Time is the most inconsistent constant in the world.

An enterprise has the same conundrum. Cash registers record time to the nearest minute. Payroll time clocks record time to the nearest one-hundredth of an hour. Asynchronous applications record time to the nearest millisecond. Database servers record time to the nearest nano-second. Each of these times is based on the clock inside each computer. A data warehouse has the task of rationalizing and reconciling all these "times" into a single cohesive representation of time within the enterprise. To do that, we need to understand why these representations of time are so different.

A cash register records time to the nearest minute because time data is a trade-off. A retail store needs to be able to identify when each transaction occurred. However, every additional byte consumed by one transaction is also consumed by millions and millions of data records. So, the cost of recording transaction times grained at the nanosecond can cost more than they are worth. Typically a fair balance is transaction time grained at the minute. Asynchronous applications and database servers also strike a balance between the cost of generating, transmitting, and storing time data and the requirement to know when an event occurred. Milliseconds and nanoseconds in billions of data records carry a cost. The inability to know when an event occurred at the nearest millisecond or nanosecond can also have a cost. In each case the enterprise must choose that balance point between the cost of owning and the cost of not having data at various levels of time granularity. These are all questions for the operational environments of the enterprise. The collective time is the representation of time in the operational environment of the enterprise. That representation of time will differ between a factory and an office, between a delivery truck and a traffic dispatcher, between an accounting application and a payroll application.

PERIODICITY

A data warehouse must represent the events from such an assortment of business units and subject areas. While doing so, the data warehouse must achieve its own balance between the cost of having data and the cost of not having data. For that decision, the data warehouse must know its own time requirements. What will the users of the data warehouse do with time grained at the nanosecond? Millisecond? Second? Minute? The answer can actually be found by answering the first half of that question: "What will the users of the data warehouse do?"

A data warehouse is a decision support system. It is not an operational support system. Rather, a data warehouse reconciles data from nonintegrated business units of the enterprise so the users of the data warehouse can see the enterprise as a cohesive integrated whole. What will the users of the data warehouse do? They will make decisions. So, will the decisions made be different if time is grained at the nanosecond, at the millisecond, at the second, or at the minute? Most probably, your decision makers will not find that their long-term strategic view of the enterprise is enhanced by data grained at the nanosecond or millisecond. They may find value in data grained at the second. The telecommunications, fast food, and call center industries might find transaction events grained at the second to be valuable in a data warehouse, because their transaction cycles occur in short periods of time. The restaurant, retail, and service industries have transaction cycles that occur in moderately longer periods of time and, therefore, would typically find value in transaction data grained at the minute rather than the second.

Notice that the decision to choose a time grain is based on the periodicity of the transaction cycles and the value that periodicity brings to the decision support. The discussion thus far has been in terms of the transactions of the enterprise (e.g., phone calls in telecommunications, retail sales, service work orders). The same thought process applies to the dimensions of the enterprise. These are the properties and attributes of the objects of the enterprise. What is the periodicity of the price of gasoline? In other words, how often does a gas station change the price of gasoline? Likewise, what is the periodicity of advertising promotions? What is the periodicity of product changes? What is the periodicity of personnel turnover? The periodicity of dimensions in an enterprise is much slower than the periodicity of transactions. While an enterprise may sell thousands of units every minute, an enterprise will not change the product, price, promotion, or placement thousands of times a minute. Typically, the shortest periodicity for the dimensions is the day. A gas station typically changes the price at the beginning of the day. A retail store may change the price at the beginning and ending of every promotion.

The periodicity of transactions is typically short. The periodicity of dimensions is typically long. The goal of a data warehouse is to rationalize the two forms of periodicity into one representation of the enterprise. This means that all the retail sales transactions of gasoline during the day of March 14 and the price of gasoline on March 14 should both have an attribute that shows they both happened on March 14. The individual sales transactions also show the time of day grained at the second and the date, which is March 14. The price dimension of that gasoline shows the price of gasoline on March 14. An integrated view of the price and sales data of that gas station would show the date and time of each individual sales transaction and the price of gasoline on that same day.

THE MORE THINGS CHANGE

In the integrated view of an enterprise that just happens to be a gas station, sales transactions throughout the day of March 14 and the price of gasoline on March 14 all indicate they occurred on March 14. If the price of gasoline in the gas station changes on March 15, then for that gasoline price and all the sales transactions that occurred throughout the day, the data warehouse would indicate they all occurred on March 15. This same pattern can repeat on March 16, 17, 18…ad infinitum. Each morning the price changes and then throughout that day the sales transactions occur, all of them indicating that day's date as the day on which they occurred. As they change every day, they stay together every day. On every day, the price of gasoline and sales transactions indicate the same date. Then, if you want to know the price of gasoline and the sales of gasoline on March 14, you could query the data warehouse for the date of March 14. If you want to know the price of gasoline and the sales of gasoline on March 15, you query the data warehouse for the date of March 15. The same is true for March 16, 17, 18…ad infinitum. That, in its simplest form, is Time Variance.

In this gas station data warehouse the price of gasoline and sale transactions of gasoline are synchronized by date, that is, Time Variance. They vary in a synchronized fashion through time. Remember that the individual sales transactions are grained at the time of day down to the second; meanwhile, the price of gasoline is grained at the date. In that way, transactions that occurred at March 14, 2011, 8:15:03; March 14, 2011, 8:15:27; and March 14, 2011, 8:16:23 all share the date March 14, 2011, with the price of gasoline on March 14, 2011. In that way, gasoline sales transactions and the price of gasoline vary together through time, even though they are grained at different levels of time granularity.

THE MORE THEY STAY THE SAME

Another simple form of Time Variance occurs when the price of gasoline doesn't change. In the imaginary gas station, the price of gasoline changed on the morning of March 14. Then gasoline sales transactions occurred throughout March 14, 15, and 16. Then, the price of gasoline changed on the morning of March 17, followed by gasoline sales transactions throughout the days of March 17, 18, and 19. In this example, the price of gasoline and sales transactions of gasoline still vary together through time. The price and sales transactions of gasoline on March 14 can still be found by querying for March 14. The price and sales transactions of gasoline on March 15 can still be found by querying for March 15. The difference in this pattern as compared to the previous pattern is that this time the price of gasoline on March 14 and 15 is the same. But, remember this is not Price of Gasoline Variance; rather, it is Time Variance. So, the price of gasoline on a date and the gasoline sales transactions throughout that date all share the same date. In that way, the price of gasoline and gasoline sales transactions both vary together through time by synchronizing on the date.

In this example of a gas station, the data warehouse has three objects. They are the price of gasoline, gasoline sales transactions, and time (i.e., the date). In this gas station data warehouse, time (i.e., the date) is the join between the price of gasoline and gasoline sales transactions. There is no other connection between the price of gasoline and gasoline sales transactions. If you want to know the gasoline sales transactions when the price of gasoline was XYZ, then you query the "price of gasoline" table for rows where the price of gasoline is XYZ, then use the date from the "price of gasoline" table to join to the "gasoline sales transactions" table. You can also query in reverse. If you want to know the price of gasoline when gasoline sales transactions occur at 11:00 p.m., then you start with the "gasoline sales transactions" table. You query the "gasoline sales transactions" table where the time of day is 11:00 p.m., then join the "gasoline sales transactions" table to the "price of gasoline" table by joining on the date. The result set will include multiple rows from the "gasoline sales transactions" table, each joined with a row from the "price of gasoline" table for the same date. Assuming gasoline sales transactions at 11:00 p.m. occurred on multiple days, that result set will include multiple days of gasoline sales transactions and different gasoline prices, but both will correspond with each other by the date. Time Variance between the price of gasoline and gasoline sales transactions allows the query result set to join them together, even when the result set includes multiple dates.

In this way, Time Variance means that Time is the key that joins rows in a fact table to rows in dimension tables. The business relevance of Time Variance is that it means the data warehouse can join transaction data with enterprise data that was in effect at the time of the transaction. For example:

- In a Telecommunications data warehouse, a phone call that occurred on Jan. 24, 2010, can be joined with…
  - The price of a phone call as of Jan 24, 2010
  - The president of the phone company on Jan. 24, 2010
  - The affiliate contract in effect on Jan. 24, 2010
  - The Consumer Price Index as of Jan. 24, 2010
  - The baud rate of the telecommunications network on Jan. 24, 2010
  - The Wimbledon Men's champion as of Jan. 24, 2010
  - Etc. etc. etc. as of Jan. 24, 2010
- In a restaurant data warehouse, a dining room meal that was served on March 18, 2011, can be joined with…
  - The price of the appetizer on March 18, 2011
  - The price of the entrée on March 18, 2011
  - The restaurant manager on March 18, 2011
  - The price of tomato sauce on March 18, 2011
  - The price of meat on March 18, 2011
  - The president of the United States on March 18, 2011
  - The Super Bowl champion as of March 18, 2011
  - Etc. etc. etc. as of March 18, 2011

Time Variance. The events and objects of the enterprise both share moments of time. In a data warehouse they can be joined together by that moment in time. A data warehouse user can ask, "Which objects, attributes, and properties were in effect at the moment of a transaction?" By joining a transaction to the enterprise objects, attributes, and properties, a data warehouse with Time Variance can show that transaction in its enterprise context at the moment of the transaction, which is the answer to the question above. By joining a large number of transactions, all transactions that occurred during the first quarter of 2011, to the enterprise objects, attributes, and properties, a data warehouse with Time Variance can show each of those transactions in their own enterprise context at the moment they occurred and yet return all that data in a single result set.

YEAR, QUARTER, MONTH, WEEK, CYCLE, DAY OF WEEK, TIME ZONE, DATE, AND TIME OF DAY

Before moving on to the next step we need to inventory what we've learned thus far about the enterprise, time, periodicity, and how these are all shared by transactions and objects within the enterprise. First, time is a concrete abstraction. We cannot touch it, yet we measure it. We cannot control it, yet we let it control us. Second, an enterprise has many, many clocks within the enterprise, and each of those clocks performs a function that is intended to meet the needs of a specific segment of the enterprise. An enterprise data warehouse must be able to reconcile all the various forms of time in the enterprise into a cohesive representation of time in the data warehouse. In doing so, the data warehouse includes transactions that are measured at a fine grain of time because those transactions happen so many times during a day; however, the data warehouse also includes objects (such as product, price, promotion, and placement) that change much less frequently, maybe as seldom as once every few years or as often as once a day. Finally, we can synchronize the state of objects in the enterprise with the transactions of the enterprise by joining those two together based on time. In the example we followed earlier in this chapter, we were able to answer the question "What sales transactions occurred when the price of gasoline was XYZ?" The answer to that question hinged on the word *when*.

You may be thinking, and you may be right, that the data from the sales transactions might have the unit price in them, and that we could then simply query the sales transactions using that data which is embedded in the sales transaction data. But then we also saw that Time Variance in a data warehouse can also allow us to join phone calls in telecommunications data with the following:

- The president of the phone company
- The affiliate contract
- The Consumer Price Index
- The baud rate of the telecommunications network

We also saw that a meal served in a restaurant could be joined through Time Variance to the following:

- The restaurant manager on March 18, 2011
- The price of tomato sauce on March 18, 2011
- The price of meat on March 18, 2011

These data points, and others like them, are not going to be in the transaction data of the enterprise. No, they can only be connected to the transaction data of the enterprise via a join based on Time Variance. Specifically, Time Variance allows a data warehouse to join the transactions of the enterprise to the objects and their properties or attributes that were in effect at that moment the transaction occurred.

Before we get too comfortable with the concept of Time Variance based on a moment in time, a data warehouse must reconcile a moment in time into multiple hierarchical groupings of a moment in time. The ubiquitous hierarchical groupings of time are those based on the standard calendar. For example 9:14 on March 14, 2011, happened within the date of March 14, 2011, which was a Monday, which happened within the month of March, which happened within a Quarter One, which happened within the year 2011. If you want to query the data warehouse to find transactions and objects and their properties or attributes in the month of March 2011, those transactions and objects and their properties or attributes will still be joined by the dates on which they occurred. In that way, the transactions on March 1, 2011, will be joined to objects and their properties or attributes as of March 1, 2011; that result set will be combined with the transactions on March 2, 2011, which will be joined to objects and their properties or attributes as of March 2, 2011; that result set will be combined with the transactions on March 3, 2011, which will be joined to objects and their properties or attributes as of March 3, 2011; and so on, until finally that result set will be combined with the transactions on March 31, 2011, which will be joined to objects and their properties or attributes as of March 31, 2011. The collective result set from those time variant result sets will represent activity within the enterprise during the month of March 2011.

Regardless of the groupings of times and dates, Time Variance still occurs at the lowest level, which is the moment in time. That moment in time, of course, is the moment the transaction occurred and the objects and their properties or attributes that were in effect as of that moment in time. So, we can gather the result sets of all those time variant joins and hierarchically group them into a calendar week, calendar month, calendar quarter, calendar year, day of week, and holiday/non-holiday. All of that can typically be found in any data warehouse. Why? Well, conveniently the calendar and hierarchical groupings of the calendar have been stable for centuries. We have gone a very long time without reordering or renaming the days of the week, days of the month, months of the year, or the number of days in a year. It would be quite feasible to populate a full set of calendar tables for the next five hundred years. Even though we can do that, we typically don't. The reasons we don't populate the calendar tables far into the future are the Left Outer Join and Transaction Summaries.

- Invariably, a data warehouse user will want to see dates when an event does and does not occur. That data warehouse customer will begin by querying a calendar table of dates and then use a Left Outer Join to join a fact table of transactions. The Left Outer Join will cause the result set to include all dates, even when there are no transactions on those dates. In that case, the transaction columns will simply be null, and the result set will extend out for five hundred years of null transactions. Rather than allow that to happen, most data warehouses simply load a much more reasonable span of future dates and date hierarchies on a periodic basis.
- Transaction Summaries are also adversely affected by the availability of five hundred years of dates for which there are no corresponding transactions. Typically, enterprise transactions are summarized by a hierarchical grouping of time (e.g., Day Summary, Week Summary, Quarter Summary). Rather than allow the summary process to

churn through five hundred years of dates for which there is no possibility of a transaction to summarize, most data warehouses simply
load a much more reasonable span of future dates and date hierarchies on a periodic basis.

In addition to calendar hierarchical groupings, every enterprise has its
own time-based business cycles. Time Variant data in a data warehouse
can also be grouped by these business cycles. For example, tourist industries have peak and off-peak periods of the year, restaurants and bars have
happy hour, retail stores have replenishment cycles, and marketing firms
have promotion cycles. The most interesting of these is the replenishment
cycle of a retail store. In a retail replenishment cycle, product orders occur
during a span of days, then product deliveries occur during a subsequent
span of days, and then product sales occur in the final span of days of that
replenishment cycle. So, product orders on March 3, product deliveries on
March 10, and product sales on March 17 could all be in a single replenishment cycle (e.g., cycle 2011–11), even though they occurred on different
days. So, for extra credit bonus points…for products in this retail store
that were sold in a transaction on March 17, what replenishment cycle was
in effect at that moment in time? The answer is replenishment cycle 2011–
11 because the product inventory level in the store was the result of product orders dated March 3, delivered March 10, and on the shelf March 17.
Coincidentally, replenishment cycle 2011–12 orders occurred on March 10
while replenishment cycle 2011–11 deliveries occurred, and replenishment
cycle 2011–13 orders occurred on March 17 while replenishment cycle
2011–12 deliveries occurred and replenishment cycle 2011–11 sales transactions occurred. In that way, three replenishment cycles occur simultaneously, yet only one of them is joined to an individual transaction.

An enterprise can, and most do, have many such business cycles occurring simultaneously. As long as a single moment in time (i.e., time of day
and/or a date) can be directly linked with one and only one member of
each hierarchical grouping of time, then the transactions and their corresponding Time Variant enterprise objects and their properties or attributes can be grouped and summed by any hierarchical grouping of time.
The best practice in data warehousing for hierarchical groupings of time
is to establish all the relationships between a single moment in time (i.e.,
time of day and/or a date) and all the hierarchical groupings of time, both
calendar and business cycle groupings of time. By guaranteeing the referential integrity of the time-based tables in the data warehouse, the data

warehouse will be able to guarantee that summaries of transactions by calendar groupings and business cycle groupings do not experience date-based anomalies. So, before joining any transactions to dates, first validate the referential integrity of all the time-based tables. Each date should join to one and only one month, each month should join to one and only one quarter, each quarter should join to one and only one year, and so on. In that way, each moment in time directly joins with one and only one member of each hierarchical grouping.

RALPH KIMBALL'S VARIATIONS OF TIME VARIANCE

Ralph Kimball, one of the pioneers of data warehousing, designed three variations of Time Variant data. They each have their application in decision support. A data warehouse may include all three or only one of these variations. Regardless, the designers of a data warehouse should understand all three to make an educated decision whether to include them.

Type 1—All History Looks Like Now

Type 1 Time Variant data is actually invariant. That is to say, the enterprise objects and their properties or attributes do not vary as time changes. Instead, all the history of the enterprise looks exactly like the enterprise looks right now. Even if you know that some aspects of the enterprise have changed, as far as Type 1 Time Variant data is concerned, nothing has ever changed. The enterprise has always been exactly as it is now.

After so much discussion of Time Variant data, including the price of gasoline and replenishment cycles, you might find the concept of Type 1 Time Variant data to be a bit curious, if not completely useless. To the contrary, Type 1 Time Variant data is indeed useful because not all decisions are made based on the objects and their properties or attributes in effect as of a moment in time. Many decisions in an enterprise are based on the current state of the enterprise. For those decisions, a data warehouse can consume significantly fewer resources by presenting the enterprise only in its current state. Rather than expend the resources necessary to join each and every transaction to the enterprise objects and their properties or attributes in effect at the moment of the transaction, a data warehouse can join all the transactions to the current set of enterprise objects and their current properties or attributes. That approach simultaneously supports decisions made in the context of the current state of the enterprise while conserving the resources of the data warehouse.

Type 2—All History in Its Own Context

Type 2 Time Variant data is the form of Time Variance discussed previously in this chapter. Every transaction is presented in its historic context. A restaurant meal is presented with the restaurant manager at the time of the meal. A retail transaction is presented with the product placement at the time of the transaction. In that way, every transaction is presented in the context in which it occurred.

Type 3—Alternate History

Type 3 Time Variant data presents enterprise transactions with an alternate history. The most common application of Type 3 Time Variant data is to reverse an enterprise reorganization. For example, if a region of stores originally had five thousand stores, and then two thousand of them were split off into a new region, Type 3 Time Variant data could bring those two thousand stores back to their original region. The reason for doing this is to present that region, throughout its history, in a comparable (i.e., apples to apples) configuration. In that way, typically Type 3 Time Variant data is used very sparingly and only for the purpose of presenting the enterprise as though the configuration or alignment of the enterprise looks exactly as it did at a moment in the past. This should not be confused with Type 1 Time Variant data, which makes the enterprise history look like the present. Rather, Type 3 Time Variant data makes the enterprise present look like the past (Kimball 1998, 2005).

Kimball envisioned this being accomplished by adding a column to a dimension table. The additional column would hold the value from a prior period, right next to the Type 1 or Type 2 value in that same dimension table row. That way, a query could leverage the dimensional data structures without modification by referencing the additional column (e.g., pre_reorg_district, conference_2003) rather than the standard column (e.g., district, conference). By referencing a Type 3 column a query can cast a dimensional structure as a date in the past. Obviously, a new column cannot be added to a dimension table every time a dimensional change occurs. Rather, a Type 3 column is added to a dimension table only when a single, moment-in-time, seismic shift in the enterprise altered the hierarchical structure such that the data prior to the shift is not comparable to the data after the shift (Kimball 2005).

TIME VARIANT DATA

So, what is Time Variant data? A data warehouse holds millions, if not billions, of transactions. A data warehouse holds hundreds, if not thousands, of objects and their properties or attributes. Time Variant data allows a data warehouse to join a transaction to an object and its properties or attributes that were in effect at the moment of the transaction. In addition, Type 1 Time Variant data allows a data warehouse to join a transaction to an object and its properties or attributes that are in effect now.

9

How Does Time Variance Produce ROI?

Time Variant data allows a data warehouse to join transactions of the enterprise to enterprise objects and their properties or attributes that were in effect at the time of the transaction. The ROI of this connection is cause and effect. Similar to the use of Market Basket Analysis to determine those enterprise behaviors that correlate with customer behaviors, Time Variant data allows a data warehouse to make a connection between the state of the enterprise and transactions of the enterprise. By understanding the enterprise objects, and their properties or attributes, as they were at the time of advantageous events and transactions, an enterprise can influence future results by mimicking those objects and their prior properties or attributes. Conversely, an enterprise can avoid negative results by avoiding the objects and their properties or attributes that were in effect at the time of previous negative results.

CAUSE AND EFFECT

The most direct application of the use of Time Variant data to study cause and effect in the enterprise applies to the four P's of marketing—Product, Price, Promotion, and Placement.

- Product—Customers may choose to accept a product and to reject another product. Like Goldilocks in the home of the three bears, one product is too hot, another is too cold, but the third product is just right. Time Variant data in the "three bears data warehouse" will show that the "hot product" and "cold product" were rejected, while the "medium product" was accepted. For a single product, the variations over time may include changes in the label, size, package type, or formula. The ability to track these changes in label, size, package type, or formula and customer responses to each of them individually can be achieved by the use of Time Variant data in a data warehouse.

- Price—Customers can reject or accept a product based solely on its price. The search for the right price point is paramount to every enterprise that can vary the price of its products. The ability to track changes in price and customer responses to each price point individually can be achieved by the use of Time Variant data in a data warehouse.
- Promotion—Promotional advertisements influence customer buying patterns...definitely...probably...we hope...we need to be sure. Promotional advertising can include a wide gamut of possibilities from radio, TV, billboards, endorsement, free gifts, price reductions, and a person in a costume waving at cars passing by. Which of these methods works? Which of these fails? Of the four P's of marketing, Promotion is the one least able to assert a direct connection between a campaign or advertisement and customer response. Maybe a prior campaign or advertisement already influenced a customer who only now has the necessary funds. Regardless, it is worthwhile to connect the Promotion occurring at the time of a transaction. Time Variant data in a data warehouse can achieve that connection between a Promotion and a transaction.
- Placement—The method by which product is placed in front of a customer can be directly associated with that customer's decision to purchase the product. If the customer intended to purchase the product prior to the transaction, then that customer went to the place where the product was found. If the customer coincidentally happened to be in the place where the product was found and then decided to purchase the product, the product was purchased in that place. Either way, the product, customer, and place are all directly linked by a transaction.

An enterprise can have many other connections between enterprise objects and their properties or attributes and transactions beyond the four P's of marketing.

- Manufacturing Foreman—A manufacturing foreman may be linked by the products manufactured during his/her shift to a reduction in product returns and rework, while another foreman may be linked to an increase in product returns and rework.

- Restaurant Manager—A restaurant manager may be linked by the meals served during his/her shift to an increase in the sale of desserts, while another restaurant manager may be linked to an increase in the sale of wine.
- Service Technician—A service technician may be linked by work orders to an increase in repeat customers, while another service technician may be linked to an increase in complaints.

The Time Variant connection between enterprise objects and transactions allows a data warehouse user to query the data warehouse looking for all events associated with a specific manufacturing foreman. The Time Variant result set will include all the transactions associated with that manufacturing foreman, regardless of the location, time, or manufacturing process for which that person was the manufacturing foreman. Likewise, all transactions associated with a restaurant manager can be found regardless of which restaurant that manager has managed. The same is true for any enterprise object directly associated with transactions via Time Variant data.

The correlation between events or transactions and enterprise objects and their properties or attributes is based on the moment in time the transaction occurred. This correlation can be similar to the correlations found in Market Basket Analysis. Customer behavior may be completely unchanged by an enterprise object and its properties or attributes. Conversely, customer behavior may vary based on another enterprise object and its properties or attributes. Time Variant data in a data warehouse allows an analyst to study these correlations based on the enterprise objects and their properties or attributes in effect at the moment of each individual transaction.

CAUSE AND EFFECT IS NOT CAUSAL ANALYSIS

Causal Analysis is an analytic discipline that has a wider scope than just the enterprise. As such, the cause and effect between enterprise objects and their properties or attributes and the results that occur within the enterprise is not really comprehensive enough to be considered Causal Analysis. The idea behind Causal Analysis is to identify and understand the conditions that caused an outcome. Thus far, this book has not proposed that

Market Basket Analysis or Time Variant data can identify what caused an event to occur, but rather those enterprise objects and their properties or attributes that correlate with an event. For that reason, the discipline of Causal Analysis goes beyond the scope and data of Time Variant data.

Causal Analysis can record and include environmental, governmental, competitive, and economic conditions that actually caused an event to occur. A data warehouse may be able to expand its scope to include these data points and may be used to facilitate Causal Analysis. However, Causal Analysis in all its meaning is a discussion for another book. The scope and context of this discussion of Time Variant data is limited to enterprise transactions and enterprise objects. As such, the set of enterprise transactions and enterprise objects does not include the hurricanes, tax breaks, competitor actions, or school activities that can affect the enterprise.

EXCEPTIONS TO THE RULE

For every rule there is an exception. Time Variant data in a data warehouse is no exception to that rule. Every enterprise has anecdotes wherein a manager benefited from the preceding manager. The preceding manager had wonderful hiring practices, productive work policies, and therefore a very productive workforce. The current manager required two whole years to dismantle that workforce into a dysfunctional and unproductive team. But, for those two years, the current manager looked very good on paper. The reverse has also been true. A new manager of a dysfunctional and unproductive team will look abysmal on paper until the results of the previous ineffectual manager can be reversed. Until then, the current manager will look bad on paper.

That sort of lagging correlation between the enterprise and its outcomes happens frequently and ubiquitously. For that reason, the presence of Time Variant data in a data warehouse is not an occasion for enterprise analysts to run their Time Variant reports and blindly draw conclusions based on the results listed in the reports. Rather, Time Variant data is a tool within a data warehouse. Like all tools, Time Variant data must be used intelligently and with an understanding and intuition of the enterprise. While Time Variant data can be very useful at finding vendors who deliver inferior product, managers who deliver productive teams, and processes that do or don't create products that will eventually require rework,

Time Variant data requires an insightful analyst to intelligently leverage its connections and correlations.

RULES TO THE EXCEPTION

Exception Reporting may be the use of Time Variant data that delivers the highest ROI. A data warehouse can be used to monitor enterprise and customer behaviors across extended periods of time. When those enterprise or customer behaviors change, to the point of being exceptional, a BI Report can be written to notice such exceptions. When these exceptions occur, that same report can be written to find the enterprise objects, properties, or attributes that changed prior to the exceptional behavior. If the enterprise and customer behaviors never changed, such a report would remain empty. However, when exceptional behavior occurs, such a report would notice the exception and the difference in enterprise objects, properties, and attributes that preceded the exceptional behavior.

Such a reporting mechanism is helpful when exceptional behavior is expected as well as when exceptional behavior is not expected. Either way, an exception report that leverages Time Variant data allows the users of a data warehouse to notice changes in the behaviors of the enterprise and its customers and the changes in the enterprise that preceded them. The ROI of Time Variant data is the ability to correlate changes in the behaviors of the enterprise or its customers and preceding changes in the enterprise.

10

Why Is Time Variance Difficult?

In my previous book, *Building and Maintaining a Data Warehouse*, I demonstrated how to build time variance into a data warehouse. In that discussion, an object in a row of a fact table joins to a dimension table via a primary key/foreign key join with an additional WHERE clause that selects the one row of the dimension table that has the Effective and Termination Dates that form a time interval that surrounds the date of the transaction in the fact table row (Silvers 2008). This and subsequent chapters constitute both a retraction and a correction of that time variant design. In practice, I have found that this model performs well at low cardinalities of data. I found that as long as the number of fact table rows is small, the number of objects joining to dimensions is small, and the number of dimension rows is small, the time variant design in Chapter 5 of *Building and Maintaining a Data Warehouse* performs satisfactorily well. If, however, any of those points of cardinality (i.e., number of fact table rows, number of objects, number of dimension table rows) increases moderately, the query performance of the data warehouse becomes less and less satisfactory as the cardinality increases. When any of those points of cardinality increases significantly, the data warehouse simply ceases to perform well at all. This conundrum was the genesis for the time variant solution design outlined in Chapter 11, "Time Variant Solution Definition."

RELATIONAL SET LOGIC

SQL queries retrieve data in sets of rows. A basic SQL query (SELECT * FROM TABLE) shows that the statement is asking for all the rows in a table. All the rows constitute a set, specifically a set of rows. The RDBMS retrieves all the rows from the table and delivers them to the user. If a query selects data from two tables, then it retrieves two sets of rows as it builds the final result set. If a query retrieves data from three tables, then it retrieves three sets of rows as it builds the final result set. If a table has an index on a column, and a query uses a WHERE clause on the specific column, the RDBMS will use the index to retrieve only the subset of rows that match the WHERE clause in the query as it builds the final result set. That subset of rows is still a set of rows. So, no matter how you write the query or index the tables, the RDBMS will always retrieve data in sets of rows. This is the set logic inherent in every RDBMS.

Set logic is a very powerful tool and an innovative leap forward past the flat file and hierarchical databases that preceded relational data structures. Prior to relational data structures, data was stored in flat files or keyed files. A procedural application was required to retrieve data from these files and databases. A business user could not submit an ad hoc query against a flat file, join that with a keyed file, and then join the result set of those two files with another keyed file. Prior to relational data structures, that technology did not exist. That technology is the relational data structures of an RDBMS. So, the set logic of an RDBMS is not a weakness. Rather, it is an innovative leap forward that suddenly made large volumes of data available to business users. Instead of waiting for an application to run a job that would create a file that was a combination of the data in two separate files, the creation of an RDBMS gave business users the ability to retrieve the data they need without waiting for a job to run a program that reads the files, combines their data, and then writes a file.

Set logic give an RDBMS the ability to manipulate large volumes of data, join separate sets of data, and combine their data into a single result set without a job running a program that generates a file. Instead, the business user submits a query and the RDBMS does all the work. When the RDBMS is finished, it passes the result set to the business user who submitted the query. For that reason, set logic is the strength of every RDBMS.

SETS—THE BANE OF TIME VARIANCE

Set logic, the strength of every RDBMS, is the bane of Time Variant data. The problem is the set of rows. All the millions of occurrences of a transaction are represented by millions of rows in a fact table. Each of those millions of rows in the fact table reference an object (probably multiple objects) in a dimension table. An attribute of an object may be prone to occasional changes. Each of those iterations of the object is represented by a row in the dimension table. Each of those dimension rows uses the Row_First_Date and Row_Last_Date columns to indicate the boundaries of the interval of time during which the data in that dimension row was in effect. Each individual row of those millions of rows of the fact table will ultimately join to only one dimension row, specifically the dimension row that was in effect at the time of the transaction represented by the fact row. However, because the RDBMS retrieves data in sets of rows, the fact table actually is joining to all the rows in the dimension table. After the join between the fact and dimension table(s) is complete, then the rows that do not match the time variant condition (i.e., Transaction Date between the Row_First_Date and Row_Last_Date) are discarded. Unfortunately, those rows had to be gathered in memory before they could be discarded. A more efficient path would be to never have gathered the rows that do not meet the time variant condition.

The example in Figure 10.1 shows that a transaction occurred on March 11, 2005. The object of that transaction has an Item Key equal to the number 4. The Transaction table on the left has one row that represents that transaction. When joining to the Item dimension table on the right, the Item Key equal to 4 joins to all the rows in the Item dimension table with an Item Key equal to 4. Then, the RDBMS inspects the set of rows that have an Item Key equal to 4, searching for the row with a time bounded by the Row_First_Date and Row_Last_Date that encompasses the Event_Date from the Transaction fact row. The final result set includes the fourth row, wherein the attribute is *yellow*.

Why is the RDBMS unable to use an index or some other relational structure to join the Transaction fact table row to the one and only Item dimension table row that has an Item Key equal to 4 and was in effect on

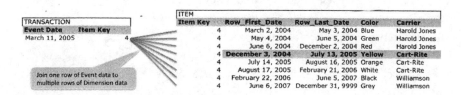

FIGURE 10.1
Time Variant set logic.

March 11, 2005? The reason is simple. No row in the Item dimension table has both the Item Key equal to 4 and the date March 11, 2005.

The example in Figure 10.1 is rather simple and small. The simplicity of that example is for introductory purposes only. Figure 10.2 extends this example to include Third Normal Form dimension tables that capture the Color Formula and Carrier Terms. Figure 10.2 shows that every row of the Item dimension table joins to every row of the Color Formula where the Color of the Item matches the Color of the Color Formula table. After each Item.Blue row joins to three Color_Formula.Blue rows, all but one row (Blue, C2387J, November 19, 2004, July 18, 2006) are discarded. After each Item.Green row joins to two Color_Formula.Green rows, all but one row (Green, UU879, February 13, 2002, July 13, 2005) are discarded. This same pattern repeats for the Red, Yellow, Orange, White, Black, and Grey colors.

The Carrier_Terms dimension table is a bit different from the Color_ Formula table in that multiple Transaction rows have the same Carrier name. All the Item rows that have the Carrier equal to "Harold Jones" join to the Carrier_Terms dimension table where the Carrier name is Harold Jones. Only after all those joins have been performed does the data warehouse attempt to discard all but one row (e.g., Harold Jones, 14:14, December 16, 2004, July 4, 2006). This also happened for the Carriers Cart-Rite and Williamson. In each case, within the join of a foreign key to a primary key, that join becomes a product (or Cartesian) join. After all the rows have been joined, only then is the Time Variant logic of the dates performed.

The example in Figure 10.2 includes only one Transaction row, only one Item with multiple Type 2 Time Variant rows, and two dimension tables (Color Formula and Carrier Terms) that join to the Item dimension table. If the Color Formula or Carrier Terms table join to more dimension tables, the collection of product joins increases with each additional Type 2 Time Variant table. As the proliferation of transaction and dimension rows increases, the performance degradation also increases. As the proliferation of levels, or layers, of dimension tables increases, the performance degradation also increases. Before long, the proliferation of tables and rows causes the performance degradation to render the data warehouse unresponsive.

The join between a fact table row and a dimension table row would work much better if it were indeed a join between a single fact table row and a single dimension table row. Unfortunately, it is a join between a fact table row and a set of dimension table rows. Multiply that join, between a row of fact data and a set of rows of dimension data, by the number of fact rows; then,

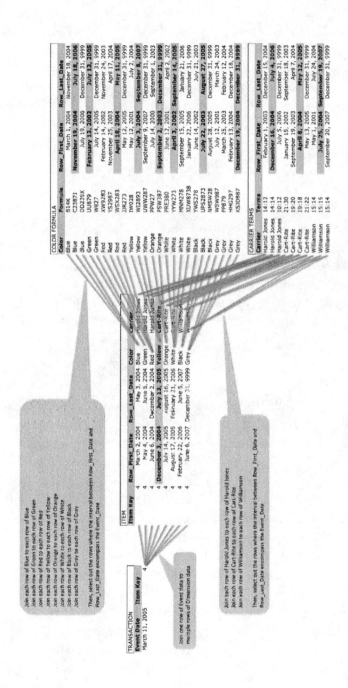

FIGURE 10.2

Time variant set logic with dimensions.

multiply that by the number of sets of dimension rows and you have a performance bottleneck on your hands. Relational data structures offer no way to index a table on dates between the Row_First_Date and Row_Last_Date because the date value between those two dates is not in the dimension table. An RDBMS cannot apply an index to data that is not there. As a result, Time Variant data, which sounds wonderful in a book or article, becomes a performance bottleneck early in the cardinality growth of the data warehouse.

OPTIONS

The search for a solution was initially guided by two questions: "What do I already possess that might solve the performance bottleneck?" and "What has someone else found that solves the performance bottleneck?" The first question led to the consideration of the RDBMS infrastructure. The stored procedure function within every RDBMS might be an option. The second question led to the discovery of temporal databases. In this context, *temporal* and *time variant* are synonymous. So, maybe someone else really did solve the performance bottleneck of Time Variant data.

Stored Procedures

Every generally available RDBMS offers the procedural functionality of a stored procedure that uses a cursor to fetch rows one at a time. That procedural cursor/fetch method works well for stored procedures because stored procedures are able to loop through millions of rows, one at a time, applying logic to each row individually. BI Reporting tools and individual data warehouse users rely on the RDBMS to perform the tasks defined in SQL queries. Unfortunately, the cursor/fetch method is not compatible with the SQL queries used by Business Intelligence Reporting (BI Reporting) tools, or the ad hoc queries written by individual data warehouse users.

If we were to use stored procedures to solve the performance bottleneck of Time Variant data, reports would be written as code in a stored procedure. A job would run the stored procedure, which could output its data in the form of a file or a table. This is eerily similar to the jobs and programs that retrieved data from flat files and keyed files prior to the advent of the RDBMS. This solution would not work for the same reason the programs that read flat files and keyed files were replaced by queries that retrieve data from one or more fact tables.

Temporal Databases

Another option is temporal databases. Temporal databases attempt to optimize the join between a fact row with a single event date and a dimension table with two date columns that form an interval (Date, Darwin, and Lorentzos 2003). That construct of a single date joining to an interval of dates is called a "tuple" (Clifford, Jajodia, and Snodgrass 1993; Date, Darwin, and Lorentzos 2003). Within the tuple construct are the two representations of time—Valid Time and Transaction Time. Valid Time is the moment or interval of time wherein the data in a row reflected the reality of the enterprise. Transaction Time is the moment or interval of time wherein a row of data was in effect. Valid Time refers to the data in the row and Transaction Time refers to the row (Clifford, Jajodia, and Snodgrass 1993; Date, Darwin, and Lorentzos 2003). The complexity of the tuple construct creates several relational integrity issues that require the enforcement of constraints by the RDBMS (Date, Darwin, and Lorentzos 2003; Gertz and Lipeck 1995).

The Tuple construct in the temporal database is not quite a Type 3 Time Variant data structure. A Tuple does not present alternate dimensions (e.g., 2001 Region, 2002 Region, 2003 Region) that exist next to the Type 1 or Type 2 Time Variant dimension value (e.g., Region). Instead, the Tuple offers multiple versions of an entity/attribute/property relationship. For example:

- On May 14, 2003, the data warehouse recorded that the Color as of May 12, 2003, was blue.
- On June 8, 2003, the data warehouse recorded that the Color as of May 12, 2003, was red.
- On July 21, 2003, the data warehouse recorded that the Color as of May 12, 2003, was green.
- On Nov. 11, 2003, the data warehouse recorded that the Color as of May 12, 2003, was white.

This has a double layered effect of Time Variance of the Time Variant data, which is not the alternate reality intended by Kimball's Type 3 Time Variant design (Kimball 2005).

The query language for these temporal tables has not yet achieved a single standard query language. One query language uses Relation Variables (RelVars) (Date, Darwin, and Lorentzos 2003). Another query language in use with temporal databases is the Historical Query Language (HSQL)

(Clifford, Jajodia, and Snodgrass 1993). A third temporal query language is the TSQL2 (Temporal SQL version 2) (Androutsopoulos, Ritchie, and Thanisch 1995; Böhlen, Jensen, and Snodgrass 1995). None of the query languages have been generally adopted. The difficulty of learning such a query syntax, lack of a standard, and lack of general adoption render the use of temporal databases rather difficult.

The relational integrity issues and relational integrity constraints work together to render the task of managing time variant data even more difficult than it was for a nontemporal RDBMS. The double layered (i.e., Valid Time & Transaction Time) Time Variant data can cause relational integrity issues that are prevented from occurring by constraints within the RDBMS (Gertz and Lipeck 1995).

The confusing query languages, none of which has yet been declared the standard, render the task of querying time variant data more difficult than it was for a nontemporal RDBMS. The tuple construct embraces the set logic inherent in an RDBMS, rather than resolve the set logic to join one row of fact data to one row of dimension data. For these reasons, a temporal database is not the solution to the performance bottleneck I was seeking.

TIME VARIANT SOLUTION DESIGN

The set logic inherent in every RDBMS causes each row of a fact table to join to all the rows of a dimension table for a given primary key. The result of that is a significant performance bottleneck. Stored procedures can retrieve one row at a time but cannot be used by business users and BI Reporting tools to query data from a data warehouse. Finally, temporal databases are a collective set of efforts to reconcile the join issue in time variant data. In the process, temporal databases actually increase the workload on the RDBMS as it enforces relational integrity constraints to avoid relational integrity issues in the temporal database. The temporal query languages are confusing and, as yet, not standardized.

So, what is the solution? How can a data warehouse present time variant data without the performance bottleneck caused by set logic, without the relational integrity issues, and without the confusing query language? Chapter 11 will present a Time Variant solution design that resolves all these design issues and delivers Time Variant data.

11

Time Variant Solution Definition

Equally important in the difficulties of Time Variance are those aspects of Time Variance that cause, and do not cause, a performance degradation. In Chapter 10, the explanation of difficulties inherent in Time Variant data did not include any confusion about time, time intervals, hierarchies, hierarchy relationships, or any other aspect of relational data or a data warehouse. That being the case, the concept of a data warehouse built on an RDBMS platform is still a sturdy architecture and has not diminished in strength or flexibility due to any concerns about Time Variant data. So, we don't need to solve the RDBMS problem, the data warehouse problem, the relational hierarchy problem, or any other such problems that do not exist. Locally, a single data warehouse implementation may contain its own self inflicted difficulties. But, as a general concept and design, the data warehouse continues to be strong and flexible. So, if nothing is broken and there's nothing to fix, what problem is solved by the Time Variant Solution Design?

TIME VARIANT PROBLEM REPRISE

Chapter 10 showed the root cause and manifestation of the Time Variant problem. The root cause is the inability of an RDBMS to join on data it does not have. A transaction occurs at a single point in time. A dimension persists for an interval of time. When attempting to join a transaction row to a dimension row, an RDBMS is peculiarly unequipped to join those two rows. Specifically, the only relational key between a Dimension_ID/Date and Dimension_ID/Interval is the Dimension_ID.

Having been half-equipped to perform such a join, the relational approach is to perform the available join on Dimension_ID and then complete the join using a WHERE clause using the statement "WHERE Date between Interval_Begin and Interval_End." This approach causes an RDBMS to assemble a superset of rows and then retain only those rows that satisfy the statement "WHERE Date between Interval_Begin and Interval_End."

The manifestation of this approach is shown in Figure 10.2. For every join to every dimension table every possible row becomes a multiplicative explosion of rows. For that reason, a Time Variant relational data warehouse quickly hits a wall. When the cardinality of a data warehouse, either in depth or breadth, exceeds the capacity of an RDBMS to handle the multiplicative explosion of rows, then that Time Variant data warehouse will cease to perform satisfactorily. The phrase "a brick" was used to describe such a data warehouse.

THE GOAL OF THIS TIME VARIANT SOLUTION DESIGN

The goal of this Time Variant Solution Design is to prevent the multiplicative explosion of data. Figure 11.1 shows how this goal, once achieved, will work for the RDBMS.

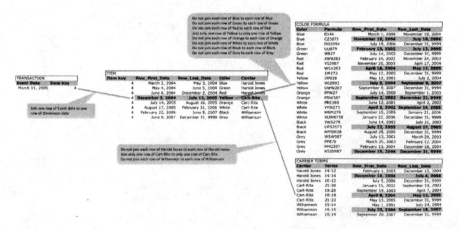

FIGURE 11.1
The goal of this Time Variant Solution Design.

The join between the Transaction and Item tables reduces from eight pairs of joined rows to one pair of joined rows. By removing extraneous pairs of joined rows from the join between the Item and Color_Formula tables, completely removing all pairs of rows joined on the colors Blue, Green, Red, Orange, White, Black, and Grey, and reducing the pairs of rows joined on the color Yellow from three to one, the pairs of joined rows reduces from twenty-six to one. By removing extraneous pairs of joined rows from the join between the Item and Carrier_Terms tables, completely removing all pairs of rows joined on the carriers Harold Jones and Williamson, and reducing the pairs of rows joined on the carrier Cart-Rite from three to one, the pairs of joined rows reduces from eleven to one. Taken together, those three joins alone reduce the number of pairs of joined rows from forty-five to three, which is a reduction by a factor of fifteen. That means that if in this example we can completely remove the multiplicative explosion of data by joining on only those rows that satisfy the conditions of the Time Variant join, the RDBMS will be required to handle one-fifteenth the volume of data it was previously required to handle.

The tuple construct of temporal databases also attempts to optimize joins within and between Time Variant data. By managing the Time Variant intersections of fact table rows, dimension table rows, and dates, temporal databases also avoid the superset of joined pairs of rows in Figure 10.2. Having never implemented a temporal database, I have no evidence in favor of, or against, temporal databases. Temporal databases may perform Time Variant joins and queries faster and more efficiently than the Time Variant Solution Design outlined in this chapter. Regardless, from researching temporal databases, I can see that temporal databases are designed to limit database activity to only those rows that apply to the query at hand, in its Time Variant context. However, temporal databases are also a departure from the relational database structure and query language of generally available relational databases. As such, I'm not yet convinced the path to the goal is in temporal databases. For those reasons, the Time Variant Solution Definition outlined in this chapter is focused solely on achieving the goal displayed in Figure 11.1 via the Time Variant Solution Design. As such, the concepts and constructs of temporal databases are not included in the remainder of this chapter. This exclusion of temporal databases is neither an implicit nor an explicit statement about temporal databases. Rather, the inclusion of the Time Variant Solution Design, to the exclusion of all other designs, only means that the Time Variant Solution Design is the singular focus of this chapter.

ONE ROW AT A TIME

The question is so simple, the answer so obvious, that it seems a trick question. When a dimension table has five million rows, and you want to join to one and only one of those five million rows, what is the fastest and most efficient way to retrieve that one and only one row? The answer is simple. Give each of those five million rows a unique identifier. Each row has one and only one unique identifier. Each unique identifier has one and only one row. It is a one-to-one relation: one row equals one unique identifier, and one unique identifier equals one row. A unique identifier can never be associated with any other row, and a row can never be associated with any other unique identifier. If a row ceases to exist, the unique identifier ceases to exist. If a unique identifier ceases to exist, the row ceases to exist.

Now, given that construct in a dimension table that has five million rows, and you want to join to one and only one of those five million rows, what is the fastest and most efficient way to retrieve that one and only one row? The answer is simple. Include a WHERE clause statement that says "WHERE unique_identifier = 12345." Such a WHERE clause will return one and only one row. No additional logic is required. No superset is required. The RDBMS does not bring five million rows into memory. Instead, the RDBMS brings only one row into memory. The goal has been achieved and we can all congratulate ourselves and call it a day...almost.

We don't query a data warehouse one table at a time. No, we query multiple tables simultaneously. When a transaction table joins to a dimension table that has five million rows, and you want to join each individual transaction row to one and only one of those five million dimension rows, what is the fastest and most efficient way to join the transaction and dimension tables such that each row of the transaction table joins to one and only one row of the dimension table? The answer is simple, and the same as before. Give each of those five million dimension rows a unique identifier. Embed that unique identifier in each row of the transaction table. Then, when each row of the transaction table is joined to the dimension table, each individual row of the transaction table will join with one and only one row of the dimension table. A query that joins the transaction and dimension tables will use that unique identifier to perform the join (i.e., Table_A JOIN Table_B on Table_A.Foreign_Key = Table_B.Unique_Identifier). No additional logic is required. No superset is required. The RDBMS does not bring five million dimension rows into memory. Instead, the RDBMS brings only one dimension row into memory for every transaction row. The goal has been achieved and we can all congratulate ourselves and call it a day…almost.

We don't query a data warehouse one dimension at a time. No, we query multiple dimension tables simultaneously. This allows a query to include a parent hierarchy or a type code lookup in conjunction with a dimension table. When a dimension table joins to another dimension table that has five thousand rows, and you want to join each individual dimension row to one and only one of those five thousand dimension rows, what is the fastest and most efficient way to join the two dimension tables such that each row of the first dimension table joins to one and only one row of the second dimension table? The answer is simple, and the same as before. Give each of those five thousand dimension rows a unique identifier. Embed that unique identifier in each row of the first dimension table. Then, when each row of the first dimension table is joined to the second dimension table, each individual row of the first dimension table will join with one and only one row of the second dimension table. The query that joins the two dimension tables will use that unique identifier to perform the join (i.e., Table_A JOIN Table_B on Table_A.Foreign_Key = Table_B.Unique_Identifier). No additional logic is required. No superset is required. The RDBMS does not bring five thousand dimension rows from the second table into memory for every row of the first dimension table. Instead, the RDBMS brings only one dimension row from the second dimension table into memory for every row from the first dimension table. The goal has been achieved and we can all congratulate ourselves and call it a day. True, assuming we can come back tomorrow and replicate this method throughout the data warehouse.

To that end, let's try to generalize what we have learned. We have learned that the fastest and most efficient method to find a row in a table is by providing each row in that table with its own unique identifier. Now we can retrieve a single row from that table, either through a direct query or through an indirect join, via the unique identifier for that row in that table. The optimal path to a single row in a table, therefore, is through a unique identifier. A query can reference the unique identifier directly or indirectly. Regardless, the fastest and most efficient path to a single row is its unique identifier.

NOT A SURROGATE KEY

At this point, some readers are one page-turn away from tossing this book into a fireplace. If a fireplace is not handy, no doubt some readers will build a fire for the sole purpose of burning this book. Why? Those readers who have a strong preference against surrogate keys may perceive this Time Variant Solution Design to be a surrogate key design by another name. That perception is a misperception but is also understandable. A unique identifier may have the look and feel of a surrogate key. However, a unique identifier does not have the purpose of a surrogate key.

Surrogate keys in a data warehouse are intended to resolve relational integrity issues caused by key collision or key confusion. Regardless, surrogate keys have been mangled and abused in many data warehouses. Some data warehouse designers prefer to avoid surrogate keys altogether simply so they can avoid the pitfalls of surrogate keys. The unique identifier in the Time Variant Solution Design is not intended to resolve relational integrity issues. The unique identifier in the Time Variant Solution Design is intended to efficiently identify a specific row in a table, which is displayed in Figure 11.1.

If a unique identifier simultaneously identifies a specific row in a table and resolves relational integrity issues, that paired coupling of features is a bonus. In that case, the unique identifier should be treated two ways, first as a unique identifier of a specific row and second as a surrogate key. These are two totally separate functions. All the data in a data warehouse is delivered by an ETL application. The functions of a unique identifier are delivered by an ETL application, which will be discussed in Chapter 13. The functions of a surrogate key are also delivered by an ETL application. You cannot simply assume that an ETL application that delivers unique identifiers also delivers surrogate keys because the concept of a unique identifier matches your implementation of surrogate keys. Such an assumption will eventually cause data quality issues as the reality of surrogate keys and the reality of unique identifiers in your data warehouse diverge into two different meanings. If you must, you probably can deliver a unique identifier and a surrogate key in the same data element. But, in doing so, the ETL application that delivers that data, and the data quality application that assesses that data, must embed the functional meaning of surrogate keys and unique identifiers into the data it delivers.

A unique identifier, therefore, is not necessarily a surrogate key. In your data warehouse implementation both the unique identifier function and the surrogate key function may be performed by the same data element; alternatively, your data warehouse may use unique identifiers with no hint of the use of surrogate keys. Surrogate keys are mentioned here only to clarify that unique identifiers and surrogate keys may be similar but are functionally different in their use and meaning within a data warehouse. So, like ducks and geese, they may look like each other, walk like each other, and fly like each other, but they are two different things.

INSTANCE KEY

The name given to the data element that serves the function of a unique identifier is Instance Key. Any one of a number of names would suffice. But, for the purposes of this explanation of this Time Variant Solution Definition, the name for the unique identifier is Instance Key. An Instance Key can take one of two forms—Simple Instance Key and Compound Instance Key. A Simple Instance Key requires only one data value to uniquely identify a row of data within a table. A Compound Instance Key requires more than one data value to uniquely identify a row of data within a table.

A Simple Instance Key, illustrated in Figure 11.2, uses a single data value to identify an individual row in a table. The simplest and cleanest method for a Simple Instance Key is a sequential numeric data element that begins with the number 1 for the first row and then increments by 1 thereafter for each additional row. A Simple Instance Key can be used when you know beyond any doubt that the number of rows in the table containing a Simple Instance Key will never exceed the positive range of the numeric data type of the Simple Instance Key. For example, the Integer data type typically has a maximum value of 2,147,483,647. If you know beyond any doubt that a dimension table, including a row for every update, will never exceed two billion rows, then you could define a Simple Instance Key for that dimension table, with the Instance Key defined as an Integer data type. A Simple Instance Key does not cause the key already assigned to an entity (i.e., the Entity Key) to become superfluous. Instead, the Entity

A Simple Instance Key never resets back to 1

COLOR FORMULA

Color	Instance Key	Formula	Row_First_Date	Row_Last_Date
Blue	1	B14K	March 1, 2004	November 18, 2004
Blue	2	C2387J	November 19, 2004	July 18, 2006
Blue	3	DD239X	July 19, 2006	December 31, 9999
Green	4	UU879	February 13, 2002	July 13, 2005
Green	5	W827	July 14, 2005	December 31, 9999
Red	6	XW9283	February 14, 2002	November 24, 2003
Red	7	YS2987	November 25, 2003	April 17, 2004
Red	8	WSX283	April 18, 2004	May 11, 2005
Red	9	JJR273	May 12, 2005	December 31, 9999
Yellow	10	IW028	May 12, 2001	July 2, 2004
Yellow	11	WI2893	July 3, 2004	September 8, 2007
Yellow	12	UWW287	September 9, 2007	December 31, 9999
Orange	13	PPW27	July 14, 2000	September 1, 2003
Orange	14	PSW387	September 2, 2003	December 31, 9999
White	15	PRE380	June 12, 2001	April 2, 2002
White	16	YYW273	April 3, 2002	September 14, 2005
White	17	MNM278	September 15, 2005	January 21, 2006
White	18	XUW8738	January 22, 2006	December 31, 9999
Black	19	YWS278	June 14, 2002	July 21, 2003
Black	20	UPS2873	July 22, 2003	August 27, 2005
Black	21	NMSW28	August 28, 2005	December 31, 9999
Grey	22	WSW987	July 12, 2001	March 24, 2003
Grey	23	PP879	March 25, 2003	February 12, 2004
Grey	24	HHG297	February 13, 2004	December 18, 2004
Grey	25	KSJD887	December 19, 2004	December 31, 9999

CARRIER TERMS

Carrier	Instance Key	Terms	Row_First_Date	Row_Last_Date
Harold Jones	1	14:12	February 1, 2003	December 15, 2004
Harold Jones	2	14:14	December 16, 2004	July 4, 2006
Harold Jones	3	10:12	July 5, 2006	December 31, 9999
Cart-Rite	4	21:30	January 15, 2002	September 18, 2003
Cart-Rite	5	19:20	September 19, 2003	April 7, 2004
Cart-Rite	6	19:18	April 8, 2004	May 12, 2005
Cart-Rite	7	21:22	May 13, 2005	December 31, 9999
Williamson	8	15:14	May 1, 2001	July 24, 2004
Williamson	9	15:15	July 25, 2004	September 19, 2007
Williamson	10	15:14	September 20, 2007	December 31, 9999

FIGURE 11.2
Simple Instance Key.

Key and the Instance Key can exist side by side without any interruption in both keys serving their individual respective purposes.

A Compound Instance Key, illustrated in Figure 11.3, uses a compound key to uniquely identify each individual row of a table. That compound key is made of the Entity Key, which is the key already assigned to an entity, and a sequential numeric Instance Key. A Compound Instance Key resets back to the value 1 for each entity within a table. The first Instance Key value for each and every individual entity is the number 1. The last Instance Key value for each and every individual entity is the number of rows assigned to each individual entity. For example, if the entity A has thirty-two rows, the Instance Key value for the first row is 1 and the

A Compound Instance Key resets back to 1 for each Entity Key

COLOR FORMULA

Color	Instance Key	Formula	Row_First_Date	Row_Last_Date
Blue	1	B14K	March 1, 2004	November 18, 2004
Blue	2	C2387J	November 19, 2004	July 18, 2006
Blue	3	DD239X	July 19, 2006	December 31, 9999
Green	1	UU879	February 13, 2002	July 13, 2005
Green	2	W827	July 14, 2005	December 31, 9999
Red	1	XW9283	February 14, 2002	November 24, 2003
Red	2	YS2987	November 25, 2003	April 17, 2004
Red	3	WSX283	April 18, 2004	May 11, 2005
Red	4	JJR273	May 12, 2005	December 31, 9999
Yellow	1	IW028	May 12, 2001	July 2, 2004
Yellow	2	WI2893	July 3, 2004	September 8, 2007
Yellow	3	UWW287	September 9, 2007	December 31, 9999
Orange	1	PPW27	July 14, 2000	September 1, 2003
Orange	2	PSW387	September 2, 2003	December 31, 9999
White	1	PRE380	June 12, 2001	April 2, 2002
White	2	YYW273	April 3, 2002	September 14, 2005
White	3	MNM278	September 15, 2005	January 21, 2006
White	4	XUW8738	January 22, 2006	December 31, 9999
Black	1	YWS278	June 14, 2002	July 21, 2003
Black	2	UPS2873	July 22, 2003	August 27, 2005
Black	3	NMSW28	August 28, 2005	December 31, 9999
Grey	1	WSW987	July 12, 2001	March 24, 2003
Grey	2	PP879	March 25, 2003	February 12, 2004
Grey	3	HHG297	February 13, 2004	December 18, 2004
Grey	4	KSJD887	December 19, 2004	December 31, 9999

CARRIER TERMS

Carrier	Instance Key	Terms	Row_First_Date	Row_Last_Date
Harold Jones	1	14:12	February 1, 2003	December 15, 2004
Harold Jones	2	14:14	December 16, 2004	July 4, 2006
Harold Jones	3	10:12	July 5, 2006	December 31, 9999
Cart-Rite	1	21:30	January 15, 2002	September 18, 2003
Cart-Rite	2	19:20	September 19, 2003	April 7, 2004
Cart-Rite	3	19:18	April 8, 2004	May 12, 2005
Cart-Rite	4	21:22	May 13, 2005	December 31, 9999
Williamson	1	15:14	May 1, 2001	July 24, 2004
Williamson	2	15:15	July 25, 2004	September 19, 2007
Williamson	3	15:14	September 20, 2007	December 31, 9999

FIGURE 11.3
Compound Instance Key.

Instance Key value for the last row is 32; if the entity B has 862 rows, the Instance Key value for the first row is 1 and the Instance Key value for the last row is 862. When joining to a table with a Compound Instance Key, likewise with any table having a compound key, the join must include the Entity Key and the Instance Key, because the combination of the Entity Key and Instance Key is required to uniquely identify an individual row.

Join to a Simple Instance Key

A join to a Simple Instance Key is achieved by embedding the Instance Key value as a foreign key. The example in Figure 11.4 shows a Transaction table that joins to a dimension table named Item. That join is achieved

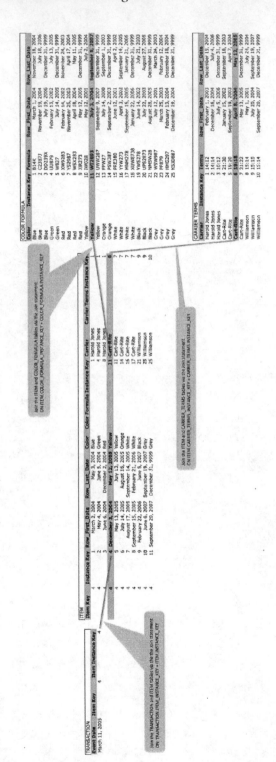

FIGURE 11.4

Transaction and Simple Instance Key.

by embedding the Item_Instance_Key as an attribute in the Transaction table. The Item_Instance_Key, which in this example has the value 4, joins to one and only one row in the Item table. That one row can be identified by the Instance_Key value equal to 4.

The Item row identified by the Instance_Key value equal to 4 has two foreign keys: Color_Formula_Instance_Key and Carrier_Terms_Instance_Key. The Color_Formula_Instance_Key value 11 joins the Item table to one and only one row in the Color Formula table. That one row in the Color Formula table is identified by the Instance Key value 11. The Carrier_Terms_Instance_Key value 6 joins the Item table to one and only one row in the Carrier Terms table. That one row in the Carrier Terms table is identified by the Instance Key value 6. In this way, the use of a Simple Instance Key satisfies the Time Variant requirement in that each row of the Transaction table joins to one and only one row of the Item table. Each row of the Item table joins to one and only one row of the Color Formula and Carrier Terms tables. When joining these tables, the RDBMS no longer need join a multitude of rows that will not be in the final result set. Instead, the RDBMS can join only those rows that will be in the final result set.

Join to a Compound Instance Key

A join to a Compound Instance Key is achieved by embedding the Entity Key and Instance Key values as foreign keys. The example in Figure 11.5 shows a Transaction table that joins to a dimension table named Item. That join is achieved by embedding the Item_Key and Item_Instance_Key as attributes in the Transaction table. The Item_Key, which has the value 4, and the Item_Instance_Key, which also has the value 4, join to one and only one row in the Item table. That one row can be identified by the Item_Key value equal to 4 and the Instance_Key value equal to 4.

The Item row identified by the Item_Key value equal to 4 and the Instance_Key value equal to 4 has two compound foreign keys: Color & Color_Formula_Instance_Key and Carrier & Carrier_Terms_Instance_Key. The Color value "Yellow" and Color_Formula_Instance_Key value 2 join the Item table to one and only one row in the Color Formula table. That one row in the Color Formula table is identified by the Color value "Yellow" and the Instance Key value 2. The Carrier value "Cart-Rite" and Carrier_Terms_Instance_Key value 3 join the Item table to one and only one row in the Carrier Terms table. That one row in the Carrier Terms table is identified by the Carrier value "Cart-Rite" and the Instance Key value 3.

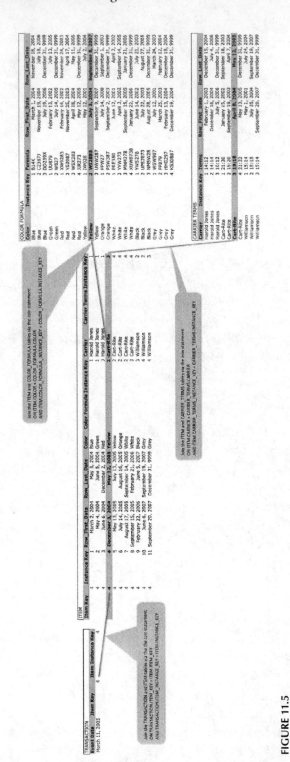

FIGURE 11.5

Transaction and Compound Instance Key.

In this way, the use of a Compound Instance Key satisfies the Time Variant requirement in that each row of the Transaction table joins to one and only one row of the Item table. Each row of the Item table joins to one and only one row of the Color Formula and Carrier Terms tables. When joining these tables, the RDBMS no longer need join a multitude of rows that will not be in the final result set. Instead, the RDBMS can join only those rows that will be in the final result set.

Cascading Instance Keys

The ex.4 also demonstrates a peculiarity of this Time Variant Solution Design. Notice in the Item table the rows identified by the Instance Key values 4 and 5 have the same attributes. The Item table rows identified by the Instance Key values 7 and 8 and the values 10 and 11 also seem to display the same attributes, yet have an incremented Item Instance Key. So, the obvious question is why. Why did the Item table increment to Instance Key 5, even though no attributes in the Item table changed? The answer is that an attribute of the Cart-Rite entity in the Carrier Terms table changed. The attribute change in the Carrier Terms table for the Cart-Rite entity caused the Carrier Terms table to increment to the next Instance Key. Coincidentally, the Item table was referencing the Cart-Rite entity in the Carrier Terms table when the Cart-Rite entity incremented to the next Instance Key. So, the Item table incorporated the new Carrier Terms Instance Key, and in the process, incremented to the next Instance Key for the Item table. Likewise, an incremented Item Instance Key was caused by the incremented Color Instance Key for the White entity in the Color Formula table. At that time the Item table was referencing the White entity of the Color Formula table. The formula for the color White changed, which caused the Color Formula table to increment to the next Color Formula Instance Key. The new Color Formula Instance Key was incorporated into the Item table, which resulted in a new Item Instance Key. The Item Instance Key 11 is also caused by a change in the Williamson entity of the Carrier Terms table. The Williamson entity of the Carrier Terms table incremented to a new Instance Key when the Terms changed. The new Carrier Instance Key for the Williamson entity cascaded down into the Item table, causing the Item table to increment to a new Item Instance Key.

The example in Figure 11.5 demonstrates the same behavior. Simple Instance Keys and Compound Instance Keys both cascade Instance Keys with identical behavior. The general rule is that any increment in the Instance

Key of a table cascades to any other table that references that table, causing an increment in the Instance Key of the referring table. A table at the top of a hierarchy structure will not experience the effect of cascading Instance Keys because a table at the top of a hierarchy structure refers to no hierarchical parents. A table at the bottom of a hierarchy structure, however, will experience significant effects from cascading Instance Keys because a table at the bottom of a hierarchy references hierarchical parents that also have hierarchical parents (and probably grandparents) of their own. A table, such as the Item table in Figure 11.4 and Figure 11.5, that refers to multiple hierarchical parents will experience cascading Instance Keys from both hierarchical parent tables.

This is the point at which this Time Variant Solution Design initially seems somewhat counterintuitive. The insertion of additional rows in a hierarchically lower table because a hierarchically higher table experienced updates seems to defy common sense. But then, a good example of why this construct succeeds can be found in the automotive insurance industry. For an example of the automotive insurance industry, we can consider a fictitious young boy named Harold.

- Harold/16 years of age—At the age of 16 years, Harold receives his driver's license. His automotive insurance company requires a very high insurance premium because Harold is 16 years of age; all 16-year-old boys are considered a very high risk.
- Harold/24 years of age—At the age of 24 years, Harold graduates from college. His automotive insurance company reduces his insurance premium because Harold is 24 year of age and has a college degree; all 24-year-old young men with a college degree are considered a moderate risk.
- Harold/35 years of age—At the age of 35 years, Harold is married and has his first child. His automotive insurance company extends its lowest possible insurance premium because Harold is 35 years of age and has a child; all 35-year-old men with a child are considered a minimal risk.

Is there a difference between Harold/16, Harold/24, and Harold/35? Yes, there is a difference. The difference is that Harold/16 is a member of a high-risk group, whereas Harold/24 is a member of a moderate-risk group and Harold/35 is a member of a low-risk group. Are Harold/16, Harold/24, and Harold/35 the same person? Yes, of course they are all Harold.

However, they are different manifestations of the one person known as Harold. Those different manifestations of Harold are Harold at different times of his life. Likewise, the incremented Instance Keys for the entities Cart-Rite, White, and Williamson mean the data is representing different manifestations of the entities Cart-Rite, White, and Williamson. In that way, Cart_Rite/3 is indeed different from Cart_Rite/4. You have to go to Cart_Rite's table, the Carrier Terms table, to find that difference. In the same way, White/2 is different from White/3, and Williamson/2 is different from Williamson/3. The Instance Keys uniquely identify the manifestations of an entity in a table. Any other table that references that entity also references a manifestation of that entity, which is identified by an Instance Key.

This is the effect of time in a data warehouse. Data modeling standard practices consider the relationship between entities with the assumption that such entity relations persist through time. If a hierarchical parent could gain and lose its relation to a hierarchical child from one day to the next, a data modeler would recognize such a condition as an error in the data model and try again. If a data model is constructed correctly, two related entities will always be related. Their relation exists today and will exist tomorrow. As such, entity relations in a data model are built with the expectation that entity relations exist at all times. Therefore, entity relations in a data model do not need to incorporate a third element (i.e., time) into their relation. However, when in a Time Variant data warehouse we add the element of time, relations between entities are affected by time. That time effect is captured in the form of Instances. That is the major difference in this Time Variant Solution Design. This Time Variant Solution Design uses Instance Keys to capture the effect of time, rather than using dates and intervals to capture the effect of time. Through the use of Instance Keys in a primary key/foreign key relation, this Time Variant Solution Design simultaneously captures the effect of time and resolves the performance problems caused by the multiplicative explosion of time variant data.

WHICH TABLES USE INSTANCE KEYS?

Every row of every table has some aspect of time. The transactions in a fact table occurred at a time. The entities in a dimension table began at a time and ended at a time. So, which of the multitude of tables in a data warehouse should include Instance Keys? The answer is any table wherein the data can be in effect over an interval, or span, of time. Transactions and events in a fact table typically occur at, or are realized as of, a single moment in time. Transactions and events that are associated with only a single moment in time do not need an Instance Key to further identify that moment in time. Entities, properties, and attributes in a dimension table typically remain in effect for a period of days, weeks, months, or years. Entities, properties, and attributes need an Instance Key to identify their existence in that interval of time in a way that can be captured in a relation between tables.

There is always an exception to the rule. Somewhere, a data warehouse has a dimension table that is specific to a single moment in time. Somewhere, another data warehouse has a fact table that has transactions that span days, weeks, months, or years. So, we cannot define the use of Instance Keys as a method dedicated solely to dimension tables, and never fact tables, in a data warehouse. If you're looking at the data model of your data warehouse wondering which tables need Instance Keys, you can probably look for dates that identify the beginning and ending of the effective span of time. If a table has such dates, that table will require an Instance Key. If a table has a time value that indicates only a moment in time, that table does not need an Instance Key.

TYPE 1 TIME VARIANCE

The Time Variant Solution Design has thus far dealt solely with Type 2 Time Variance. Type 2 Time Variance places all transactions and events in their original historical context. This Time Variant Solution Design also includes a solution for Type 1 Time Variance. The difference between Type 1 and Type 2 Time Variance is, therefore, the historic context in time. Type 2 Time Variance achieves the historic context by the inclusion of all history rows, each of which is uniquely identified by Instance Keys, either Simple or Compound. Type 1 Time Variance can also be achieved by reversing both those features. In Figure 11.6, the history rows are removed, retaining only those rows that are the most recent for each entity. The notations in Figure 11.6 also show that all joins are achieved by way of the entity keys.

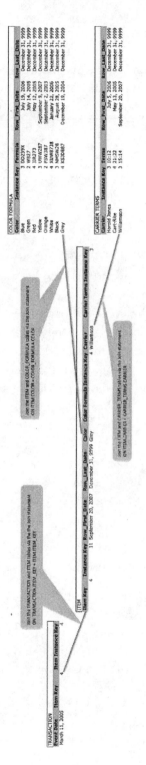

FFIGURE 11.6

Transaction and Type 1 Time Variance with Simple Instance Keys.

The tables in Figure 11.6 avoid the multiplicative explosion of rows by retaining only one row for each entity. In Chapter 10, the joins using entity keys caused the multiplicative explosion of rows because the dimension tables had multiple rows for the same entity key. The dimension tables in Figure 11.6, however, have only one row for each entity key. So, you could say the tables in Figure 11.6 also experience the multiplicative explosion of rows, and the multiplicative factor is the number of rows per entity, which would be a factor of 1.

Also notice that the dimension tables in Figure 11.6 retain their Instance Keys. The inclusion of the instance keys facilitates a data quality assessment of the parity between the Type 2 and Type 1 tables. The ability to match the entity keys, instance keys, and attributes for each entity in each dimension table in the Type 1 and Type 2 sets of data increases the level of confidence in the parity between the two sets of data, as compared to matching only the entity keys and attributes.

The tables in Figure 11.7 are very similar to the tables in Figure 11.6. The one difference is the instance keys. The instance keys in Figure 11.7 are based on rows from a dimension table that was built using Compound Instance Keys. The resulting data is the same. The only difference is the key structure that returned that data. The data from the Type 2 tables in Figure 11.4 and Figure 11.5 associated the transaction with a yellow item delivered by Cart-Rite. However, the data from the Type 1 tables in Figure 11.6 and Figure 11.7 associated the transaction with a gray item delivered by Williamson. Which answer is correct? They are both correct...for their respective time variant context.

TYPE 1 AND TYPE 2 COMBINED

A data warehouse can incorporate both forms of time variance. The existence of the Type 1 time variant dimension tables does not preclude the existence of Type 2 time variant dimension tables. A transaction or dimension table is able to join to them both, as can be seen in Figures 11.4, 11.5, 11.6, and 11.7. So, there really is no reason to choose one form of time variance at the exclusion of the other.

Figure 11.8 shows a single transaction table (in the middle of the figure) that joins to Type 2 dimension tables (in the top of the figure) and Type 1 dimension tables (in the bottom of the figure). This approach leverages a

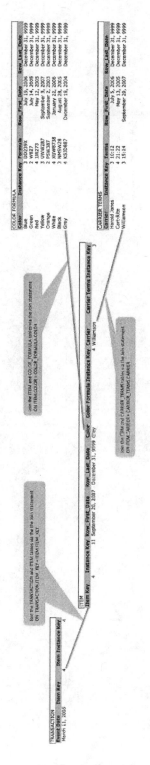

FIGURE 11.7

Transaction and Type 1 Time Variance with Compound Instance Keys.

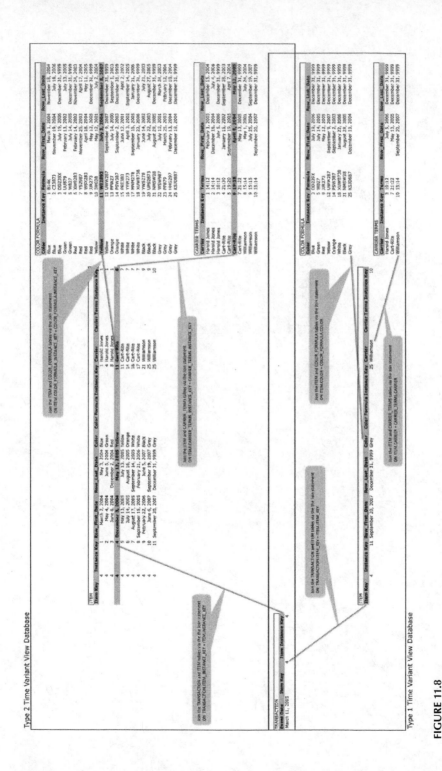

FIGURE 11.8

Transaction and Type 1 and 2 Time Variance with Simple Instance Keys.

single set of transaction, or fact, tables that can join to both Type 1 dimension tables and Type 2 dimension tables.

The only caveat here is the possibility to cause confusion. When joining the Transaction table to the Item table, which Item table do I join to the Transaction table? The answer, which will be discussed in further detail in Chapter 12, is to use three databases. The first database holds only the transaction, or fact, tables. The second database holds the Type 1 dimension tables and views to the transaction, or fact, tables. In that Type 1 database, the Transaction table can join to only one Item table because the Type 1 database has only one Item table. The third database holds the Type 2 dimension tables and views to the transaction, or fact, tables. In that Type 2 database, the Transaction table can join to only one Item table because the Type 2 database has only one Item table. So, if you want to view the data warehouse in the Type 1 time variant context, you query the Type 1 database; if you want to view the data warehouse in the Type 2 time variant context, you query the Type 2 database.

Figure 11.9 shows the combination of Type 1 and Type 2 databases, using Compound Instance Keys to uniquely identify the Type 2 dimension rows. The dimension rows in Figure 11.8 used Simple Instance Keys to uniquely identify every dimension row. The combination of Type 1 and Type 2 dimension tables works equally well with Simple Instance Keys and Compound Instance Keys. Both forms of combined time variance avoid the multiplicative explosion of rows that is the root cause of the performance degradation associated with a time variant data warehouse. Data warehouse customers who wish to see enterprise transactions in their historical context can query the Type 2 database. Data warehouse customers who wish to see enterprise transactions in the present context of the enterprise can query the Type 1 database. The query language used to query both databases is the standard relational SQL. By using this Time Variant Solution Design, a data warehouse can simultaneously deliver Type 1 and Type 2 time variant data, without the performance degradation associated with time variance via date logic.

SUMMARY TABLES

Transaction tables contain data from individual transactions. For a shipping company a Transaction table could hold all the shipping orders,

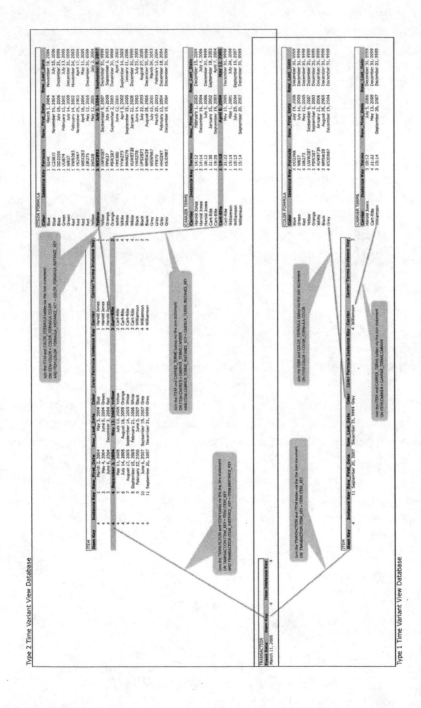

FIGURE 11.9

Transaction and Type 1 & 2 Time Variance With Compound Instance Keys.

deliveries, and confirmations. For a restaurant a Transaction table could contain all the dining orders. For a retail company a Transaction table could contain all the sales details that occurred. Granular detailed data is a valuable asset to a data warehouse, unless you need a weekly sales report. When you need to know how many pounds of potatoes sold every week for the past two years, granular transaction data about the individual sale of potatoes only causes the data warehouse RDBMS to work harder to provide a weekly sales report. For that reason, the most obvious performance optimization for a data warehouse is Summary tables.

Summary tables hold the result set of an Insert/Select query that sums the additive quantitative portions of a Transaction table. A summation query also includes a GROUP BY statement. The GROUP BY statement defines the level of granularity of the Summary table. If the summation query groups retail locations by a geographic area (i.e., region), then the geographic granularity of the Summary table will be the region, whereas the geographic granularity of the Transaction table was the retail location. If the summation query groups products by a hierarchy (i.e., department), then the hierarchical granularity of the Summary table will be the department, whereas the hierarchical granularity of the Transaction table was the individual product.

Summary tables can, and often are, a summation of time. All the transactions that occurred during a day can be summarized to the level of granularity of a day (i.e., day-level summary), week (i.e., week-level summary), or any other time cycle within the enterprise. The time period of a Summary table may, or may not, override the time variance of the data included in the Summary table. If, for example, a Summary table is defined as a week-level summary, that table would summarize all the transactions that occurred from Sunday through Saturday. Suppose a product in those transactions was blue on Sunday, green on Monday, red on Tuesday, yellow on Wednesday, black on Thursday, white on Friday, and mauve on Saturday. So for the week-level summary of transactions including that product, what is the color of that product for the week? Is it the first color? Is it the last color?

The answer is based on the time variance of the Summary table. If the Summary table is a Type 1 Summary table, then all dimensions will be represented by their Entity Key. The product in question, which seems to change color daily, will be represented by its Entity Key. What is its color? It is the color it is right now. Because it is a Type 1 Summary table, by definition the Type 1 dimensions can represent only their properties and attributes in effect now.

If, however, the Summary table is a Type 2 Summary table, then all the dimensions will be represented by their Instance Key. The product in question, which seems to change color daily, will be represented by all its Instance Keys—all seven of them, one for each color. Because it is a Type 2 Summary table, by definition the Type 2 dimensions can represent their properties and attributes in effect at the time of the original transaction or event. Even when summed up by the week all the "green" rows sum together, all the "red" rows sum together, all the "yellow" rows sum together, and so on.

The result is that a Type 1 Summary table will have one row for each GROUP BY key including the Entity_Key, regardless of the time variant changes in the dimensions referenced by the GROUP BY statement, which included the Entity_Key. However, a Type 2 Summary table for the same GROUP BY key including the Instance_Key will have one row for each time variant change in the dimensions referenced by the GROUP BY statement, which included the Instance_Key.

ETL Cycles

ETL cycles are the frequency, or schedule, by which the ETL jobs run. If the ETL jobs run once a day, then the ETL cycle is the day. If the ETL jobs run once a week, then the ETL cycle is the week. The ETL cycle determines how often the data warehouse "sees" the enterprise. If the enterprise changes the color of a product nine times every day, and the ETL application for a data warehouse extracts the color of that product only once in a day, then the data warehouse will be aware of only one color update per day. The other eight color updates per day will never be seen in the data warehouse. In that example the ETL cycle is a day.

The ETL cycle determines the smallest possible interval of time in a dimension table. For example, if the ETL cycle runs once per day at 5:00 a.m., then the smallest interval of time for that dimension table is the day (e.g., 5:00 a.m. today through 5:00 a.m. tomorrow). So, if the ETL cycle for the color of a product runs at 5:00 a.m. every day, then the smallest time interval for the product color table would be a 24-hour day. So, the Instance Key value 1357 would indicate that the color of the product was blue from Sunday 5:00 a.m. through Monday 5:00 a.m. The time interval indicated by an Instance Key in that table, therefore, would be Sunday

5:00 a.m. through Monday 5:00 a.m., which is a day. In that example, the Instance Key represents a day.

If an ETL application extracts data once per week on Tuesday morning at 8:00 a.m., then the ETL cycle would be from Tuesday 8:00 a.m. through the following Tuesday 8:00 a.m. The smallest interval of time for which a dimension update could exist in that data warehouse would be from Tuesday 8:00 a.m. through the following Tuesday 8:00 a.m. The Instance Key for that dimension table would indicate the time period Tuesday 8:00 a.m. through the following Tuesday 8:00 a.m.

If an ETL application extracts data once per month on the fifth of the month, then the ETL cycle would be from the fifth of the month through the fifth of the following month. The smallest interval of time for which a dimension update could exist in that data warehouse would be from the fifth of the month through the fifth of the following month. The Instance Key for that dimension table would indicate the time period the fifth of the month through the fifth of the following month.

Therefore, the ETL cycle determines the smallest time interval that can be represented by an Instance Key. So, if you want the Instance Keys to represent dates, then ETL cycle must run once per day. If you want the Instance Keys to represent weeks, then the ETL cycle must run once per week. Time-based Summary tables can summarize at a time hierarchy level equal to the time interval represented by the Instance Keys. However, time-based Summary tables cannot summarize at a level more granular than the time interval represented by the Instance Keys.

Instance Keys

The time interval between ETL cycles is the time interval represented by an Instance Key. In that way, the ETL cycle defines the periodicity of the Instance Keys. If the ETL cycle occurs every twenty-four hours, and an update with an incremented Instance Key occurs every twenty-four hours, then the interval represented by each Instance Key is twenty-four hours. That means that all rows in a Transaction table representing that twenty-four hour period will share the same Instance Key.

A time variant data warehouse works best when the entire data warehouse shares the same ETL Cycle, and therefore, the same periodicity. A shared common periodicity avoids difficult time variant conversions and the same relational integrity issues that arise in the presence of differing time frames. By defining the periodicity of the ETL cycle and Instance

Keys, a data warehouse is able to be time variant in a single consistent unit of time. The unit of time chosen for a specific data warehouse is a judgment decision based on the transactions and activity within the enterprise.

REAL TIME AND TIME VARIANCE

At first glance, Real Time and Time Variance would seem to go hand in hand. They are both about time, and they both have a wow factor of 9+. So, they should go together, right? Actually, no, Real Time and Time Variance do not go together.

The goal of Time Variance is to synchronize enterprise events in the past with the state of the enterprise at that moment in the past. A time variant data warehouse will be able to synchronize events on July 21, 2001, with the state of the enterprise on July 21, 2001. Time Variance adds value by increasing the span of time during which transactions and dimensions can be synchronized. The reason Time Variance is so difficult is that there is so much history to synchronize. Looking back in time, the history begins yesterday and continues as far as the enterprise can see.

Real Time, on the other hand, could be renamed as Right Now. The focus of Real Time is the "right now" time frame. Real Time is not focused on the five, ten, or fifteen years leading up to today. Instead, Real Time is focused on today. That being the case, the "time" in Real Time is right now, whereas the "time" in Time Variant is all of history. These two time frames contrast drastically with each other.

The enterprise knows the properties and attributes of a product today. The enterprise also knows the properties and attributes of that same product as of yesterday. So, time variant data about transactions and dimensions that occurred today, or yesterday, do not add much value. However, a data warehouse that can synchronize enterprise transactions and dimensions for the past five, ten, or fifteen years adds value through its time variant data. As such, time variant data about today's transactions is not as helpful as time variant data about transactions from the past fifteen years.

The distinction between time variant data for the past fifteen years and real-time data for the past fifteen hours is the distinction between strategic and tactical data. Strategic data provides the big picture, far distant horizon, and holistic perspective of the enterprise. Tactical data provides the current, up-to-the minute, "right now" perspective of the enterprise. Strategic data can identify trends and patterns that can only be seen by looking at multiple years of data. Tactical data can tell you the state of the enterprise right now, this minute, which has changed since you began reading this paragraph...see, it changed again.

If that tactical, "right now" time frame is your requirement, then you need an operational data store. An operational data store is both. It is operational. It is a data store. An operational data store provides an interface into the operational data of a single business unit. The data is grained at the lowest level available in the operational system. The data retention period is very short, possibly as short as days, or as long as weeks. The ETL process for an operational data store updates the data frequently—if not real time, then near real time. The lowest-level granularity, short retention period, frequent updates, and single business unit focus all together indicate the tactical nature of an operational data store.

The operational data store is explained in Chapter 5 of *Building and Maintaining a Data Warehouse*. The architectural considerations that lead to the creation of an operational data store are similar to the distinction between a delivery truck and an ice cream truck. They both serve their individual purposes very well. They do not, however, serve both purposes simultaneously well at all. For that reason, real-time up-to-the-minute data is best presented in an operational data store, while long-range time variant data is best presented in a data warehouse.

FIRST TIME VARIANT SUBJECT AREA

Your first time variant data warehouse subject area should be small... smaller than that...still smaller. That is because your first time variant subject area will include the initial creation of all things time variant: tables, keys, ETL, views, BI reports, data quality, metadata. The scope of your first time variant subject area will be more about time variance than about the subject area. Unfortunately, you don't get to under-deliver the subject area. So, the safest plan is to convert a reasonably small subject area that is already mature in the data warehouse. Your ability to recognize mistakes will be improved when you're looking at data you can recognize. For that reason, begin with a subject area with which you are experienced. This will initially seem counterintuitive. However, for that first time variant subject area the new deliverable is time variance. Delivering a time variant version of a mature subject area allows you to focus more on the time variant structures and infrastructures. For the second time variant subject area, all those structures and infrastructures will already be in place.

12

Time Variant Database Definition

If this Time Variant Solution Design has taken you out of your comfort zone, then please pause, breathe deeply, and get ready to go back to your comfort zone. This database design is more about fitting Instance Keys and indexes into an existing data warehouse design than it is about creating a new data warehouse design. If you're waiting for this chapter to tell you to throw everything away and prepare to start over, you're going to wait a very long time. Rather than throw away everything you know about your data warehouse, including all those little idiosyncrasies that only a handful of people know about, this chapter will assume that you have maintained your data warehouse to the best of your ability and that your data warehouse is the best it can be. For that reason, obviously you're not trying to solve a data model or ETL problem with a Time Variant design. You are simply trying to integrate Time Variance into an existing data warehouse.

If, however, you're starting from the beginning, please be aware that everything in this chapter comes after the source system analysis, conceptual data model, logical data model, and the first physical data model. Time variance should be introduced somewhere around the second physical data model. All these analysis and design methods are explained in *Building and Maintaining a Data Warehouse*. This discussion of time variance in a data warehouse does not bypass or replace any of the analysis and design methods that are key to the success of every data warehouse. Rather, this discussion of time variance in a data warehouse is in addition to the data warehouse analysis and design methods. For that reason, this discussion of data warehousing assumes a shared level of knowledge. If this is your first book on data warehousing, please have a copy of *Building and Maintaining a Data Warehouse* handy for reference purposes.

TABLES OF TYPES AND TYPES OF TABLES

This Time Variant Solution Design is a method for defining table keys and optimizing joins to those table keys. Fact tables are still fact tables. Dimension tables are still dimension tables. Dimensional data models are still dimensional data models. In addition, Third Normal Form retains its present form. This Time Variant Solution Design is not intended to change any of the data warehousing data modeling methods. Instead, this Time Variant Solution Design is intended to optimize joins within those data models when they are intended to reflect the passage of time.

The genius of the fact, dimension, and summary table concepts is rendered more obvious in the presence of this Time Variant Solution Design. Rather than modify their purpose and function, the addition of time variance to fact, dimension, and summary tables only increases their effectiveness in achieving their individual goals and purposes. We don't need to force fact, dimension, and summary tables to a new and unfamiliar purpose, like a square peg in a round hole. Instead, we expand the value achieved by fact, dimension, and summary tables in a data warehouse by incorporating time variance into their current design.

TYPE 2 TIME VARIANT DIMENSION TABLES

Dimension tables present the properties and attributes of an entity. Time variance expands that definition to…present the properties and attributes of an entity as of a moment in time. Without time variance a dimension table is a two-way join between an entity and a property or attribute. The addition of time variance creates a three-way join that now includes the time interval during which the two-way join between an entity and a property or attribute was in effect. That three-way join has been the cause of significant performance issues in relational data warehouses.

The performance degradation is resolved by the use of an Instance Key that uniquely identifies a single row of a dimension table. In that way, an Instance Key uniquely identifies the row that presents the two-way join between an entity and its attributes and properties as of a specific moment in time. An Instance Key is a sequential numeric column in a dimension table. A Simple Instance Key is composed of only that sequential numeric column of data in a dimension table. A Compound Instance Key is composed of an Entity Key and a sequential numeric column of data that resets back to the value 1 for every new Entity Key.

Figure 11.4 shows a set of time variant dimension tables that join by Simple Instance Keys. Figure 11.5 shows a set of time variant dimension tables that join by Compound Instance Keys. Both sets of tables follow the same query paths, which can go in two directions. The query can begin with fact table rows and then join up to the dimension tables. The query can also begin with a parent dimension table rows and then join down to the fact table. Instance Keys are intended to optimize the joins in query paths in both directions.

A query that begins with a fact table will join up to the dimension tables. More specifically, a query that begins with a row of data from a fact table will join up to a single row in a dimension table. The optimization of this Time Variant Solution Design is achieved by optimizing the join between a row of a fact table and a row of a dimension table. To that end, the Instance Key is the primary key (or primary index) of a Type 2 time variant dimension table. When the Instance Key of a dimension table is also the primary key (or primary index) of a table, a join to that table via the Instance Key becomes the fastest join path to that table. To make that happen, the Instance Key of every dimension table is also the primary key (or primary index) of every Type 2 time variant dimension table. For these tables, that means the Instance Key is the fastest possible join path to each table. When the Instance Key of a table is a Simple Instance Key, the primary key of that table is that single column which is the Instance Key. When the Instance Key of a table is a Compound Instance Key, the primary key of that table is the pair of columns that are the Entity Key and the Instance Key, which together form the Compound Instance Key.

A query that begins with a fact table joins to a dimension table and then joins dimension tables to dimension tables. As shown in Figure 11.4 and Figure 11.5, a time variant join can occur between dimensions. Figure 11.4 shows the dimension table Item joins to the Color_Formula and Carrier_ Terms tables by referencing the single column that is the Instance Key of the Color_Formula table and the single column that is the Instance Key of the Carrier_Terms table. Figure 11.5 shows the dimension table Item joins to the Color_Formula and Carrier_Terms tables by referencing the two columns that are the Entity Key and Instance Key of the Color_Formula table and the two columns that are the Entity Key and Instance Key of the Carrier_Terms table. Every dimension table has its own Instance Key, which is its primary key.

The query path from a fact table begins with the fact table. A foreign key column in the fact table joins to the Instance Key of a dimension table. In Figure 11.4 the fact table foreign key joins to a Simple Instance Key in the Item table. In Figure 11.5 the fact table foreign key joins to a Compound Instance Key in the Item table. Then a dimension table continues the query path by joining, via Instance Keys, to other dimension tables. In Figure 11.4 the Item table joins to the Color_Formula and Carrier_Terms tables via Simple Instance Keys. In Figure 11.5 the Item table joins to the Color_Formula and Carrier_Terms tables via Compound Instance Keys.

The query path that begins with a fact table and then joins to dimension tables usually is the result of a question that begins with the transactions in the fact table. The query path can also begin with a dimension table. A Department summary would begin with the Department dimension table. A Region summary would begin with a Region dimension table. Or, in the case of the example in Figure 11.4 and Figure 11.5, a Carrier_Terms summary would begin with the Carrier_Terms table; a Color_Formula summary would begin with the Color_Formula table.

To optimize the join path from a dimension table (e.g., Carrier_Terms or Color_Formula) backward toward the fact table, the foreign key Instance Keys in all dimension tables will be indexed as a secondary index. In Figure 11.4 and Figure 11.5, the join path from the Color_Formula table "backward" to the Item table will be optimized by a secondary index on the Color_Formula Instance Key in the Item table; in addition, the join path from the Carrier_Terms table "backward" to the Item table will be optimized by a secondary index on the Carrier_Terms Instance Key in the Item table. So, when the query path goes "backward" from a dimension table, through other dimension tables, down to the fact table, the primary keys and foreign keys reverse. The join from the Carrier_Terms table down to the Item table finds the applicable rows in the Item table by finding the Item rows wherein the Carrier_Terms Instance Key matches the Carrier_ Terms Instance Key of the Carrier_Terms table. The join from the Color_ Formula table down to the Item table finds the applicable rows in the Item table by finding the Item rows wherein the Color_Formula Instance Key matches the Color_Formula Instance Key of the Color_Formula table. To optimize this join path, the Color_Formula Instance Key in the Item table is covered by a secondary index, and the Carrier_Terms Instance Key in the Item table is also covered by a secondary index. When the Instance Keys are Simple Instance Keys, the covering secondary index is an index of only the one Instance Key column. When the Instance Keys are Compound Instance Keys, the covering secondary index is an index of the two Instance Key columns.

To summarize the design of a Type 2 dimension table:

- The Instance Key is a numeric sequential unique identifier for every row of a dimension table.
- A Simple Instance Key is made of only a single numeric column within a dimension table.
- A Compound Instance Key is made of an Entity Key and a single numeric sequential column of data that resets back to 1 for every new entity.
- A dimension table's Instance Key is the primary key, or primary index, of that table.
- A dimension table has foreign Instance Keys which should be covered as a secondary index.
- For some RDBMS platforms, foreign key/primary key relations perform more efficiently when all instances of the key are the same data type.
- Figure 11.4 and Figure 11.5 display foreign key/primary key relations in a Type 2 time variant data warehouse.

TYPE 1 AND TYPE 2 TIME VARIANT DIMENSION TABLES IN A SHARED ENVIRONMENT

Type 2 Time Variance is achieved by connecting every row of a fact table to the dimension rows that were in effect at the time of the transaction presented in that row. Type 1 Time Variance is achieved by connecting every row of a fact table to the dimension rows that are in effect right now. This will create two representations of the enterprise. One is a Type 1 "present state" representation of the enterprise. The other is a Type 2 "historic state" representation of the enterprise. Figure 11.8 (showing Simple Instance Keys) and Figure 11.9 (showing Compound Instance Keys) give a big picture view of how these two representations work together in one data warehouse. As a DBA, you choose how to present these two sets of dimensions (present state and historic state). The possibilities include two separate databases, two schemas, or some other demarcation. The goal of that demarcation is to allow the users of the data warehouse to know which set of dimensions they are using. They need to know that when they are in the "Present State" demarcation, their query results will reflect only the present state of the enterprise. Likewise, the data warehouse users need to know that when they are in the "Historic State" demarcation, their query results will reflect only the historic state of the enterprise.

Figure 11.8 and Figure 11.9 show that both the Type 1 Time Variance dimension tables and the Type 2 Time Variance dimension tables share the same set of fact tables. The sharing of fact tables avoids unnecessary resource consumption by doubling the disk capacity of the fact tables via replicated tables and avoids the possibility of differing total quantities when comparing Type 1 and Type 2 result sets (and yes, everyone will compare the Type 1 and Type 2 data).

Having established the concept and implementation of Instance Keys, Type 2 Time Variance is easy to understand. The remaining challenge is to build the Type 1 Time Variant dimension tables and the fact tables, so that the Type 1 and Type 2 dimension tables can share the same fact tables.

TYPE 1 TIME VARIANT DIMENSION TABLES

A data warehouse presents enterprise events in both their historic context and their present context. Ralph Kimball dubbed the presentation of enterprise events in their present context as Type 1 Time Variance, and Kimball dubbed the presentation of enterprise events in their historic context as Type 2 Time Variance. The discussion of Type 1 Time Variance versus Type 2 Time Variance is a discussion of the presentation of dimensions in the data warehouse. The previous section explained the concepts underlying relational structures that would achieve Type 2 Time Variance. This section will explain the concepts underlying relational structures that would achieve Type 1 Time Variance.

The historic context of Type 2 Time Variant dimension tables is achieved by joining on Instance Keys. Instance Keys synchronize the rows that were in effect as of a moment in time. The present context of Type 1 Time Variant dimension tables is achieved by joining on Entity Keys. Entity Keys ignore the possibility that a row of dimension data might not have been in effect as of a moment in the past, because the Type 1 dimension tables cannot see the past.

All the Same Columns

The Type 1 dimension tables have all the same columns as the Type 2 dimension tables, including the Instance Keys. Retaining all the columns allows the queries and BI reports using the Type 2 "historic context" dimension to be as similar as possible to the queries and BI reports using the Type 1 "historic context" dimensions. The same columns also make management of the two sets of dimension tables easier and cleaner. Also, retaining the Instance Keys, Row_First_Date, and Row_Last_Date columns in the Type 1 "present state" dimension tables strengthens the effect of the data quality assessment that will verify that the Type 1 dimension tables do indeed have only the most recent dimension row for each entity. So, while it may seem strange at first to retain all the time variant columns in the Type 1 dimension tables, that design approach adds more value than the disk space it consumes.

Only the Row in Effect Right Now

The Type 1 Time Variant dimension table will avoid any possible confusion about historic dimension rows by presenting only the row in effect right now for a given entity. Figure 11.6 and Figure 11.7 display how this would look in the example of a transaction involving Item Key 4. In that example, Item Key is the Entity Key, and Item Key 4 is the entity. Since the example includes only one item (Item 4), the Type 1 Item table includes only one row. If the example were expanded to include four hundred items, then the Type 1 Item table would include four hundred rows.

The other obvious observation is that the Type 1 dimension tables have fewer rows than their Type 2 dimension table counterparts. Obviously, the Type 1 dimension tables have fewer rows because they do not include any history rows.

Entity Primary Keys

The primary key in Type 1 Time Variant dimension tables is a structural Data Definition Language (DDL) change compared to the primary keys of the Type 2 Time Variant dimension tables. In Type 1 Time Variant dimension tables the Entity Key is the primary key. This is different because in a Type 1 Time Variant dimension you are not joining to an entity as of a moment in the past. Instead, you are joining to an entity...period. In a

Type 1 Time Variant dimension there is no representation of the past. So, there is no need to try to join to the past. Instead, each entity has only one row, and that one row is the goal of a join to that entity.

When the query path goes from a fact table to a Type 1 dimension table, the fact table joins to an Entity Key in a dimension table. That dimension table joins to another dimension table via the Entity Key of the second dimension table. The second dimension table joins to a third dimension table via the Entity Key of the third dimension table, and so on.

Entity Foreign Keys

When the query path goes from a Type 1 dimension table to a fact table, the dimension table joins to the fact table via a foreign Entity Key. A Type 1 dimension table can join to a second Type 1 dimension table by finding its Entity Key as a foreign key in the second dimension table. The second dimension table can also join to a third dimension table by finding its Entity Key as a foreign key in the third dimension table, and so on. Finally, the lowest-level Type 1 dimension table joins to a fact table by finding its Entity Key as a foreign key in the fact table.

To optimize the performance of these joins from a Type 1 dimension table to another Type 1 dimension table, or a fact table, the foreign Entity Keys should be covered by a secondary index. By joining to the secondary index, the join from one dimension table to another dimension table should be able to find a more efficient explain than a full table scan.

FACT TABLES

The rows of a fact table represent individual enterprise events or transactions. In a data warehouse, the fact tables represent the business functions of the data warehouse. The rows of the fact tables represent the individual occurrences of those business functions. The Entity Keys and Instance Keys in a fact table identify the individual enterprise entities involved in the business function.

The primary key of a fact table has no relevance to this Time Variant Solution Design. So, the primary key should be designed to optimize BI reports that query large numbers of fact rows. The foreign keys that join to dimension tables, however, are relevant to this Time Variant Solution

Design. To optimize the performance of queries that begin from the dimension tables, the Entity Keys that join to Type 1 dimension tables should each be covered by a secondary index, and the Instance Keys that join to Type 2 dimension tables should each be covered by a secondary index.

TIME SUMMARY TABLES

The detailed and granular data in a fact table can be summarized by any dimension hierarchy referenced in that fact table. Transactions can be summarized by a Product hierarchy up to the Department level of that hierarchy. Events can be summarized by a Labor hierarchy up to the Skill level of that hierarchy. The Time hierarchy is a ubiquitous summary scheme. Typically, a data warehouse will summarize individual transactions up to the Day and Week. From those two Time summaries, other less frequent Time summaries can be performed at run time.

The "Summary Tables" section of Chapter 11 explained that Time summaries in this Time Variant Solution Design can be defined as either Type 1 Summary tables or Type 2 Summary tables. A Type 1 Summary table is different from its source Fact table in that a Type 1 Summary table has only Entity Keys and no Instance Keys. A Type 2 Summary table is different from its source Fact table in that a Type 2 Summary table has only Instance Keys and no Entity Keys.

A Type 2 Summary table could serve both purposes as a Type 1 and Type 2 Summary table by retaining both the Entity Keys and Instance Keys. Such a hybrid Type 1/Type 2 Summary table is feasible because hierarchically all Instance Keys for an Entity Key are contained within that Entity Key. When a hybrid Type 1/Type 2 Summary table joins to a Type 1 Dimension table, a summation operation must occur again to sum the quantitative measurements up to the Entity Keys in the Summary table. When a hybrid Type 1/Type 2 Summary table joins to a Type 2 Dimension table, no additional summation operation is required to sum the quantitative measurements up to the Instance Keys in the Summary table.

The decision to deploy a Type 1 Summary table, Type 2 Summary table, or hybrid Type 1/Type 2 Summary table is a judgment call between the requirements, disk capacity, and CPU and I/O capacity of the data warehouse RDBMS.

CONCLUSION

Figure 11.8, using Simple Instance Keys, and Figure 11.9, using Compound Instance Keys, display a data warehouse that has a set of Type 1 "present state" dimension tables, a set of Type 2 "historic state" dimension tables, and a fact table that joins to both sets of dimension tables. The Type 1 "present state" dimension tables join via Entity Keys. The Type 2 "historic state" dimension tables join via Instance Keys. The fact and summary tables join via the method indicated by the set of dimension tables to which they join in an individual query. The result of these three sets of tables is a data warehouse that can present the events and transactions of the enterprise in their present and historic context.

Conceivably, a data warehouse can use a mixture of Simple and Compound Instance Keys. In practice, such a mixture of Simple and Compound Instance Keys can be very confusing. For that reason, if possible, a data warehouse should be designed using only Simple Instance Keys or only Compound Instance Keys. If that unilateral design is not an option, then a naming standard should be adopted to identify the time variant key of each table. Because every dimension table, including each Type 1 table and every Type 2 table, will retain its Entity Key and Instance Key, a table with a Simple Instance Key will look very similar to a table with a Compound Instance Key. The data warehouse users should not be required to profile the data in every dimension table to determine its key structure before using each table. For that reason, the best approach is to unilaterally use one Instance Key design (either Simple or Compound) or a naming standard that distinguishes the two from each other.

13

ETL into a Time Variant Data Warehouse

The purpose of an Extract, Transform, and Load (ETL) application is to bring data from the enterprise into a data warehouse. That may sound rather simplistic. However, the simplicity of that statement belies the complexities of ETL. In *Building and Maintaining a Data Warehouse*, Chapter 6 explains the analysis, architecture, design, development, and implementation of an ETL application. If you are reading this chapter intending to learn all you need to know about ETL, please refer to Chapter 6 of *Building and Maintaining a Data Warehouse*. For a data warehouse rookie, the text of that chapter will provide the foundation information necessary to understand and incorporate the Time Variant ETL design discussed in this chapter. The fundamental ETL concepts included in this chapter include Changed Data Capture (CDC) and ETL Key. The Time Variant ETL design will build on these two concepts.

CHANGED DATA CAPTURE

Entities

The CDC function applies specifically to dimension tables. Remember, dimension tables contain the entities of the enterprise. Those entities can include the products, locations, personnel, vendors, customers, formulas, transportation vehicles, and so on. Entities are those things that are somehow involved in the business processes of the enterprise.

For example, the manufacture of a product might include the following entities:

- Factory Worker: The person performing or monitoring the manufacture of a product
- Raw Materials: The physical inputs into the manufacture process
- Location: The factory in which the manufacture occurred
- Formula: The algorithm by which raw materials are combined into a finished product

Each of those entities could be described, or further defined, by other entities:

- Factory Worker: The person performing or monitoring the manufacture of a product
  - Certification: The jobs that a factory worker is educated to perform
  - Safety Rating: The safety risk level associated with a worker based on past history
- Raw Materials: The physical inputs into the manufacture process
  - Supplier: The vendor who provided a raw material to the enterprise
  - Quality: The level of rejected raw materials associated with the Supplier and that specific raw material based on past history
- Location: The factory in which the manufacture occurred
  - Geography: The physical region wherein the factory is located
  - Hierarchy: The organizational placement of the factory within the enterprise
- Formula: The algorithm by which raw materials are combined into a finished product
  - Fail Rate: The percentage of rework associated with a specific formula
  - Skill Set: The abilities required to perform the manufacture process with a specific formula

Attributes

When an entity describes or defines another entity (e.g., Certification and Safety Rating describe Factory Worker), that describing and defining entity is an attribute of the described or defined entity. In the example above, Certification and Safety Rating are attributes of Factory Worker; Supplier and Quality are attributes of Raw Material; Geography and

Hierarchy are attributes of Location; and Fail Rate and Skill Set are attributes of Formula.

An attribute entity can be described or further defined by another attribute entity. For example, Certification might be further described by Certification Board, Accreditation Date, and Test Criteria. In that example Certification Board is an attribute of Certification, which is an attribute of Factory Worker. The same can also be true for all other entities. The Raw Material entity is defined by its Supplier, which could be further described by the Credit Terms of the Supplier. In this way an entity of the enterprise can be both an entity and an attribute of an entity, and an attribute of an entity can have its own attributes that are also entities of the enterprise.

The role of a CDC function is to identify changes in each individual entity and integrate those changes into the data warehouse. Table 13.1 displays the comparison performed by a CDC function. Obviously, a CDC function does not operate on one Factory Worker, one Raw Material, one Location, and one Formula. Instead, a CDC function focuses on all Factor Workers, another CDC function focuses on all Raw Materials, another CDC function focuses on all Locations, and another CDC function focuses on all Formulas. The example here in Table 13.1 is presented in this form for continuity throughout this chapter.

The "Change?" results for Factory Worker, Raw Material, Location, and Formula are all equal to the value "n/a." This happens because the Factory Worker's name is Fred. Fred's name identifies Fred and is therefore the

TABLE 13.1

Changed Data Capture

Dimension	Attribute	Previous Value	Present Value	Change?
Factory Worker		Fred	Fred	n/a
	Certification	Craftsman	Craftsman	No
	Safety Rating	AA+	AA+	No
Raw Material		Iron Ore	Iron Ore	n/a
	Supplier	Hess Ironworks	Hess Ironworks	No
	Quality	95%	96%	Yes
Location		Atlanta Iron 35	Atlanta Iron 35	n/a
	Geography	Atlanta, GA	Atlanta, GA	No
	Hierarchy	Metals	Metals	No
Formula		RWU987	RWU987	n/a
	Fail Rate	4%	2%	Yes
	Skill Set	Iron Craftsman	Iron Craftsman	No

ETL Key by which a CDC function will identify changes in Fred's attributes. Fred's name does not define or describe Fred. We can garner no information about Fred by Fred's name, not even Frederica's gender, or Frederick's gender. The attributes Certification and Safety Rating provide some information about Fred. A CDC function compares entity attributes as they presently exist in the source system to the comparable set of entity attributes in the data warehouse. The output of a CDC comparison process can only identify four scenarios, explained here in the context of Fred, the factory worker:

- New: Fred was not in the enterprise previously.
- Update: Fred was in the enterprise previously, but now has a different attribute(s).
- Discontinue: Fred was in the enterprise previously, but is no longer in the enterprise.
- Continue: Fred was in the enterprise, and continues to exist in the enterprise with the same attributes.

ETL Cycle and Periodicity

Chapter 11 presented the concepts of ETL Cycle and Periodicity. The ETL Cycle and the periodicity it creates are an integral element of the ETL design. An ETL application includes three major functions:

- Extract: This function retrieves data from an operational source system. In the context of Table 13.1, one Extract function retrieves all Factory Workers from the Personnel system; another retrieves all Raw Materials from the Buying system, all Locations from the Facilities system, and all Formulas from the Manufacturing system.
- Transform: This function performs the CDC function that identifies new, updated, discontinued, or continued entities within a set of entities (e.g., all Factory Workers, all Raw Materials).
- Load: This function incorporates the output of the Transform function into the data of the data warehouse.

If an ETL application performs these three functions (Extract, Transform, and Load) every fifteen minutes, then the periodicity of the data warehouse is in fifteen-minute increments. If the periodicity of the data warehouse is in fifteen-minute increments, then the time variant metadata of each row of dimension data must be expressed in fifteen-minute increments. That would mean every row of dimension data would be able to identify the moment that row came into effect, and out of effect, in fifteen-minute increments. Fifteen-minute periodicity would also mean the ETL application is reading all Factory Worker values, all Raw Material values, all Location values, and all Formula values every fifteen minutes. Typically, the managers of most operational systems do not appreciate that sort of resource consumption every fifteen minutes, every hour, or any other frequency other than that source system's down time.

Typically, every operational system has its own resource consumption peaks and valleys. During the resource consumption peaks, an operational system is busy performing its primary function for the enterprise. During that time, the managers of an operational system typically prefer to focus all resources on that primary function. During the resource consumption valleys, an operational system has a higher level of availability to deliver its data to an Extract function. Chapter 11 discussed the architectural considerations for a real-time ETL application versus a periodic batch ETL application. Those considerations, coupled with the resource availability of operational source systems, would indicate that the Extract function will happen on a regular periodic frequency that will be synchronized with the resource consumption valleys of the operational source system. That regular periodic frequency is most often an ETL Cycle that occurs once every 24 hours (i.e., once daily).

Time Variant Metadata

When the ETL Cycle for a dimension table occurs once per day, the time variance for that dimension table is at the day level. That means that a row of data in a dimension table begins on a day and ends on a day, rather than beginning as of a minute of a day and then ending as of an hour of a day, or rather than beginning as of a week of a year and then ending as of a month of a year. Time variance for a dimension table at the minute, hour, week, and month is irregular and rather absurd. An ETL Cycle of a minute would mean repeating the ETL application and all its functions every minute. An ETL Cycle of an hour would mean repeating the ETL application and all its functions every hour. An ETL Cycle of a week would mean waiting seven days to repeat the ETL application. Finally, an ETL Cycle of a month would mean waiting a month to repeat the ETL application.

Considering these ETL Cycles, and their consequences, highlights the regular and reasonable nature of a twenty-four-hour ETL Cycle.

Each row of a dimension table should contain its time variant metadata. Specifically, that is the time at which the row of data came into effect and the time at which the row of data discontinued its effect. For every entity, no time gaps should be allowed. This also is a consideration in the decision to choose an ETL Cycle, and therefore the periodicity, of a dimension table. If the periodicity is at the level of the day, then the first time a row came into effect is a date; the time when a dimension row was discontinued is also a date. Chapter 12 referred to these dates as Row_First_Date and Row_Last_Date. For continuity, these names will be used in this chapter to identify the first date a row came into effect and the date when a row discontinued its effect.

Also the SQL BETWEEN statement is inclusive. That means the statement "between Row_First_Date and Row_Last_Date" includes both Row_First_Date and Row_Last_Date within the set of dates that satisfy the BETWEEN condition. For that reason, the dates in time variant metadata work best and easiest when the Row_First_Date and Row_Last_Date are inclusive, meaning the Row_First_Date is the first date on which a row is in effect and the Row_Last_Date is the last date on which a row is in effect.

Having defined the time variant metadata concept, the time variant metadata concept can be applied to the example in Table 13.1. In that example, the Quality rating of the Iron Ore changed from 95% to 96%. This is indeed a change. A row in the Raw Materials table might look like the row in Table 13.2.

Table 13.2 shows that the first row of data for Iron Ore came into effect on March 14, 2006. The Row_Last_Date value of Dec. 31, 9999, is a high-values date, which means that the row's last, or discontinuation, date is not yet known because it has not yet occurred.

Table 13.3 shows that the Quality rating for Iron Ore changed on May 12, 2010. That means that the last date on which the first row that shows the 95% Quality rating was in effect was May 11, 2010. The second Iron

TABLE 13.2

Raw Material

Name	Supplier	Quality	Row_First_Date	Row_Last_Date
Iron Ore	Hess Ironworks	95%	March 14, 2006	Dec. 31, 9999

TABLE 13.3

Raw Material Changed

Name	Supplier	Quality	Row_First_Date	Row_Last_Date
Iron Ore	Hess Ironworks	95%	March 14, 2006	May 11, 2010
Iron Ore	Hess Ironworks	96%	May 12, 2010	Dec. 31, 9999

TABLE 13.4

Formula

Name	Fail Rate	Skill Set	Row_First_Date	Row_Last_Date
RWU987	4%	Iron Craftsman	Jan. 20, 2005	Dec. 31, 9999

Ore row, which came into effect on May 12, 2010, now has the high-values Row_Last_Date value of Dec. 31, 9999.

The Row_Last_Date value for the first row was updated by the Load function. The output of the Transform function identified the row that discontinued as of May 11, 2010, and the row that began as of May 12, 2010. The best practice is to transform these dates in one unit of work to avoid creating any gaps in the time variant metadata.

The other attribute that changed in Table 13.1 was the Fail Rate of the RWU987 formula. Table 13.4 shows how the initial row of dimension data for the RWU987 formula might have looked. Formula RWU987 came into effect on Jan. 20, 2005, and has yet to discontinue.

Table 13.5 shows the dimension table updates that occur when extracting Formula data; as of Nov. 25, 2008, the Fail Rate for formula RWU987 was observed to be 2%, which is different from the previous value of 4%.

The Transform function identifies the entity that changed, the row of Formula dimension data that has discontinued as of Nov. 24, 2008, and the row of Formula dimension data that has become effective as of Nov. 25, 2008. The Load function applies the update to the Row_Last_Date of the first row, and inserts the new row, in the Formula dimension table.

Back to the Original Problem

Yes, this explanation of CDC and the application of time variant metadata look very similar to the data displayed in Figure 10.1 and Figure 10.2. That similarity is no accident. The data in Table 13.3 and Table 13.5 is built on the same programming logic that would have built the data in

TABLE 13.5

Formula Changed

Name	Fail Rate	Skill Set	Row_First_Date	Row_Last_Date
RWU987	4%	Iron Craftsman	Jan. 20, 2005	Nov. 24, 2008
RWU987	2%	Iron Craftsman	Nov. 25, 2008	Dec. 31, 9999

Figure 10.1 and Figure 10.2. So, yes, we have come full circle back to the original problem.

If you already have an ETL application that feeds dimensional data to a data warehouse, then you probably already have an ETL application, including the CDC function, that uses programming logic very similar to the discussion thus far in this chapter. The logic explained thus far is the basic fundamental logic of all ETL applications, CDC functions, and Load functions.

The ETL portion of this Time Variant Solution Design does not remove any logic or functionality already included in the ETL application, the CDC function, or the Load function. All the functions, features, and homegrown gems already included in the ETL application can remain. So, if you already have an ETL application, then you still have an ETL application—in fact, the same ETL application. And, if you are planning your first ETL application, nothing is lost as all that you intended to include in the ETL application can still be included.

INSTANCE KEYS IN DIMENSION ETL

This Time Variant Solution Design requires the addition of Instance Keys to all dimension tables. The following sections will explain the logic by which Instance Keys are generated and incorporated into the data that is then loaded into a dimension table. The examples below provide a mix of Simple Instance Keys and Compound Instance Keys. That mixture of Simple and Compound Instance Keys is for discussion purposes only. In practice, such a mixture of Simple and Compound Instance Keys can be very confusing. For that reason, if possible, a data warehouse should be designed using only Simple Instance Keys or only Compound Instance Keys. If that unilateral design is not an option, then a naming standard should be adopted to identify the time variant key of each table. Because every dimension table will retain its Entity Key and Instance Key, a table with a Simple Instance Key will look very similar to a table with a Compound Instance Key. You don't want to force the data warehouse users to profile the data in every dimension table to determine its key structure before using each table. For that reason, the best approach is to unilaterally use one Instance Key design (either Simple or Compound) or a naming standard that distinguishes the two from each other.

New Row

A new row of dimension data occurs when an entity, which did not exist before, has been discovered to exist now. The CDC function compared the set of Entity Keys extracted from the operational source system to the set of Entity Keys already in the data warehouse and found a new Entity Key. Table 13.6 and Table 13.7 both show this scenario. If the dimension table is designed to use Simple Instance Keys, then the Transform function, in addition to all the other work it performs, finds the maximum Instance Key value in the dimension table and then increments by one the Instance Key value (e.g., max(Instance Key) + 1) for every Insert row. The row of dimension data in Table 13.6 could be the first row of dimension data for the entity Iron Ore. The Instance Key value 385 would indicate that the Raw Material table previously had 384 rows and that the new Iron Ore row is the 385th row.

If the dimension table is designed to use Compound Instance Keys, then the Transform function, in addition to all the other work it performs, finds the maximum Instance Key value for that Entity Key in the

TABLE 13.6

Raw Material with a Simple Instance Key

Name	Supplier	Quality	Row_First_Date	Row_Last_Date	Instance Key
Iron Ore	Hess Ironworks	95%	March 14, 2006	Dec. 31, 9999	385

TABLE 13.7

Formula with a Compound Instance Key

Name	Fail Rate	Skill Set	Row_First_Date	Row_Last_Date	Instance Key
RWU987	4%	Iron Craftsman	Jan. 20, 2005	Dec. 31, 9999	1

dimension table and then increments by one the Instance Key value (e.g., max(Instance Key) + 1) for the Insert row for that Entity Key. Finding no previously existing row of dimension data for that Entity Key, the Transform function will assign the value one (e.g., 1). The row of dimension data in Table 13.7 could be the first row of dimension data for the entity RWU987. The Instance Key value 1 would indicate that the Formula table previously had no rows for the RWU987 entity and that the new row is the first row for RWU987.

Updated Row

An updated row of dimension data occurs when an entity, which did exist before and does exist now, has been discovered to have a different attribute value. The CDC function compared the set of Entity Keys extracted from the operational system to the set of Entity Keys already in the data warehouse and found an Entity Key that exists in both sets. The row of dimension data extracted from the operational source system is, however, different from the row of dimension data in the data warehouse in that the two rows have a different attribute value. This means that within the operational source system that attribute value has changed since the previous ETL Cycle.

The Transform function will write a record that will cause the Load function to update the Row_Last_Date of the existing row. That will have the effect of discontinuing the existing row of dimension data. The Transform function will also write a record that will cause the Load function to insert a new row of data for the Iron Ore entity. Table 13.8 shows the final result for the Iron Ore entity.

The update to the Row_Last_Date of the row previously in effect performed no operation on the Instance Key. The Transform function may include the Instance Key of the row in which the Row_Last_Date will be updated. The Instance Key would allow the Load function to find the

TABLE 13.8

Raw Material Changed with Simple Instance Keys

Name	Supplier	Quality	Row_First_Date	Row_Last_Date	Instance Key
Iron Ore	Hess Ironworks	95%	March 14, 2006	May 11, 2010	385
Iron Ore	Hess Ironworks	96%	May 12, 2010	Dec. 31, 9999	482

updated row more efficiently. Because the Raw Material table uses Simple Instance Keys, the Transform function performs the same algorithm to find the maximum Instance Key value for the table and then increments by one the Instance Key value (e.g., max(Instance Key) + 1) for every Insert row. Every dimension update is composed of a record that discontinues the previously effective row and another record that creates a new Insert row.

The function of defining a new Insert record exists in the Transform output for both New and Updated rows. For that reason, the Instance Key incrementer (e.g., max(Instance Key) + 1) should take as its input data the Insert records from the New and Updated rows. This will allow the Transform function to find the maximum Instance Key and increment the Instance Key in only one iteration rather than two.

An updated row of dimension data with Compound Instance Keys is very similar to an updated row of dimension data with Simple Instance Keys. The CDC function compared the set of Entity Keys extracted from the operational system to the set of Entity Keys already in the data warehouse and found an Entity Key that exists in both sets. The row of dimension data extracted from the operational source system is, however, different from the row of dimension data in the data warehouse in that the two rows have a different attribute value. This means that within the operational source system that attribute value has changed since the previous ETL Cycle.

The Transform function will write a record that will cause the Load function to update the Row_Last_Date of the existing row. That will have the effect of discontinuing the existing row of dimension data. The Transform function will also write a record that will cause the Load function to insert a new row of data for the RWU987 entity. Table 13.9 shows the final result for the RWU987 entity.

If the dimension table is designed to use Compound Instance Keys, then the Transform function, in addition to all the other work it performs, finds the maximum Instance Key value for that Entity Key in the

TABLE 13.9

Formula Changed with Compound Instance Keys

Name	Fail Rate	Skill Set	Row_First_Date	Row_Last_Date	Instance Key
RWU987	4%	Iron Craftsman	Jan. 20, 2005	Nov. 24, 2008	1
RWU987	2%	Iron Craftsman	Nov. 25, 2008	Dec. 31, 9999	2

dimension table and then increments by one the Instance Key value (e.g., max(Instance Key) + 1) for the Insert row for that Entity Key. The row of dimension data in Table 13.9 could be the initial and second row of dimension data for the entity RWU987. In the second row, the Instance Key value 2 would indicate that the Formula table previously had one row for the RWU987 entity and that the new row is the second row for RWU987.

Discontinued Row

The major difference between the standard CDC logic and this Time Variant Solution Design CDC logic is the case of the Discontinued Row. To avoid any gaps in the time frames for an entity, there must be a time frame for the occurrence when an entity ceases to exist. An argument can be made that if an entity ceases to exist, then no enterprise events or transactions will reference it. Any queries that join the nonexistent fact rows to the nonexistent dimension rows will experience no data fallout, as the data doesn't exist. While this argument may seem true in some level of theory, it does not work well in practice.

The dimension attributes will need a data value that equates to the meaning of "this dimension entity attribute no longer exists." This is a data model and data design decision. Attributes that are character-based (i.e., alpha characters) can often use the value "n/a." Attributes that are numeric, with all the arithmetic properties of numeric data, often opt for the null value to avoid any relevance to arithmetic operations. The Row_First_Date and Row_Last_Date will reflect the time frame during which the nonexistent row of dimension data does not exist. If the nonexistence began on Nov. 24, 2010, and continues to persist, then the Row_First_Date would be Nov. 24, 2010, and the Row_Last_Date would be the high-values Dec. 31, 9999, value.

Having established how to present the nonexistence of an Entity Key for a period of time, the CDC function will treat a discontinued entity as an updated entity. For the row previously in effect, a record will be written that will cause the Load function to update the Row_Last_Date of that effective row, rendering it discontinued. For the nonexistence of the entity, an Insert record will be written wherein the attributes are all the "this dimension entity attribute no longer exists" value, the Row_First_Date is the first date on which the Entity Key ceased to exist, and the Row_Last_Date is the high-values Dec. 31, 9999, value.

The Load function will treat the Update row as an update to a previously existing row. The Load function will treat the Insert row as a new row to be inserted. The net effect will be a row for the next time frame that indicates that the entity attributes no longer exist. Even that row, the row that shows the nonexistence of the Entity Key, will have its own Instance Key.

Cascading Instance Keys

Chapter 11 explained the concept of Cascading Instance Keys. Dimension tables relate to other dimension tables via a foreign key/primary key relation. A foreign key that is embedded in a first dimension table will directly join to the primary key of a second dimension table. Figure 11.4 and Figure 11.5 display this design.

Typically the dimension tables that do not have a foreign key to another dimension table are those dimension tables that are at the top of their hierarchies and those dimension tables that are lookup tables. Lookup tables provide a textual description of a cryptic code or indicator value. The vast majority of dimension tables in a data warehouse will reference another dimension table. The Entity Key and Instance Key of a lookup table, which is referenced by a dimension table, will be embedded in the dimension table. The Entity Key and Instance Key of a hierarchical dimension table, which is referenced by a lower hierarchical dimension table, will be embedded in the lower hierarchical table. This is true for both Type 1 and Type 2 time variant dimension tables.

For the purposes of dimension CDC this foreign key/primary key aspect of this Time Variant Solution Design is very important. Cascading Instance Keys dictate the sequence of the ETL jobs for dimension tables. A dimension table can reference the Instance Key of a second dimension table only after the Instance Key for the second dimension table has been generated. That means the ETL jobs cannot be run at random. Instead, the ETL job for a dimension table can only run after the ETL jobs for all tables referenced by that first table have run, including the generation of Instance Keys. For example, if Table A references Table B, and Table B references Table C, then the sequence of ETL jobs would populate Table C, then Table B, and finally Table A. In the case of a lookup table, the ETL job for a lookup table must complete before the ETL jobs for dimension tables that reference that lookup table can run.

That is why Cascading Instance Keys dictate the sequence of ETL jobs. An ETL job flow will typically begin with lookup tables and top-level hierarchy tables. Then, the ETL jobs for the next lower hierarchy level can run, and then the next lower level, and so on, until all the dimension ETL jobs have run. The dimension ETL jobs must complete before a fact ETL job can reference the Instance Keys of the dimension tables.

Dimension Load

The Load function in an ETL application, every ETL application, should contain the least application logic possible. A Load function is like a hinge in a piece of furniture. It is exercised often while also being simultaneously the weakest and most vulnerable link in the piece. For that reason a Load function is optimized by minimizing the application logic, which reduces the number of moving and integrated elements. For that reason, the general rule of Load jobs is that simpler is better. For that reason a Dimension Load should perform only three functions—Delete, Update, and Insert.

Delete

The Delete function is used when a Type 1 dimension row has changed. Because a Type 1 dimension table does not retain history, it also does not retain history rows. For that reason, when an entity is updated, the Load function will delete the previously existing row from a Type 1 dimension table.

The key by which the Delete function can occur is the Entity Key. In a Type 1 dimension table, the Entity Key is the primary key of the table. So, the optimal path by which to delete a row from a Type 1 dimension table is to delete any row from the Type 1 dimension table where the Entity Key of the Type 1 dimension table equals the Entity Key of the Update record written by the CDC function.

Update

The Update function is used when a Type 2 dimension row has changed. The Update function specifically applies a new value to the Row_Last_ Date. For a given ETL Cycle the discontinuation of a row is achieved by updating the Row_Last_Date to the date immediately prior to the date for which the ETL Cycle is running. The ETL Cycle may be running for yesterday, two days ago, or any number of days ago. Sometimes an operational source system may delay the availability of data to the Extract function. Such a delay will cause a lag between the date of the ETL Cycle and the date on which the ETL Cycle actually runs. Regardless, the Update function updates the Row_Last_Date to the value of the ETL Cycle date minus one time period, that is, minus one day.

The key by which the Update function can occur is the Instance Key. In a Type 2 dimension table, the Instance Key is the primary key of the table. So, the optimal path by which to update a row from a Type 2 dimension table is to update any row from the Type 2 dimension table where the Instance Key of the Type 2 dimension table equals the Instance Key of the Update record written by the CDC function.

The update function for Type 1 dimension tables and the Update function for Type 2 dimension tables can use the same Update record written by a CDC function. Sharing the Update record with the Delete and Update functions is preferred as it limits the possibility that the Delete and Update functions might use different data. Using the same Update record increases the possibility that corresponding Type 1 and Type 2 dimension tables will stay in synch with each other.

Insert

The Insert function is used in both Type 1 and Type 2 dimension tables. In a Type 1 dimension table an updated entity consists of a Delete function, which removes any previously existing row, and an Insert function, which incorporates the updated dimension row into the Type 1 dimension table. In a Type 2 dimension table an updated entity consists of an Update function, which discontinues the previously existing rows by changing its Row_Last_Date, and an Insert function, which incorporates the updated dimension row into the Type 2 dimension table. Regardless, whether in a Type 1 or Type 2 dimension table, the Insert function does one thing: it inserts. No more, no less, simple and elegant—an Insert function only inserts rows from an Insert record written by the CDC function.

Data Quality

This Time Variant solution has a small margin for error. If your data warehouse has not incorporated an active data quality program into the ETL application, the moment when Type 1 and Type 2 time variant dimension tables are created is the perfect time to incorporate an active data quality program. Data quality is best assessed at all the junctures in an ETL application. The junctures listed thus far, and their potential data quality assessments, are the following:

- Extract—After the Extract function retrieves rows from the source system, use an alternate data retrieval method to profile the data that should have been extracted. Compare the data profile to a comparable profile of the Extract file.
- Transform—After the Transform function writes the Update/Delete and Insert files:
  - Verify that the Entity Keys in the Update/Delete file, but not in the Insert file, are in the data warehouse but not in the Extract file.
  - Verify that the Entity Keys in the Insert file, but not in the Update/Delete file, are in the Extract file but not in the data warehouse.
  - Verify that the Instance Key of an Entity Key in the Insert file is greater than the maximum Instance Key for the same Entity Key in the data warehouse.
- Load—After the Load function has updated the data warehouse from the Update/Delete and Insert files:
  - Verify that for every Entity Key, exactly one Instance Key applies to each time frame, so that no time frame exists without an Instance Key, which will cause confusion as to which Type 2 time variant dimension row applies to a moment in the past. If the answer is zero Type 2 time variant dimension rows, that's the wrong answer.
  - Verify that for every Entity Key, only one Instance Key applies to each time frame, so that no Instance Keys overlap, which will cause confusion as to which Type 2 time variant dimension row applies to a moment in the past. If the answer is two Type 2 time variant dimension rows, that's the wrong answer.
  - Verify that for every Entity Key, the row in the Type 1 dimension table is identical to the most recent row in the Type 2 dimension table.

Data quality is a seldom understood, and less frequently implemented, function of an ETL application. The data quality assessments listed above are among the most basic and rudimentary.

Additional data quality assessments are available in Chapter 8 of *Building and Maintaining a Data Warehouse*. If a time variant data warehouse experiences data quality issues, the potential for data corruption is immense. The best defense against data quality issues is a good offense. The data quality assessments listed above can be the beginnings of a good data quality offense.

Metadata

The simplest form of metadata for a Dimension ETL application is a log table. Each ETL Cycle for each Extract function is assigned a batch number, which is the primary key of the log table. As the extracted data flows through the Transform and Load functions, updates are applied to a series of columns in the log file. Those columns could include such metrics as the following:

- Timestamp of the beginning of the Extract function
- Number of rows extracted
- Timestamp of the ending of the Extract function
- Timestamp of the beginning of the Transform function
- Number of rows received by the Transform function
- Number of "Insert" rows delivered by the CDC function
- Number of "Update/Delete" rows delivered by the CDC function
- Timestamp of the ending of the Transform function
- Timestamp of the beginning of the Load function
- Number of "Insert" rows received by the Load function
- Number of "Update/Delete" rows received by the Load function
- Number of rows inserted
- Number of rows updated
- Number of rows deleted
- Timestamp of the ending of the Load function

The "log table" method is a simple metadata method. The log table method and other metadata measurements are available in Chapter 9 of *Building and Maintaining a Data Warehouse*. A time variant data warehouse has many moving parts. The time variant aspect renders questions about the data in the data warehouse more difficult to answer. A metadata function will eventually be required when questions arise about how a row, or set of rows, arrived into a dimension table. Chapter 9 of *Building and Maintaining a Data Warehouse* provides a more comprehensive explanation of the metadata measurements that can render a Type 2 time variant data warehouse easier to understand.

FACT ETL

A Fact table presents the occurrence of an enterprise performing its business functions. Retail sales transactions are extracted from the Retail system, transformed, and then loaded into a Sales table. Manufacturing checkpoints are extracted from the Manufacturing system, transformed, and then loaded into a Manufacturing table. The addition of this Time Variant Solution Design to the Dimension ETL application added the logic to create new Instance Keys. Likewise, the addition of this Time Variant Solution Design to the Fact ETL will only add logic to find existing Instance Keys.

An Extract function retrieves data from the occurrences of a business function. The Transform function identifies the entities involved in that business function. Using the sample data in Table 13.10, a manufacture process includes four data elements—Factory Worker, Raw Material, Location, and Formula—and a quantitative measure of the manufactured output called Quantity. That data will become a row of data in a fact table that presents occurrences of a manufacturing process involving iron ore. For that reason, this sample table might be named Manufacture_Metals_Detail. That row of data in the Manufacturing fact table could look like the data in Table 13.10.

Instance Keys in Fact ETL

The addition of Instance Keys to a Fact ETL application changes very little about that ETL application. The source system is still the source system. The business process is still the business process. The entities, quantitative measurements, attributes, and general meaning of rows delivered by a Fact ETL application remain unchanged. Therefore, all the concepts,

TABLE 13.10

Manufacture_Metals_Detail

Date	Time	Factory Worker	Raw Material	Location	Formula	Quantity
Aug. 27, 2008	13:42	Fred	Iron Ore	Atlanta Iron 35	RWU987	16
Aug. 27, 2008	14:52	Fred	Iron Ore	Atlanta Iron 35	RWU987	12
Aug. 27, 2008	15:03	Fred	Iron Ore	Atlanta Iron 35	RWU987	17
Aug. 27, 2008	16:25	Fred	Iron Ore	Atlanta Iron 35	RWU987	21

principles, and best practices already built into an ETL application continue to be the concepts, principles, and best practices…with the addition of Instance Keys.

Every entity in a Fact row is presented by an Entity Key. The Manufacture_Metals_Detail presented in Table 13.10 includes four entities. Those entities are Factory Worker, Raw Material, Location, and Formula. The entity Factory Worker has the Entity Key value of "Fred." The entity Raw Material has the Entity Key value of "Iron Ore." The entity Location has the Entity Key value of "Atlanta Iron 35." The entity Formula has the Entity Key value "RWU987." Admittedly, these Entity Key values would never actually be used in a data warehouse. They are used here simply to contrast the Instance Key values.

A Fact ETL application incorporates Instance Keys by looking them up. For every entity, the Entity Key and date of the transaction or event represented in the Fact table row are used in a lookup of the dimension table for that entity. First, match on the Entity Key to find all rows for that entity. Then, having identified all rows for that entity, use the date of the transaction or event to find the row of dimension data that matches the Entity Key of that entity and has Row_First_Date and Row_Last_Date values that encompass the date of the transaction or event. Having found the one row of dimension data that matches the Entity Key and encompasses the date of the transaction or event, return the Instance Key in that row of dimension data. That Instance Key will uniquely identify the occurrence of that entity in that dimension table that was effective within the enterprise at the time of the transaction or event.

The Fact ETL does not simply use Type 1 dimension tables for this lookup. To do so would assume that all Fact table data presented to the Fact ETL application can only have occurred during the most recent periodicity time frame of the data warehouse. Such an assumption is most probably completely invalid. So, since we cannot assume that all Fact data presented to the Fact ETL application occurred during the most recent periodicity time frame of the data warehouse, instead we look up the occurrences of each dimension table to avoid placing the time variant entities of a row of Fact table data in the wrong time frame.

Data Quality in Fact ETL

This method must be supported by an attention to data quality. Within a single dimension, for each individual Entity Key, only one Instance Key can apply to each individual time frame. A Dimension ETL post-load data quality assessment should be used to verify that for a single Entity Key, and a single moment in time, exactly one Type 2 time variant dimension row applies to that Entity Key and moment in time. Otherwise, the result set to this lookup operation will cause the Fact ETL application to fail. If the result set has zero rows, the row of Fact data will fail to find a Type 2 Instance Key. If the result set has multiple rows, the Fact ETL will be unequipped to resolve the overlapping dimension rows.

The best-laid plans of ETL analysts and developers often go astray at such junction points between Dimensions and Facts in Fact ETL. You can either programmatically enforce the data quality and integrity of Dimension data in the Dimension ETL or Fact ETL. The alternative is to manually monitor and repair the Fact ETL when it encounters data anomalies. Despite the best efforts to the contrary, data anomalies occur. Data anomalies can be detected and mitigated with the least impact during the Dimension ETL. If they are not mitigated during Dimension ETL, they will reveal themselves during Fact ETL. Data anomalies are most impactful when encountered during Fact ETL.

It is a simple case of "Garbage in...garbage out." If the Dimension data is certified to be clean before the Fact ETL, the Fact ETL will encounter significantly fewer problems. Chapter 8 of *Building and Maintaining a Data Warehouse* explained methods for assessing, tracking, and delivering data quality. Data quality does not have to be the vague area south of Mordor. The impact of good and poor data quality is quite tangible and real. The management of data quality can be equally tangible and real. Time variant Fact ETL does not require the use of a data quality program, including data quality assessments, metrics, thresholds, and so on. However, a time variant Fact ETL application will increase in effectiveness, efficiency, and ROI as the quality of its input data increases.

Metadata in Fact ETL

A Fact table may include billions or trillions of rows of data. Business Intelligence (BI) reports wait for that data to arrive. BI applications wait for that data to arrive. Downstream ETL processes wait for that data to arrive. Likewise, a Fact ETL application will need to know its predecessor Dimension ETL applications have completed and the quality of the data delivered by its predecessors. These are the reasons to apply controls to ETL applications, both Dimension ETL and Fact ETL. That level of control is delivered via metadata. Metadata identifies an ETL application job and the data created by that ETL application job. A Metadata application can then inform downstream ETL applications that their predecessors and thresholds have, or have not, been met.

Mistakes happen. When they happen you may need to revise rows of a Fact table. When you need to revise a set of rows of a Fact table you will need a method that will identify that set of Fact rows separately from all other rows of the same Fact table. Again, that level of control is delivered via Metadata. Metadata allows you to identify a specific set of rows of a table that were created by a specific ETL application executed by a specific ETL job. Once the errant rows in a Fact table have been identified, they can be re-created and validated in a separate table. The same dimension lookup function that yielded an incorrect Instance Key previously can be repeated. The corrected and validated rows can be repeated using a corrected Dimension table, yielding corrected results. Once the Fact rows have been re-created and validated in a separate table, they can replace the errant rows in the Fact table.

The textbook definition of Metadata (data about data) is cryptic and uninformative. A better definition of Metadata should include the control, management, and manipulation of data, ETL processes, BI processes, and data quality. These functions, features, and methods are explained in Chapter 9 of *Building and Maintaining a Data Warehouse*. Time variant ETL does not require Metadata. However, the support of a time variant data warehouse is almost impossible without a Metadata application. So, while Metadata does not inherently create time variance, Metadata enables a data warehouse to control and manage the data and processes in a data warehouse.

Instance Keys—The Manufacturing Example

Before we can incorporate sample data from the Iron Ore manufacturing process first presented in Table 13.10, we need to resolve all the sample Instance Keys to either Simple Instance Keys or Compound Instance Keys. Table 13.11 presents all the Instance Keys as Simple Instance Keys. The Instance Keys in Table 13.11 will be used in the following examples of the Fact table Manufacture_Metals_Detail.

Table 13.12 includes the Fact table rows found in Table 13.10, with the addition of Instance Keys for the entities Factor Worker, Raw Material, Location, and Formula. The Instance Keys, which are Simple Instance Keys in this example, come from Table 13.11.

TABLE 13.11

Manufacturing Dimensions with Simple Instance Keys

Factory Worker

Name	Certification	Safety Rating	Row_First_Date	Row_Last_Date	Instance Key
Fred	Craftsman	AA+	April 14, 2007	Dec. 31, 9999	942

Raw Material

Name	Supplier	Quality	Row_First_Date	Row_Last_Date	Instance Key
Iron Ore	Hess Ironworks	95%	March 14, 2006	May 11, 2010	385
Iron Ore	Hess Ironworks	96%	May 12, 2010	Dec. 31, 9999	482

Location

Name	Geography	Hierarchy	Row_First_Date	Row_Last_Date	Instance Key
Atlanta Iron 35	Atlanta, GA	Metals	Feb. 6, 1998	Dec. 31, 9999	234

Formula

Name	Fail Rate	Skill Set	Row_First_Date	Row_Last_Date	Instance Key
RWU987	4%	Iron Craftsman	Jan. 20, 2005	Nov. 24, 2008	294
RWU987	2%	Iron Craftsman	Nov. 25, 2008	Dec. 31, 9999	762

- The Factory Worker entity Fred has the Instance Key 942 because the dimension row for Fred in the Factory Worker table with the Instance Key value 942 has the Row_First_Date and Row_Last_Date values of April 14, 2007, and Dec. 31, 9999, which inclusively surround the Fact row date of Aug. 27, 2008.
- The Raw Material entity Iron Ore has the Instance Key 385 because the dimension row for Iron Ore in the Raw Material table with the Instance Key value 385 has the Row_First_Date and Row_Last_Date values of March 14, 2006, and May 11, 2010, which inclusively surround the Fact row date of Aug. 27, 2008.
- The Location entity Atlanta Iron 35 has the Instance Key 234 because the dimension row for Atlanta Iron 35 in the Location table with the Instance Key value 234 has the Row_First_Date and Row_Last_Date values of Feb. 6, 1998, and Dec. 31, 9999, which inclusively surround the Fact row date of Aug. 27, 2008.
- The Formula entity RWU987 has the Instance Key 294 because the dimension row for RWU987 in the Formula table with the Instance Key value 294 has the Row_First_Date and Row_Last_Date values of Jan. 20, 2005, and Nov. 24, 2008, which inclusively surround the Fact row date of Aug. 27, 2008.

A Fact ETL application will perform all the lookup operations described in this chapter to find the Instance Keys shown in Table 13.12. If the quality of the Dimension data has been assessed and certified, the Fact ETL lookup processes can be that simple. The lookup processes repeat for every row of data processed by a Fact ETL application.

Most ETL tools include an optimized lookup operation. Often the dimension values are stored in memory so that the lookup operation experiences I/O only on the first "read" operation against a disk drive. Every "read" operation in the lookup that occurs thereafter is a "read" from memory and not from disk. A hand-coded ETL application can achieve the same result by reading all the dimension values into an internal memory array. Then, perform all the lookup operations against the internal memory array rather than against a dimension table stored on disk.

To see time vary, we must vary time. Table 13.13 presents another set of Manufacture_Metals_Detail rows. The set of rows in Table 13.13 occurred on Jan. 20, 2011. The Instance Keys, again in this example, come from Table 13.11.

TABLE 13.12

Manufacture_Metals_Detail Aug 2008

Date	Time	Factory Worker	Factory Worker IK	Raw Material	Raw Material IK	Location	Location IK	Formula	Formula IK	Quantity
Aug. 27, 2008	13:42	Fred	942	Iron Ore	385	Atlanta Iron 35	234	RWU987	294	16
Aug. 27, 2008	14:52	Fred	942	Iron Ore	385	Atlanta Iron 35	234	RWU987	294	12
Aug. 27, 2008	15:03	Fred	942	Iron Ore	385	Atlanta Iron 35	234	RWU987	294	17
Aug. 27, 2008	16:25	Fred	942	Iron Ore	385	Atlanta Iron 35	234	RWU987	294	21

TABLE 13.13

Manufacture_Metals_Detail Jan 2011

Date	Time	Factory Worker	Factory Worker IK	Raw Material	Raw Material IK	Location	Location IK	Formula	Formula IK	Quantity
Jan. 20, 2011	9:35	Fred	942	Iron Ore	482	Atlanta Iron 35	234	RWU987	762	21
Jan. 20, 2011	10:02	Fred	942	Iron Ore	482	Atlanta Iron 35	234	RWU987	762	25
Jan. 20, 2011	10:49	Fred	942	Iron Ore	482	Atlanta Iron 35	234	RWU987	762	19
Jan. 20, 2011	11:14	Fred	942	Iron Ore	482	Atlanta Iron 35	234	RWU987	762	24

- The Factory Worker entity Fred has the Instance Key 942 because the dimension row for Fred in the Factory Worker table with the Instance Key value 942 has the Row_First_Date and Row_Last_Date values of April 14, 2007, and Dec. 31, 9999, which inclusively surround the Fact row date of Jan. 20, 2011.
- The Raw Material entity Iron Ore has the Instance Key 482 because the dimension row for Iron Ore in the Raw Material table with the Instance Key value 482 has the Row_First_Date and Row_Last_Date values of May 12, 2010, and Dec. 31, 9999, which inclusively surround the Fact row date of Jan. 20, 2011.
- The Location entity Atlanta Iron 35 has the Instance Key 234 because the dimension row for Atlanta Iron 35 in the Location table with the Instance Key value 234 has the Row_First_Date and Row_Last_Date values of Feb. 6, 1998, and Dec. 31, 9999, which inclusively surround the Fact row date of Jan. 20, 2011.
- The Formula entity RWU987 has the Instance Key 294 because the dimension row for RWU987 in the Formula table with the Instance Key value 294 has the Row_First_Date and Row_Last_Date values of Nov. 25, 2008, and Dec. 31, 9999, which inclusively surround the Fact row date of Jan. 20, 2011.

From the Fact rows in Table 13.12 to the Fact rows in Table 13.13, the Instance Key for Raw Material changed from 385 to 482, and the Instance Key for Formula changed from 294 to 762. They would not, however, exist in two separate Fact tables. Instead, they would exist side by side in a single Fact table, which is shown in Table 13.14.

Type 1 Time Variance

Type 1 Time Variance views all the history of the enterprise as it is now. Chapter 12 provided a solution for organizing the Type 1 dimension tables and views so that they join well with a Fact table that supports both Type 1 and Type 2 time variant dimensions.

- A Type 1 query of all the Manufacture_Metals_Detail rows that include the Factory Worker entity named "Fred" will return all the rows in Table 13.14.

TABLE 13.14

Manufacture_Metals_Detail Combined

Date	Time	Factory Worker	Factory Worker IK	Raw Material	Raw Material IK	Location	Location IK	Formula	Formula IK	Quantity
Aug. 27, 2008	13:42	Fred	942	Iron Ore	385	Atlanta Iron 35	234	RWU987	294	16
Aug. 27, 2008	14:52	Fred	942	Iron Ore	385	Atlanta Iron 35	234	RWU987	294	12
Aug. 27, 2008	15:03	Fred	942	Iron Ore	385	Atlanta Iron 35	234	RWU987	294	17
Aug. 27, 2008	16:25	Fred	942	Iron Ore	385	Atlanta Iron 35	234	RWU987	294	21
Jan. 20, 2011	9:35	Fred	942	Iron Ore	482	Atlanta Iron 35	234	RWU987	762	21
Jan. 20, 2011	10:02	Fred	942	Iron Ore	482	Atlanta Iron 35	234	RWU987	762	25
Jan. 20, 2011	10:49	Fred	942	Iron Ore	482	Atlanta Iron 35	234	RWU987	762	19
Jan. 20, 2011	11:14	Fred	942	Iron Ore	482	Atlanta Iron 35	234	RWU987	762	24

- A Type 1 query of all the Manufacture_Metals_Detail rows that include the Raw Material entity named "Iron Ore" will return all the rows in Table 13.14.
- A Type 1 query of all the Manufacture_Metals_Detail rows that include the Location entity named "Atlanta Iron 35" will return all the rows in Table 13.14.
- A Type 1 query of all the Manufacture_Metals_Detail rows that include the Formula entity named "RWU987" will return all the rows in Table 13.14.

Type 1 time variant queries make no mention of Instance Keys. Instance Keys provide a join strategy for time variant data. For that reason, Type 1 time variant queries do not need to include Instance Keys.

Type 2 Time Variance

Type 2 time variant queries, however, use only Instance Keys (unless, of course, the Instance Key is a Compound Instance Key that includes the Entity Key). This example uses Simple Instance Keys. So, in this example Type 2 time variant queries use only Instance Keys, and never use Entity Keys.

- A Type 2 query of all the Manufacture_Metals_Detail rows that include the Factory Worker Instance Key 942 will return all the rows in Table 13.14.
- A Type 2 query of all the Manufacture_Metals_Detail rows that include the Raw Material "Iron Ore" with a Quality rating of 95%, which is in the Raw Material row with Instance Key 385, will return the rows in Table 13.14 dated Aug. 27, 2008.
- A Type 2 query of all the Manufacture_Metals_Detail rows that include the Raw Material "Iron Ore" with a Quality rating of 96%, which is in the Raw Material row with Instance Key 482, will return the rows in Table 13.14 dated Jan. 20, 2011.
- A Type 2 query of all the Manufacture_Metals_Detail rows that include the Location Instance Key 234 will return the rows in Table 13.14.
- A Type 2 query of all the Manufacture_Metals_Detail rows that include the Formula "RWU987" with a Fail Rate of 4%, which is in the Formula row with Instance Key 294, will return the rows in Table 13.14 dated Aug. 27, 2008.

- A Type 2 query of all the Manufacture_Metals_Detail rows that include the Formula "RWU987" with a Fail Rate of 2%, which is in the Formula row with Instance Key 762, will return the rows in Table 13.14 dated Jan. 20, 2011.

The Dimension and Fact tables have no direct connection between a Quality rating of 95% and Aug. 27, 2008, between a Quality rating of 96% and Jan. 20, 2011, between a Fail Rate of 4% and Aug. 27, 2008, or between a Fail Rate of 2% and Jan. 20, 2011. The connection between these dimension attributes and dates in a Fact table is the Instance Keys that are embedded in a row of Fact data by the Fact ETL. Those Instance Keys in a row of Fact data join directly to one, and only one, row of Dimension data. Each row of Dimension data is uniquely identified by an Instance Key because the Dimension ETL application that populated that Dimension table assigned that Instance Key to one, and only one, row of that Dimension table.

Obviously, therefore, all the Dimension ETL must be complete (meaning the Dimension tables have been populated with data) before the Fact ETL can begin. Otherwise, the Instance Key lookup operation will not have a current set of Instance Keys to look up.

SUMMARY ETL

After a Fact ETL application has completed the updates to a Fact table, a Summary application can summarize data from that Fact table. Summaries in a data warehouse are created for performance reasons. If data warehouse users consistently query a Fact table, summing by one of its dimensions, a Summary process can remove that resource consumption from the data warehouse by performing that sum operation once and then storing the result set in a separate table. Thereafter, data warehouse customers need only query the separate summary table. That reduces the occurrence of the sum operation from near ad infinitum throughout the day to once during off-peak hours.

The phrase "summing by one of its dimensions" is a reference to both the structure of a Fact table and the structure of the SQL in a query. In its simplest form, a summing query will include a SUM clause and a GROUP BY clause, as shown in Figure 13.1.

The possible dimensions in Table 13.14, which could be included in a Sum operation, are Factory Worker, Raw Material, Location, and Formula.

```
SELECT
DIMENSION
, SUM(QUANTITATIVE VALUE)
FROM FACT_TABLE
GROUP BY
DIMENSION
```

FIGURE 13.1
SUM SQL.

The only quantitative value in Table 13.14 is the column named Quantity. The Fact table in Table 13.14 presents both Entity Keys and Instance Keys. So, it is possible that a summation operation can leverage either the Entity Keys or the Instance Keys.

Type 1 Summary ETL

Entity Keys are associated with Type 1 Time Variance. A Summary ETL application is a Type 1 Summary ETL application when it references Entity Keys, rather than Instance Keys. Figure 13.2 shows a summation query that references only Entity Keys. The result set will include only Entity Keys and will therefore be a Type 1 result set.

Type 2 Summary ETL

Instance Keys are associated with Type 2 Time Variance. A Summary ETL application is a Type 2 Summary ETL application when it references Instance Keys, rather than Entity Keys. Figure 13.3 shows a summation query that references only Instance Keys. The result set will include only Instance Keys and will therefore be a Type 2 result set.

From the perspective of a Summary ETL application, a Type 2 Summary table and a hybrid Type 1/Type 2 Summary table are extremely similar. A hybrid Type 1/Type 2 Summary table contains both the Entity Key and the Instance Key for each dimension. Therefore, the SQL in the Summary ETL for a hybrid Type 1/Type 2 Summary table, shown in Figure 13.4, includes both the Entity Key and the Instance Key for every dimension. Because the Instance Key is the lower granularity of the two keys, the Instance Key, rather than the Entity Key, determines the cardinality of the summation operation and the output result set.

```
SELECT
Entity_Key
, SUM(QUANTITATIVE VALUE)
FROM FACT_TABLE
GROUP BY
Entity_Key
```

FIGURE 13.2
Type 1 Time Variant SUM SQL.

```
SELECT
Instance_Key
, SUM(QUANTITATIVE VALUE)
FROM FACT_TABLE
GROUP BY
Instance_Key
```

FIGURE 13.3
Type 2 Time Variant SUM SQL.

```
SELECT
Entity_Key
, Instance_Key
, SUM(QUANTITATIVE VALUE)
FROM FACT_TABLE
GROUP BY
Entity_Key
, Instance_Key
```

FIGURE 13.4
Hybrid Type 1/Type 2 Time Variant SUM SQL.

Metadata, Data Quality, and the Like

All the Metadata processes included in Dimension and Fact ETL are also included in Summary ETL. Summary ETL processes require the same level of management, control, and quality assessment as other ETL processes. Rather than repeat the previous descriptions of Metadata and Data Quality processes already covered, please refer back to Chapters 8 and 9 of *Building and Maintaining a Data Warehouse*, as both the Metadata and Data Quality applications are explained there.

14

Market Basket Analysis in a Time Variant Data Warehouse

HIGH-LEVEL REVIEW

Chapters 2 through 7 presented a method for delivering Market Basket Analysis via a data warehouse. Chapters 8 through 13 presented a method for delivering capitalize data in a data warehouse. Chapter 14 combines those two methods into a unified method that can deliver Market Basket Analysis within a Time Variant context. Before we merge these two sets of methods into one single unified method, we need to review at a high level the Market Basket Analysis method and the Time Variance method. Then we can merge the two methods at a high level to create an initial expectation of Market Basket Analysis in a Time Variant context.

Market Basket Analysis at a High Level

Market Basket Analysis is a two-step method built around a recursive SQL statement. The recursive SQL, shown in Figure 5.2, juxtaposes the objects within an individual Itemset against all the other objects in the same Itemset. The key structure of the Market Basket Table, shown in Table 5.1, optimizes the recursive Market Basket Query so that a significant quantity of Itemsets can be included in an iteration of the Market Basket Query. The result set of the Market Basket Query is loaded into the Market Basket BI Table, shown in Table 5.3.

The Market Basket Analysis BI View, shown in Figure 5.7, sums the quantitative measurements (e.g., Quantity and Dollars) and the count of Itemsets in the Market Basket BI Table. The cumulative result provides data necessary to answer the question in the Market Basket Scope Statement, shown in Figure 5.1: "When Driver Object A is in an Itemset, what Correlation Object B is in, or not in, the Itemset?"

Time Variance at a High Level

The Time Variant Solution Design in Chapters 8 through 13 is built around a join strategy. The optimal join strategy between two tables is a primary key/foreign key relation. For that reason, the Time Variant Solution Design uses a primary key/foreign key relation to optimize the join between a Fact table and time variant Dimension tables.

The two forms of Time Variance included in the Time Variant Solution Design are Type 1 and Type 2 Time Variance. Ralph Kimball created these two concepts of time variance and their names. Type 1 Time Variance is the frame of reference wherein all events in the past are perceived in the present context of the enterprise. Type 2 Time Variance is the frame of reference wherein all events in the past are perceived in the historical context of the enterprise at the time of the transaction or event represented by each individual row of a Fact table.

The join strategy in a Type 1 Time Variant context, casting all past events in the present context of the enterprise, is based on Entity Keys. Every entity in a Type 1 dimension table has one, and only one, row that is uniquely identified by an Entity Key that operates as a primary key to a Type 1 dimension table. An Entity Key from the Type 1 dimension table is embedded as a foreign key in each row of a Fact table. When the Fact table is joined via the Entity Key to a Type 1 dimension table, the result set presents the rows of that Fact table in the present context of the enterprise.

The join strategy in a Type 2 Time Variant context, casting all past events in the context in which they occurred, is based on Instance Keys. Every instance of every entity in a Type 2 dimension table has one, and only one, row that is uniquely identified by an Instance Key that operates as a primary key to a Type 2 dimension table. An Instance Key from the Type 2 dimension table is embedded as a foreign key in each row of a Fact table. When the Fact table is joined via the Instance Key to a Type 2 dimension table, the result set presents the rows of that Fact table in their historical context at the time they occurred.

Market Basket Analysis in a Time Variant Context at a High Level

The Driver Objects and Correlation Objects of Market Basket Analysis are dimensions. Typically we think of them as products in a shopping cart, services in a work order, or menu items in a dinner. However, from the broad perspective of Market Basket Analysis, they are dimensions. The Time Variant Solution Design embeds two expressions of dimensions in a Fact table. The Type 1 time variant expression of a dimension in a Fact table is the Entity Key that joins to a Type 1 dimension table. The Type 2 time variant expression of a dimension in a Fact table is the Instance Key that joins to a Type 2 dimension table.

A Driver Object can be an Entity Key or an Instance Key. A Correlation Object can also be an Entity Key or an Instance Key. When the Driver Object and Correlation Objects are Entity Keys, the Market Basket Analysis considers both entities without any time variant context. When the Driver Object and Correlation Object are Instance Keys, the Market Basket Analysis considers both entities in their time variant contexts.

The time variant contexts of the Driver and Correlation Objects can juxtapose each other. When the Driver Object is an Instance Key and the Correlation Object is an Entity Key, the Market Basket Analysis considers each individual occurrence of the Driver Object against the whole universe of occurrences of the Correlation Object. When the Driver Object is an Entity Key and the Correlation Object is an Instance Key, the Market Basket Analysis considers the whole universe of occurrences of the Driver Object against each individual occurrence of the Correlation Object.

ELEMENTS OF TIME VARIANT MARKET BASKET ANALYSIS

We divulged the plot, including the big finish wherein we juxtapose the time variant contexts of Itemsets. Now that all the secrets are on the table, the first order of business is to define the elements of the Market Basket Analysis. Chapter 5 defined the Market Basket Solution in terms of an Itemset and Objects. The Itemset and Objects, therefore, are the elements that must be defined in terms of the Time Variant Solution Design.

Itemset

In Chapter 5, the "Definition of an Itemset" section explained that every enterprise has moments when the business performs its business functions. Unfortunately, there is no universal Transaction Key. Unlike the Entity Key, which is based on the data modeling concept of an entity, and the Instance Key, which is based on individual iterations of an entity, there is no data modeling concept that encompasses the individual transactions of a restaurant, retail store, and service provider. For that reason, the label Itemset cannot be replaced by something else that is universally recognized as the unique identifier for transactions or Itemsets.

That being the case, the definition of an Itemset is unique to each enterprise. For a Fact table to represent the Itemsets of the enterprise to a Market Basket Analysis application, that Fact table must also be able to represent each individual transaction so that each individual transaction can be identified separately from all other transactions. The first Market Basket ETL function will extract data from a Fact table and then load that data into a Market Basket Table. Within the Market Basket Table, each individual Itemset may be identified by a compound key composed of various entities, such as a date, time, place, station, and person, or by a simple unique sequential key.

Object

The Objects of a Market Basket Analysis application are also the Objects of a Time Variant Market Basket Analysis application. The difference is time variance, which means that Objects in a Market Basket Analysis application are represented simultaneously by their Type 1 Entity Key and by their Type 2 Instance Key in a single Fact table row.

Chapter 7 (Market Basket ETL) presented two hierarchical levels of object. At the lower hierarchical level, the Object_Key represented an individual object. At the higher hierarchical level, the Hierarchy_Key represented a grouping or class of objects. Both Object_Keys and Hierarchy_Keys were incorporated into the Market Basket Analysis application. The concept of juxtaposing an object and a class of objects was presented for two reasons. The first reason is that such a juxtaposition is a value-adding practice within Market Basket Analysis. The second reason is that it provides the conceptual foundation for Time Variant Market Basket Analysis.

Unlike the multiple hierarchical levels of objects in an enterprise, only two hierarchical levels exist in a Time Variant data warehouse. The lowest level presents each individual occurrence of an object: Halloween candy and Holiday candy are individual occurrences of candy. An individual object, therefore, has two hierarchical levels of the time variant occurrences: the individual instance of an object, which is represented by the Instance_Key (i.e., Halloween candy, Holiday candy, Supplier A milk from 2009 and Supplier B milk from 2010), and the universe of all occurrences of an object represented by the Entity_Key of the same object (i.e., all iterations of candy and all iterations of milk).

FORMS OF TIME VARIANT MARKET BASKET ANALYSIS

The forms of Time Variant Market Basket Analysis are the permutations of Object (Driver and Correlation) and Key (Instance_ and Entity_). This should sound very similar to the permutations of Object (Driver and Correlation) and Key (Object_ and Hierarchy_) in Chapter 7, because they are conceptually the same. The hierarchy between an Object_Key and its hierarchical parent Hierarchy_Key is the same relationship as that between an Instance_Key and its hierarchical parent Entity_Key.

- Instance Driver Object and Instance Correlation Object—This form of Time Variant Market Basket Analysis will juxtapose each occurrence of Driver Object (e.g., Halloween candy, Holiday candy, Supplier A milk from 2009 and Supplier B milk from 2010) with each occurrence of Correlation Object (e.g., Halloween candy, Holiday candy, Supplier A milk from 2009 and Supplier B milk from 2010).
  - Halloween candy juxtaposed with…
    - Holiday Candy
    - Supplier A milk from 2009
    - Supplier B milk from 2010
  - Holiday candy juxtaposed with…
    - Halloween Candy
    - Supplier A milk from 2009
    - Supplier B milk from 2010
  - Supplier A milk from 2009 juxtaposed with…
    - Halloween Candy

- Holiday Candy
- Supplier B milk from 2010
- Supplier B milk from 2010 juxtaposed with...
  - Halloween Candy
  - Holiday Candy
  - Supplier A milk from 2009
- Instance Driver Object and Entity Correlation Object—This form of Time Variant Market Basket Analysis will juxtapose each occurrence of Driver Object (e.g., Halloween candy, Holiday candy, Supplier A milk from 2009 and Supplier B milk from 2010) with the universe of occurrences of Correlation Objects (e.g., all candy and all milk).
  - Halloween candy juxtaposed with...
    - Milk (regardless of the supplier A from 2009 or Supplier B from 2010)
  - Holiday candy juxtaposed with...
    - Milk (regardless of the supplier A from 2009 or Supplier B from 2010)
  - Supplier A milk from 2009 juxtaposed with...
    - Candy (regardless of the Halloween or Holiday occurrence of the candy)
  - Supplier B milk from 2010 juxtaposed with...
    - Candy (regardless of the Halloween or Holiday occurrence of the candy)
- Entity Driver Object and Instance Correlation Object—This form of Time Variant Market Basket Analysis will juxtapose the universe of occurrences of Driver Objects (e.g., all candy and all milk) with each occurrence of Correlation Object (e.g., Halloween candy, Holiday candy, Supplier A milk from 2009 and Supplier B milk from 2010).
  - Milk (regardless of the supplier A from 2009 or Supplier B from 2010) juxtaposed with...
    - Halloween Candy
    - Holiday Candy
  - Candy (regardless of the Halloween or Holiday occurrence of the candy) juxtaposed with...
    - Supplier A milk from 2009
    - Supplier B milk from 2010
- Entity Driver Object and Entity Correlation Object—This form of Time Variant Market Basket Analysis will juxtapose the universe of

occurrences of Driver Objects (e.g., all candy and all milk) with the universe of occurrences of Correlation Object (e.g., all candy and all milk).

- Milk (regardless of the supplier A from 2009 or Supplier B from 2010) juxtaposed with...
  - Candy (regardless of the Halloween or Holiday occurrence of the candy)
- Candy (regardless of the Halloween or Holiday occurrence of the candy) juxtaposed with...
- Milk (regardless of the Supplier A milk from 2009 or Supplier B from 2010)

Sample Data

The four permutations of Time Variant Market Basket Analysis are discussed below using the sample data in Table 14.1. The products in Table 14.1 are Toothpaste, Mouthwash, and Dental Floss. The product Toothpaste has two rows of time variant data. Both the Mouthwash and Dental Floss have three rows each of time variant data.

The three products are included in five transactions in Table 14.2. Notice that the Entity_Key and Instance_Key columns are both in the Fact table. This is a difference between the hierarchical relationship in Table 7.1 and Table 14.2. In Table 7.1, the Hierarchy_Key (hierarchical parent to the Object_Key) had to be joined relationally to the Fact table. In Table 14.2, the Entity_Key (hierarchical parent to the Instance_Key) is already in the Fact table and therefore does not need to be joined to the Fact table.

The Entity_Key and Instance_Key are both included in a Fact table to facilitate joins to a Type 1 dimension table and to a Type 2 dimension table. Time is the only stable hierarchy such that July 12, 2011, 6:32 a.m. will always reside in the July 12, 2011, 6:00 a.m. hour, which will always reside in July 12, 2011, which will always reside in July 2011, which will always reside in Quarter Three 2011, which will always reside in the year 2011, which will always reside in the twenty-first century. Hierarchical groupings of products, subdepartments, departments, and other such hierarchies in an enterprise are not so stable. So, while embedding a Hierarchy_Key in a Fact table would be risky at best, embedding an Entity_Key next to an Instance_Key in a Fact table will work so long as time is a stable hierarchy.

TABLE 14.1

Product Dimension

Instance Key	Entity Key	Row First Date	Row Last Date	Description
0	0	January 1, 2000	December 31, 9999	SINGLE OBJECT ITEMSET
78	1124	May 11, 2008	November 24, 2009	TOOTHBRUSH—blue and white
98	1124	November 25, 2009	December 31, 9999	TOOTHBRUSH—purple
16	6543	May 12, 2008	August 27, 2009	MOUTHWASH—mint
43	6543	August 28, 2009	January 20, 2010	MOUTHWASH—aqua blast
64	6543	January 21, 2010	December 31, 9999	MOUTHWASH—spring fever
15	9792	March 17, 2008	October 31, 2009	DENTAL FLOSS—plain
57	9792	November 1, 2009	April 21, 2010	DENTAL FLOSS—cinnamon
87	9792	April 22, 2010	December 31, 9999	DENTAL FLOSS—lavender

Instance Driver Object and Instance Correlation Object

The first function of the Time Variant Market Basket ETL, shown in Figure 14.1, is to extract data from a fact table and then load it into the Market Basket Table. A time variant Market Basket Table can also have the case of a Single Object Itemset. In a Single Object Itemset, the Entity_Key and Instance_Key of a Single Object Itemset are assigned the value zero. As mentioned in Chapter 7, this will provide the Correlation Object in the Single Object Itemset that will allow the object to join to its own Itemset as the Driver Object.

The result set of the SQL in Figure 14.1, which will be loaded into the Market Basket Table, is shown in Table 14.3. Both the Entity_Key and Instance_Key are included in the Market Basket Table. However, because the Instance_Key is a lower hierarchical grain than the Entity_Key, the Instance_Key within each Itemset is the time variant hierarchical grain at which the Itemsets are summarized. In a later ETL step, the Instance_Key will be discarded, which will leave the Entity_Key as the lowest time variant hierarchical grain.

The second step in the Time Variant Market Basket ETL, shown in Figure 14.2, juxtaposes the Instance_Keys of each Itemset with each other.

TABLE 14.2

Fact Table

Itemset Key	Transaction Date	Instance Key	Entity Key	Quantity	Dollars
1	June 30, 2008	15	9792	1	$15.31
1	June 30, 2008	15	9792	1	$15.31
2	February 14, 2009	15	9792	1	$15.31
2	February 14, 2009	15	9792	1	$15.31
2	February 14, 2009	16	6543	1	$12.21
2	February 14, 2009	78	1124	1	$13.44
2	February 14, 2009	78	1124	1	$13.44
2	February 14, 2009	78	1124	1	$13.44
3	December 1, 2009	43	6543	1	$14.32
3	December 1, 2009	43	6543	1	$14.32
3	December 1, 2009	43	6543	1	$14.32
3	December 1, 2009	57	9792	1	$9.09
3	December 1, 2009	57	9792	1	$9.09
3	December 1, 2009	57	9792	1	$9.09
3	December 1, 2009	57	9792	1	$9.09
3	December 1, 2009	98	1124	1	$2.45
3	December 1, 2009	98	1124	1	$2.45
4	March 14, 2010	57	9792	1	$9.09
4	March 14, 2010	57	9792	1	$9.09
4	March 14, 2010	64	6543	1	$12.37
4	March 14, 2010	64	6543	1	$12.37
4	March 14, 2010	64	6543	1	$12.37
4	March 14, 2010	98	1124	1	$2.45
4	March 14, 2010	98	1124	1	$2.45
5	July 1, 2010	64	6543	1	$12.37
5	July 1, 2010	64	6543	1	$12.37
5	July 1, 2010	87	9792	1	$16.87

This is a recursive join on Itemset_Key (A.ITEMSET_KEY = B.ITEMSET_KEY). The database design that optimized the recursive join of Figure 7.2 also applies to the recursive join in Figure 14.2. The Itemset_Key is the recursive join key on which the Market Basket Table will optimize the recursive join in Figure 14.2.

The result set, shown in Table 14.4, includes both the Instance_Key and Entity_Key. As mentioned previously, the Entity_Key draws its stability from the stability of time as a dimension. It will facilitate subsequent iterations of Market Basket Analysis at the level of Type 1 Time Variance.

```
DELETE FROM
MARKET_BASKET_TABLE
;
INSERT INTO MARKET_BASKET_TABLE
(ITEMSET_KEY
,INSTANCE_KEY
,ENTITY_KEY
,QUANTITY
,DOLLARS)
SELECT
ITEMSET_KEY
,INSTANCE_KEY
,ENTITY_KEY
,SUM(QUANTITY) AS QUANTITY_SUM
,SUM(DOLLARS) AS DOLLARS_SUM
FROM FACT_TABLE
GROUP BY
ITEMSET_KEY
,INSTANCE_KEY
,ENTITY_KEY
;
```

FIGURE 14.1

Load Market Basket Table.

TABLE 14.3

Market Basket Table

Itemset_Key	Instance_Key	Entity_Key	Quantity	Dollars
1	0	0	0	$0.00
1	15	9792	2	$30.62
2	15	9792	2	$30.62
2	16	6543	1	$12.21
2	78	1124	3	$40.32
3	43	6543	3	$42.96
3	57	9792	4	$36.36
3	98	1124	2	$4.90
4	57	9792	2	$18.18
4	64	6543	3	$37.11
4	98	1124	2	$4.90
5	64	6543	2	$24.74
5	87	9792	1	$16.87

The Market Basket BI Table is queried using the SQL in Figure 14.3. This SQL is analogous to the SQL in Figure 7.4. The Instance_Key, like the Object_Key in Figure 7.4, is the lowest hierarchical level. So, the inequality (DRIVER.DRIVER_INSTANCE_KEY = CORR.DRIVER_INSTANCE_KEY) prevents each row from joining to itself. The output of this SQL is shown in Table 14.5.

```
DELETE FROM MARKET_BASKET_BI_TABLE
;
INSERT INTO MARKET_BASKET_BI_TABLE
( ITEMSET_KEY
, DRIVER_INSTANCE_KEY
, DRIVER_ENTITY_KEY
, DRIVER_QUANTITY
, DRIVER_DOLLARS
, DRIVER_COUNT
, CORR_INSTANCE_KEY
, CORR_ENTITY_KEY
, CORR_QUANTITY
, CORR_DOLLARS
, CORR_COUNT)
SELECT
A.ITEMSET_KEY
, A.INSTANCE_KEY AS DRIVER_INSTANCE_KEY
, A.ENTITY_KEY AS DRIVER_ENTITY_KEY
, A.QUANTITY AS DRIVER_QUANTITY
, A.DOLLARS AS DRIVER_DOLLARS
, 1 AS DRIVER_COUNT
, B.INSTANCE_KEY AS CORR_INSTANCE_KEY
, B.ENTITY_KEY AS CORR_ENTITY_KEY
, B.QUANTITY AS CORR_QUANTITY
, B.DOLLARS AS CORR_DOLLARS
, 1 AS CORR_COUNT
FROM MARKET_BASKET_TABLE A
INNER JOIN MARKET_BASKET_TABLE B
ON A.ITEMSET_KEY = B.ITEMSET_KEY
WHERE A.INSTANCE_KEY <> B.INSTANCE_KEY
AND A.INSTANCE_KEY <> 0
;
```

FIGURE 14.2
Load Market Basket BI Table.

Instance Driver Object and Entity Correlation Object

The next step in the Market Basket ETL uses the data already in the Market Basket BI Table to populate a second Market Basket BI Table that correlates Entity_Keys rather than Instance_Keys. The SQL in Figure 14.4 is very similar to the SQL in Figure 7.4. By changing the grain of the Correlation Object from the Instance_Key to the Entity_Key, the output shown in Table 14.6 juxtaposes each time variant occurrence of the Driver Object with the universe of occurrences of the Correlation Object.

The SQL in Figure 14.4 uses data already juxtaposed in the Market Basket BI Table. For that reason, the SQL does not need to use the recursive join that created the data in the Market Basket BI Table. That is the advantage of this stepped approach to Market Basket Analysis.

TABLE 14.4

Market Basket BI Table

Itemset Key	Driver Instance Key	Driver Entity Key	Driver Quantity	Driver Dollars	Driver Count	Corr Instance Key	Corr Entity Key	Corr Quantity	Corr Dollars	Corr Count
1	15	9792	2	$30.62	1	0	0	0	$0.00	1
2	15	9792	2	$30.62	1	16	6543	1	$12.21	1
2	15	9792	2	$30.62	1	78	1124	3	$40.32	1
2	16	6543	1	$12.21	1	15	9792	2	$30.62	1
2	16	6543	1	$12.21	1	78	1124	3	$40.32	1
2	78	1124	3	$40.32	1	15	9792	2	$30.62	1
2	78	1124	3	$40.32	.1	16	6543	1	$12.21	1
3	43	6543	3	$42.96	1	57	9792	4	$36.36	1
3	43	6543	3	$42.96	1	98	1124	2	$4.90	1
3	57	9792	4	$36.36	1	43	6543	3	$42.96	1
3	57	9792	4	$36.36	1	98	1124	2	$4.90	1
3	98	1124	2	$4.90	1	43	6543	3	$42.96	1
3	98	1124	2	$4.90	1	57	9792	4	$36.36	1
4	57	9792	2	$18.18	1	64	6543	3	$37.11	1
4	57	9792	2	$18.18	1	98	1124	2	$4.90	1
4	64	6543	3	$37.11	1	57	9792	2	$18.18	1
4	64	6543	3	$37.11	1	98	1124	2	$4.90	1
4	98	1124	2	$4.90	1	57	9792	2	$18.18	1
4	98	1124	2	$4.90	1	64	6543	3	$37.11	1
5	64	6543	2	$24.74	1	87	9792	1	$16.87	1
5	87	9792	1	$16.87	1	64	6543	2	$24.74	1

```
SELECT
DRIVER.DRIVER_INSTANCE_KEY
, CORR.CORR_INSTANCE_KEY
, DRIVER.DRIVER_QUANTITY_SUM
, DRIVER.DRIVER_DOLLARS_SUM
, DRIVER.DRIVER_COUNT_SUM
, CORR.CORR_QUANTITY_SUM
, CORR.CORR_DOLLARS_SUM
, CORR.CORR_COUNT_SUM
, CORR.CORR_QUANTITY_SUM/DRIVER.DRIVER_QUANTITY_SUM AS QUANTITY_RATIO
, CORR.CORR_DOLLARS_SUM/DRIVER.DRIVER_DOLLARS_SUM AS DOLLARS_RATIO
, CORR.CORR_COUNT_SUM/DRIVER.DRIVER_COUNT_SUM AS COUNT_RATIO
FROM
(SELECT
DRIVER_INSTANCE_KEY
,SUM(DRIVER_QUANTITY) AS DRIVER_QUANTITY_SUM
,SUM(DRIVER_DOLLARS) AS DRIVER_DOLLARS_SUM
,SUM(DRIVER_COUNT) AS DRIVER_COUNT_SUM
FROM(SELECT
ITEMSET_KEY
,DRIVER_INSTANCE_KEY
,DRIVER_QUANTITY
,DRIVER_DOLLARS
,DRIVER_COUNT
FROM MARKET_BASKET_BI_TABLE
GROUP BY
ITEMSET_KEY
,DRIVER_INSTANCE_KEY
,DRIVER_QUANTITY
,DRIVER_DOLLARS
,DRIVER_COUNT)
GROUP BY
DRIVER_INSTANCE_KEY)DRIVER
INNER JOIN
(SELECT
DRIVER_INSTANCE_KEY
,CORR_INSTANCE_KEY
,SUM(CORR_QUANTITY) AS CORR_QUANTITY_SUM
,SUM(CORR_DOLLARS) AS CORR_DOLLARS_SUM
,SUM(CORR_COUNT) AS CORR_COUNT_SUM
FROM MARKET_BASKET_BI_TABLE
GROUP BY
DRIVER_INSTANCE_KEY
,CORR_INSTANCE_KEY)CORR
ON DRIVER.DRIVER_INSTANCE_KEY = CORR.DRIVER_INSTANCE_KEY
ORDER BY
DRIVER.DRIVER_INSTANCE_KEY
, CORR.CORR_INSTANCE_KEY
```

FIGURE 14.3
Market Basket Analysis BI View.

Rather than trying to achieve all the data transformations in one step, the Market Basket ETL steps achieve the data transformations in controlled batches.

The inequality statement (DRIVER_ENTITY_KEY <> CORR_ENTITY_KEY) causes each Instance_Key to never juxtapose with its

TABLE 14.5

Market Basket Analysis BI View

Driver Instance Key	Corr Instance Key	Driver Quantity Sum	Driver Dollars Sum	Driver Count Sum	Corr Quantity Sum	Corr Dollars Sum	Corr Count Sum	Quantity Ratio	Dollars Ratio	Count Ratio
15	0	4	$61.24	2	0	$0.00	1	0.0000%	0.0000%	50.0000%
15	16	4	$61.24	2	1	$12.21	1	25.0000%	19.9379%	50.0000%
15	78	4	$61.24	2	3	$40.32	1	75.0000%	65.8393%	50.0000%
16	15	1	$12.21	1	2	$30.62	1	200.0000%	250.7781%	100.0000%
16	78	1	$12.21	1	3	$40.32	1	300.0000%	330.2211%	100.0000%
43	57	3	$42.96	1	4	$36.36	1	133.3333%	84.6369%	100.0000%
43	98	3	$42.96	1	2	$4.90	1	66.6667%	11.4060%	100.0000%
57	43	6	$54.54	2	3	$42.96	1	50.0000%	78.7679%	50.0000%
57	64	6	$54.54	2	3	$37.11	1	50.0000%	68.0418%	50.0000%
57	98	6	$54.54	2	4	$9.80	2	66.6667%	17.9685%	100.0000%
64	57	5	$61.85	2	2	$18.18	1	40.0000%	29.3937%	50.0000%
64	87	5	$61.85	2	1	$16.87	1	20.0000%	27.2757%	50.0000%
64	98	5	$61.85	2	2	$4.90	1	40.0000%	7.9224%	50.0000%
78	15	3	$40.32	1	2	$30.62	1	66.6667%	75.9425%	100.0000%
78	16	3	$40.32	1	1	$12.21	1	33.3333%	30.2827%	100.0000%
87	64	1	$16.87	1	2	$24.74	1	200.0000%	146.6509%	100.0000%
98	43	4	$9.80	2	3	$42.96	1	75.0000%	438.3673%	50.0000%
98	57	4	$9.80	2	6	$54.54	2	150.0000%	556.5306%	100.0000%
98	64	4	$9.80	2	3	$37.11	1	75.0000%	378.6735%	50.0000%

```
DELETE FROM MARKET_BASKET_BI_TABLE_CORR_ENTITY
;
INSERT INTO MARKET_BASKET_BI_TABLE_CORR_ENTITY
(ITEMSET_KEY
, DRIVER_INSTANCE_KEY
, DRIVER_QUANTITY
, DRIVER_DOLLARS
, DRIVER_COUNT
, CORR_ENTITY_KEY
, CORR_QUANTITY
, CORR_DOLLARS
, CORR_COUNT)
SELECT
ITEMSET_KEY
, DRIVER_INSTANCE_KEY
, DRIVER_QUANTITY
, DRIVER_DOLLARS
, DRIVER_COUNT
, CORR_ENTITY_KEY
, SUM(CORR_QUANTITY) AS CORR_QUANTITY_SUM
, SUM(CORR_DOLLARS) AS CORR_DOLLARS_SUM
, 1 AS CORR_COUNT
FROM MARKET_BASKET_BI_TABLE
WHERE
DRIVER_ENTITY_KEY <> CORR_ENTITY_KEY
GROUP BY
ITEMSET_KEY
, DRIVER_INSTANCE_KEY
, DRIVER_QUANTITY
, DRIVER_DOLLARS
, DRIVER_COUNT
, CORR_ENTITY_KEY
ORDER BY
DRIVER_INSTANCE_KEY
, CORR_ENTITY_KEY
;
```

FIGURE 14.4
Load Market Basket BI Table with Correlation Entity.

time variant parent Entity_Key. If that inequality statement were changed to DRIVER_INSTANCE_KEY<>DRIVER_INSTANCE_KEY, then each Instance_Key would be juxtaposed with its time variant parent Entity_Key, excluding its own portion of that Entity_Key. This is a subtlety that can cause more confusion than any value it adds for analysts who don't understand the presence of a row juxtaposing an Instance_Key and its parent Entity_Key. For that reason, and the limited value it provides, the inequality statement DRIVER_ENTITY_KEY <> CORR_ENTITY_KEY is often the preferred approach.

TABLE 14.6

Market Basket BI Table with Correlation Entity

Itemset Key	Driver Instance Key	Driver Quantity	Driver Dollars	Driver Count	Corr Entity Key	Corr Quantity	Corr Dollars	Corr Count
1	15	2	$30.62	1	0	0	$0.00	1
2	15	2	$30.62	1	1124	3	$40.32	1
2	15	2	$30.62	1	6543	1	$12.21	1
2	16	1	$12.21	1	1124	3	$40.32	1
2	16	1	$12.21	1	9792	2	$30.62	1
2	78	3	$40.32	1	6543	1	$12.21	1
2	78	3	$40.32	1	9792	2	$30.62	1
3	43	3	$42.96	1	1124	2	$4.90	1
3	43	3	$42.96	1	9792	4	$36.36	1
3	57	4	$36.36	1	1124	2	$4.90	1
3	57	4	$36.36	1	6543	3	$42.96	1
3	98	2	$4.90	1	6543	3	$42.96	1
3	98	2	$4.90	1	9792	4	$36.36	1
4	57	2	$18.18	1	1124	2	$4.90	1
4	57	2	$18.18	1	6543	3	$37.11	1
4	64	3	$37.11	1	1124	2	$4.90	1
4	64	3	$37.11	1	9792	2	$18.18	1
4	98	2	$4.90	1	6543	3	$37.11	1
4	98	2	$4.90	1	9792	2	$18.18	1
5	64	2	$24.74	1	9792	1	$16.87	1
5	87	1	$16.87	1	6543	2	$24.74	1

The SQL in Figure 14.5 uses the Instance_Key as the Driver Object by joining on the Instance_Key in the Driver_Object and Correlation Object (DRIVER.DRIVER_INSTANCE_KEY = CORR.DRIVER_INSTANCE_KEY). The SQL in Figure 14.5 is analogous to the SQL in Figure 7.5. The SQL in Figure 7.5 juxtaposed the Driver Object_Key with the Correlation

```
SELECT
DRIVER.DRIVER_INSTANCE_KEY
, CORR.CORR_ENTITY_KEY
, DRIVER.DRIVER_QUANTITY_SUM
, DRIVER.DRIVER_DOLLARS_SUM
, DRIVER.DRIVER_COUNT_SUM
, CORR.CORR_QUANTITY_SUM
, CORR.CORR_DOLLARS_SUM
, CORR.CORR_COUNT_SUM
, CORR.CORR_QUANTITY_SUM/DRIVER.DRIVER_QUANTITY_SUM AS QUANTITY_RATIO
, CORR.CORR_DOLLARS_SUM/DRIVER.DRIVER_DOLLARS_SUM AS DOLLARS_RATIO
, CORR.CORR_COUNT_SUM/DRIVER.DRIVER_COUNT_SUM AS COUNT_RATIO
FROM
(SELECT
DRIVER_INSTANCE_KEY
,SUM(DRIVER_QUANTITY) AS DRIVER_QUANTITY_SUM
,SUM(DRIVER_DOLLARS) AS DRIVER_DOLLARS_SUM
,SUM(DRIVER_COUNT) AS DRIVER_COUNT_SUM
FROM(SELECT
ITEMSET_KEY
,DRIVER_INSTANCE_KEY
,DRIVER_QUANTITY
,DRIVER_DOLLARS
,DRIVER_COUNT
FROM MARKET_BASKET_BI_TABLE_CORR_ENTITY
GROUP BY
ITEMSET_KEY
,DRIVER_INSTANCE_KEY
,DRIVER_QUANTITY
,DRIVER_DOLLARS
,DRIVER_COUNT)
GROUP BY
DRIVER_INSTANCE_KEY)DRIVER
INNER JOIN
(SELECT
DRIVER_INSTANCE_KEY
,CORR_ENTITY_KEY
,SUM(CORR_QUANTITY) AS CORR_QUANTITY_SUM
,SUM(CORR_DOLLARS) AS CORR_DOLLARS_SUM
,SUM(CORR_COUNT) AS CORR_COUNT_SUM
FROM MARKET_BASKET_BI_TABLE_CORR_ENTITY
GROUP BY
DRIVER_INSTANCE_KEY
,CORR_ENTITY_KEY)CORR
ON DRIVER.DRIVER_INSTANCE_KEY = CORR.DRIVER_INSTANCE_KEY
ORDER BY
DRIVER.DRIVER_INSTANCE_KEY
, CORR.CORR_ENTITY_KEY
```

FIGURE 14.5
Market Basket Analysis BI View with Correlation Entity.

Hierarchy_Key. The SQL in Figure 14.5 juxtaposes the Driver Instance_Key with the Correlation Entity_Key.

The output shown in Table 14.7 is likewise analogous to the output in Table 7.8. The lower hierarchical level is the Driver Object while the higher hierarchical level is the Correlation Object.

Entity Driver Object and Instance Correlation Object

The next step in the Time Variant Market Basket ETL is to juxtapose the Itemsets by using the Entity_Key as the Driver Object and the Instance_Key as the Correlation Object. The SQL in Figure 14.6 uses the data already juxtaposed in the Market Basket BI Table in another controlled batch of Market Basket ETL.

The inequality statement (DRIVER_ENTITY_KEY <> CORR_ENTITY_KEY) causes an Entity_Key to never juxtapose with any of its hierarchically subordinate Instance_Keys. Unlike the previous Market Basket ETL step, which could change the inequality to DRIVER_INSTANCE_KEY<>DRIVER_INSTANCE_KEY, this Market Basket ETL step cannot change the inequality to DRIVER_INSTANCE_KEY<>DRIVER_INSTANCE_KEY. To do so would cause the juxtaposition of Driver Entity_Key to Correlation Instance_Key to only apply to the Driver Entity_Key, rather than the Entity_Key of each row of the Market Basket BI Table, which would generate bogus results.

The SQL in Figure 14.6 is analogous to the SQL in Figure 7.6. The output in Table 14.8 is analogous to the output in Table 7.9. The "1 AS DRIVER_COUNT" statement resets the count of Itemsets back to one because the count of Itemsets is not additive. In the transformation of the grain of the Driver Object from Instance_Key to Entity_Key, the count of Itemsets cannot be summed. Instead, in this ETL step, the count of Itemsets can only be reset to one. The Quantity and Dollars metrics, however, are additive and can be summed in the transformation from Instance_Key to Entity_Key.

The SQL in Figure 14.7 is analogous to the SQL in Figure 7.7. In both SQL statements the parent hierarchy is the Driver Object and the child hierarchy is the Correlation Object because the Driver and Correlation subqueries join on their Driver_Entity_Keys (DRIVER.DRIVER_ENTITY_KEY = CORR.DRIVER_ENTITY_KEY). The output in Table 14.9 is analogous to the output in Table 14.10.

TABLE 14.7

Market Basket Analysis BI View with Correlation Entity

Driver Instance Key	Corr Entity Key	Driver Quantity Sum	Driver Dollars Sum	Driver Count Sum	Corr Quantity Sum	Corr Dollars Sum	Corr Count Sum	Quantity Ratio	Dollars Ratio	Count Ratio
15	1124	4	$61.24	2	3	$40.32	1	75.0000%	65.8393%	50.0000%
15	6543	4	$61.24	2	1	$12.21	1	25.0000%	19.9379%	50.0000%
15	0	4	$61.24	2	0	$0.00	1	0.0000%	0.0000%	50.0000%
16	1124	1	$12.21	1	3	$40.32	1	300.0000%	330.2211%	100.0000%
16	9792	1	$12.21	1	2	$30.62	1	200.0000%	250.7781%	100.0000%
43	9792	3	$42.96	1	4	$36.36	1	133.3333%	84.6369%	100.0000%
43	1124	3	$42.96	1	2	$4.90	1	66.6667%	11.4060%	100.0000%
57	6543	6	$54.54	2	6	$80.07	2	100.0000%	146.8097%	100.0000%
57	1124	6	$54.54	2	4	$9.80	2	66.6667%	17.9685%	100.0000%
64	1124	5	$61.85	2	2	$4.90	1	40.0000%	7.9224%	50.0000%
64	9792	5	$61.85	2	3	$35.05	2	60.0000%	56.6694%	100.0000%
78	6543	3	$40.32	1	1	$12.21	1	33.3333%	30.2827%	100.0000%
78	9792	3	$40.32	1	2	$30.62	1	66.6667%	75.9425%	100.0000%
87	6543	1	$16.87	1	2	$24.74	1	200.0000%	146.6509%	100.0000%
98	9792	4	$9.80	2	6	$54.54	2	150.0000%	556.5306%	100.0000%
98	6543	4	$9.80	2	6	$80.07	2	150.0000%	817.0408%	100.0000%

```
DELETE FROM MARKET_BASKET_BI_TABLE_DRIVER_ENTITY
;
INSERT INTO MARKET_BASKET_BI_TABLE_DRIVER_ENTITY
(ITEMSET_KEY
,DRIVER_ENTITY_KEY
,DRIVER_QUANTITY
,DRIVER_DOLLARS
,DRIVER_COUNT
,CORR_INSTANCE_KEY
,CORR_QUANTITY
,CORR_DOLLARS
,CORR_COUNT)
SELECT
ITEMSET_KEY
, DRIVER_ENTITY_KEY
, SUM(DRIVER_QUANTITY) AS DRIVER_QUANTITY_SUM
, SUM(DRIVER_DOLLARS) AS DRIVER_DOLLARS_SUM
, 1 AS DRIVER_COUNT
, CORR_INSTANCE_KEY
, CORR_QUANTITY
, CORR_DOLLARS
, CORR_COUNT
FROM MARKET_BASKET_BI_TABLE
WHERE
DRIVER_ENTITY_KEY <> CORR_ENTITY_KEY
GROUP BY
ITEMSET_KEY
, DRIVER_ENTITY_KEY
, CORR_INSTANCE_KEY
, CORR_QUANTITY
, CORR_DOLLARS
, CORR_COUNT
ORDER BY
ITEMSET_KEY
, DRIVER_ENTITY_KEY
, CORR_INSTANCE_KEY
;
```

FIGURE 14.6
Load Market Basket BI Table with Driver Entity.

Entity Driver Object and Entity Correlation Object

In this final step of the Market Basket ETL, both the Driver Object and the Correlation Object are Entity_Keys. This step goes all the way back to the source Fact table for two reasons. First, the transformation of the grain of both the Driver_Instance_Key and the Corr_Instance_Key hierarchically up to the level of their respective Entity_Keys causes the data to be a transformation of a transformation. Rather than use a transformation of

TABLE 14.8

Market Basket BI Table with Driver Entity

Itemset Key	Driver Entity Key	Driver Quantity	Driver Dollars	Driver Count	Corr Instance Key	Corr Quantity	Corr Dollars	Corr Count
1	9792	2	$30.62	1	0	0	$0.00	1
2	1124	3	$40.32	1	15	2	$30.62	1
2	1124	3	$40.32	1	16	1	$12.21	1
2	6543	1	$12.21	1	15	2	$30.62	1
2	6543	1	$12.21	1	78	3	$40.32	1
2	9792	2	$30.62	1	16	1	$12.21	1
2	9792	2	$30.62	1	78	3	$40.32	1
3	1124	2	$4.90	1	43	3	$42.96	1
3	1124	2	$4.90	1	57	4	$36.36	1
3	6543	3	$42.96	1	57	4	$36.36	1
3	6543	3	$42.96	1	98	2	$4.90	1
3	9792	4	$36.36	1	43	3	$42.96	1
3	9792	4	$36.36	1	98	2	$4.90	1
4	1124	2	$4.90	1	57	2	$18.18	1
4	1124	2	$4.90	1	64	3	$37.11	1
4	6543	3	$37.11	1	57	2	$18.18	1
4	6543	3	$37.11	1	98	2	$4.90	1
4	9792	2	$18.18	1	64	3	$37.11	1
4	9792	2	$18.18	1	98	2	$4.90	1
5	6543	2	$24.74	1	87	1	$16.87	1
5	9792	1	$16.87	1	64	2	$24.74	1

```
SELECT
DRIVER.DRIVER_ENTITY_KEY
, CORR.CORR_INSTANCE_KEY
, DRIVER.DRIVER_QUANTITY_SUM
, DRIVER.DRIVER_DOLLARS_SUM
, DRIVER.DRIVER_COUNT_SUM
, CORR.CORR_QUANTITY_SUM
, CORR.CORR_DOLLARS_SUM
, CORR.CORR_COUNT_SUM
, CORR.CORR_QUANTITY_SUM/DRIVER.DRIVER_QUANTITY_SUM AS QUANTITY_RATIO
, CORR.CORR_DOLLARS_SUM/DRIVER.DRIVER_DOLLARS_SUM AS DOLLARS_RATIO
, CORR.CORR_COUNT_SUM/DRIVER.DRIVER_COUNT_SUM AS COUNT_RATIO
FROM
(SELECT
DRIVER_ENTITY_KEY
,SUM(DRIVER_QUANTITY) AS DRIVER_QUANTITY_SUM
,SUM(DRIVER_DOLLARS) AS DRIVER_DOLLARS_SUM
,SUM(DRIVER_COUNT) AS DRIVER_COUNT_SUM
FROM(SELECT
ITEMSET_KEY
,DRIVER_ENTITY_KEY
,DRIVER_QUANTITY
,DRIVER_DOLLARS
,DRIVER_COUNT
FROM MARKET_BASKET_BI_TABLE_DRIVER_ENTITY
GROUP BY
ITEMSET_KEY
,DRIVER_ENTITY_KEY
,DRIVER_QUANTITY
,DRIVER_DOLLARS
,DRIVER_COUNT)
GROUP BY
DRIVER_ENTITY_KEY)DRIVER
INNER JOIN
(SELECT
DRIVER_ENTITY_KEY
,CORR_INSTANCE_KEY
,SUM(CORR_QUANTITY) AS CORR_QUANTITY_SUM
,SUM(CORR_DOLLARS) AS CORR_DOLLARS_SUM
,SUM(CORR_COUNT) AS CORR_COUNT_SUM
FROM MARKET_BASKET_BI_TABLE_DRIVER_ENTITY
GROUP BY
DRIVER_ENTITY_KEY
,CORR_INSTANCE_KEY)CORR
ON DRIVER.DRIVER_ENTITY_KEY = CORR.DRIVER_ENTITY_KEY
ORDER BY
DRIVER.DRIVER_ENTITY_KEY
, CORR.CORR_INSTANCE_KEY
```

FIGURE 14.7

Market Basket Analysis BI View with Driver Entity.

a transformation when the original source data is available, this step goes back to the original source table, which is a best practice in ETL.

The SQL in Figure 14.8 excludes Instance_Keys so that the grain of the output, shown in Table 14.10, will be at the Entity_Key hierarchical level. The transformation in this ETL step still accounts for the Single Object Itemset. So, the first Itemset, which is a Single Object Itemset, is accompanied by a zero-filled row in the Market Basket Table.

TABLE 14.9

Market Basket Analysis BI View with Driver Entity

Driver Entity Key	Corr Instance Key	Driver Quantity Sum	Driver Dollars Sum	Driver Count Sum	Corr Quantity Sum	Corr Dollars Sum	Corr Count Sum	Quantity Ratio	Dollars Ratio	Count Ratio
1124	15	7	$50.12	3	2	$30.62	1	28.5714%	61.0934%	33.3333%
1124	16	7	$50.12	3	1	$12.21	1	14.2857%	24.3615%	33.3333%
1124	43	7	$50.12	3	3	$42.96	1	42.8571%	85.7143%	33.3333%
1124	57	7	$50.12	3	6	$54.54	2	85.7143%	108.8188%	66.6667%
1124	64	7	$50.12	3	3	$37.11	1	42.8571%	74.0423%	33.3333%
6543	15	9	$117.02	4	2	$30.62	1	22.2222%	26.1665%	25.0000%
6543	57	9	$117.02	4	6	$54.54	2	66.6667%	46.6074%	50.0000%
6543	78	9	$117.02	4	3	$40.32	1	33.3333%	34.4556%	25.0000%
6543	87	9	$117.02	4	1	$16.87	1	11.1111%	14.4163%	25.0000%
6543	98	9	$117.02	4	4	$9.80	2	44.4444%	8.3746%	50.0000%
9792	0	11	$132.65	5	0	$0.00	1	0.0000%	0.0000%	20.0000%
9792	16	11	$132.65	5	1	$12.21	1	9.0909%	9.2047%	20.0000%
9792	43	11	$132.65	5	3	$42.96	1	27.2727%	32.3860%	20.0000%
9792	64	11	$132.65	5	5	$61.85	2	45.4545%	46.6265%	40.0000%
9792	78	11	$132.65	5	3	$40.32	1	27.2727%	30.3958%	20.0000%
9792	98	11	$132.65	5	4	$9.80	2	36.3636%	7.3879%	40.0000%

```
DELETE FROM MARKET_BASKET_TABLE_ENTITIES
;

INSERT INTO MARKET_BASKET_TABLE_ENTITIES
(ITEMSET_KEY
,ENTITY_KEY
,QUANTITY
,DOLLARS)
SELECT
ITEMSET_KEY
,ENTITY_KEY
,SUM(QUANTITY) AS QUANTITY_SUM
,SUM(DOLLARS) AS DOLLARS_SUM
FROM FACT_TABLE
GROUP BY
ITEMSET_KEY
,ENTITY_KEY
;
```

FIGURE 14.8
Load Market Basket Table with Entities.

TABLE 14.10

Market Basket Table with Entities

Itemset_Key	Entity_Key	Quantity	Dollars
1	0	0	$0.00
1	9792	2	$30.62
2	1124	3	$40.32
2	6543	1	$12.21
2	9792	2	$30.62
3	1124	2	$4.90
3	6543	3	$42.96
3	9792	4	$36.36
4	1124	2	$4.90
4	6543	3	$37.11
4	9792	2	$18.18
5	6543	2	$24.74
5	9792	1	$16.87

The SQL in Figure 14.9 is very simple compared to the previous recursive join SQL statements. Because both the Driver Object and the Correlation Object are at the parent hierarchy level, there is no question that the inequality (A.ENTITY_KEY <> B.ENTITY_KEY) will also be at the parent hierarchy level.

The result set in Table 14.11 is smaller than previous Market Basket BI Tables because both the Driver Object and the Correlation Object are at

```
DELETE FROM MARKET_BASKET_BI_TABLE_ENTITIES
;
INSERT INTO MARKET_BASKET_BI_TABLE_ENTITIES
( ITEMSET_KEY
, DRIVER_ENTITY_KEY
, DRIVER_QUANTITY
, DRIVER_DOLLARS
, DRIVER_COUNT
, CORR_ENTITY_KEY
, CORR_QUANTITY
, CORR_DOLLARS
, CORR_COUNT)
SELECT
A.ITEMSET_KEY
, A.ENTITY_KEY AS DRIVER_ENTITY_KEY
, A.QUANTITY AS DRIVER_QUANTITY
, A.DOLLARS AS DRIVER_DOLLARS
, 1 AS DRIVER_COUNT
, B.ENTITY_KEY AS CORR_ENTITY_KEY
, B.QUANTITY AS CORR_QUANTITY
, B.DOLLARS AS CORR_DOLLARS
, 1 AS CORR_COUNT
FROM MARKET_BASKET_TABLE_ENTITIES A
INNER JOIN MARKET_BASKET_TABLE_ENTITIES B
ON A.ITEMSET_KEY = B.ITEMSET_KEY
WHERE A.ENTITY_KEY <> B.ENTITY_KEY
AND A.ENTITY_KEY <> 0
;
```

FIGURE 14.9
Load Market Basket BI Table with Entities.

their parent hierarchy level. As these Market Basket BI Tables move up their respective hierarchies, the number of rows will decrease while the values in the additive metrics will increase. If this pattern is followed up hierarchical levels, soon the number of rows would be small, the values would be large, and the ROI of the exercise would be questionable.

The SQL in Figure 14.10 is the simplest Market Basket Analysis BI View for the same reason. By querying a table with only one hierarchical level, the SQL has no options for the hierarchical grain of the Driver Object and Correlation Object. The Driver Object and Correlation Object are joined at the Entity_Key (DRIVER.DRIVER_ENTITY_KEY = CORR.DRIVER_ENTITY_KEY).

The output result set in Table 14.12 is the smallest result set yet from a Market Basket Analysis BI View in this discussion of Time Variant Market Basket Analysis. As mentioned previously, by moving the grain of the Market Basket Analysis up hierarchical levels, the number of rows gets smaller, the additive values get bigger, and the ROI decreases. For that

TABLE 14.11

Market Basket BI Table with Entities

Itemset Key	Driver Entity Key	Driver Quantity	Driver Dollars	Driver Count	Corr Entity Key	Corr Quantity	Corr Dollars	Corr Count
1	9792	2	$30.62	1	0	0	$0.00	1
2	1124	3	$40.32	1	6543	1	$12.21	1
2	1124	3	$40.32	1	9792	2	$30.62	1
2	6543	1	$12.21	1	1124	3	$40.32	1
2	6543	1	$12.21	1	9792	2	$30.62	1
2	9792	2	$30.62	1	1124	3	$40.32	1
2	9792	2	$30.62	1	6543	1	$12.21	1
3	1124	2	$4.90	1	6543	3	$42.96	1
3	1124	2	$4.90	1	9792	4	$36.36	1
3	6543	3	$42.96	1	1124	2	$4.90	1
3	6543	3	$42.96	1	9792	4	$36.36	1
3	9792	4	$36.36	1	1124	2	$4.90	1
3	9792	4	$36.36	1	6543	3	$42.96	1
4	1124	2	$4.90	1	6543	3	$37.11	1
4	1124	2	$4.90	1	9792	2	$18.18	1
4	6543	3	$37.11	1	1124	2	$4.90	1
4	6543	3	$37.11	1	9792	2	$18.18	1
4	9792	2	$18.18	1	1124	2	$4.90	1
4	9792	2	$18.18	1	6543	3	$37.11	1
5	6543	2	$24.74	1	9792	1	$16.87	1
5	9792	1	$16.87	1	6543	2	$24.74	1

```
SELECT
DRIVER.DRIVER_ENTITY_KEY
, CORR.CORR_ENTITY_KEY
, DRIVER.DRIVER_QUANTITY_SUM
, DRIVER.DRIVER_DOLLARS_SUM
, DRIVER.DRIVER_COUNT_SUM
, CORR.CORR_QUANTITY_SUM
, CORR.CORR_DOLLARS_SUM
, CORR.CORR_COUNT_SUM
, CORR.CORR_QUANTITY_SUM/DRIVER.DRIVER_QUANTITY_SUM AS QUANTITY_RATIO
, CORR.CORR_DOLLARS_SUM/DRIVER.DRIVER_DOLLARS_SUM AS DOLLARS_RATIO
, CORR.CORR_COUNT_SUM/DRIVER.DRIVER_COUNT_SUM AS COUNT_RATIO
FROM
(SELECT
DRIVER_ENTITY_KEY
,SUM(DRIVER_QUANTITY) AS DRIVER_QUANTITY_SUM
,SUM(DRIVER_DOLLARS) AS DRIVER_DOLLARS_SUM
,SUM(DRIVER_COUNT) AS DRIVER_COUNT_SUM
FROM(SELECT
ITEMSET_KEY
,DRIVER_ENTITY_KEY
,DRIVER_QUANTITY
,DRIVER_DOLLARS
,DRIVER_COUNT
FROM MARKET_BASKET_BI_TABLE_ENTITIES
GROUP BY
ITEMSET_KEY
,DRIVER_ENTITY_KEY
,DRIVER_QUANTITY
,DRIVER_DOLLARS
,DRIVER_COUNT)
GROUP BY
DRIVER_ENTITY_KEY)DRIVER
INNER JOIN
(SELECT
DRIVER_ENTITY_KEY
,CORR_ENTITY_KEY
,SUM(CORR_QUANTITY) AS CORR_QUANTITY_SUM
,SUM(CORR_DOLLARS) AS CORR_DOLLARS_SUM
,SUM(CORR_COUNT) AS CORR_COUNT_SUM
FROM MARKET_BASKET_BI_TABLE_ENTITIES
GROUP BY
DRIVER_ENTITY_KEY
,CORR_ENTITY_KEY)CORR
ON DRIVER.DRIVER_ENTITY_KEY = CORR.DRIVER_ENTITY_KEY
ORDER BY
DRIVER.DRIVER_ENTITY_KEY
, CORR.CORR_ENTITY_KEY
```

FIGURE 14.10
Market Basket Analysis BI View with Entities.

reason, a Market Basket Analysis effort is a search for, among other things, those hierarchical level of analyses where the result sets can be understood and value-added at the same time. You don't want to stare at the bark on the trees. However, you also don't want to view the forest from far away. A successful Market Basket Analysis application will find those hierarchical grains at which the analysts can understand the results and the enterprise can implement a response.

TABLE 14.12
Market Basket Analysis BI View with Entities

Driver Entity Key	Corr Entity Key	Driver Quantity Sum	Driver Dollars Sum	Driver Count Sum	Corr Quantity Sum	Corr Dollars Sum	Corr Count Sum	Quantity Ratio	Dollars Ratio	Count Ratio
1124	6543	7	$50.12	3	7	$92.28	3	100.0000%	184.1181%	100.0000%
1124	9792	7	$50.12	3	8	$85.16	3	114.2857%	169.9122%	100.0000%
6543	1124	9	$117.02	4	7	$50.12	3	77.7778%	42.8303%	75.0000%
6543	9792	9	$117.02	4	9	$102.03	4	100.0000%	87.1902%	100.0000%
9792	0	11	$132.65	5	0	$0.00	1	0.0000%	0.0000%	20.0000%
9792	1124	11	$132.65	5	7	$50.12	3	63.6364%	37.7836%	60.0000%
9792	6543	11	$132.65	5	9	$117.02	4	81.8182%	88.2171%	80.0000%

CONCLUSION

This chapter is a synthesis of the concepts and methods presented in the previous chapters. The Market Basket Analysis methods can be implemented on their own without any intention to incorporate time variance. Likewise, the Time Variant methods can be implemented without any use of the Market Basket Analysis methods. The combination of the Market Basket Analysis and Time Variant methods is a powerful tool in a data warehouse.

All three of these methods (Market Basket Analysis, Time Variance, and Time Variant Market Basket Analysis) are complete applications. All three include database design, ETL design, and a set of Business Intelligence views. The database design optimizes the ETL design, which delivers data in a form optimal to a Business Intelligence layer of views. All three applications can operate within a BI Analysis context or a BI Reporting context.

If when you first looked over the table of contents you were disappointed that none of the three applications are as simple as a set of BI views, then hopefully you were pleasantly surprised to realize that the Business Intelligence portion is as simple as a set of BI views. If, also, when you first looked over the table of contents you were disappointed that the applications designs seem rather specific, then hopefully you were also pleasantly surprised to realize all the designs are flexible to any data model or platform. The intention here is to provide a set of concepts and methods that can be incorporated into any data warehouse, so that when someone questions the ROI of your data warehouse you have an answer…a very good answer.

References

Androutsopoulos, J., G. D. Ritchie, and P. Thanisch. 1995. Experience Using TSQL2 in a Natural Language Interface. In *Recent Advances in Temporal Databases*, ed. J. Clifford, and A. Tuzhilin, 113–132. Great Britain: British Computer Society.

Böhlen, M. H., C. S. Jensen, and R. T. Snodgrass. 1995. Evaluating the Completeness of TSQL2. In *Recent Advances in Temporal Databases*, ed. J. Clifford, and A. Tuzhilin, 153–174. Great Britain: British Computer Society.

Clifford, T., G. Jajodia, and S. Snodgrass. 1993. *Temporal Databases—Theory, Design and Implementation*. Redwood City: Benjamin/Cummings.

Date, C. J., H. Darwin, and N. Lorentzos. 2003. *Temporal Data and the Relational Model*. San Francisco: Morgan Kaufmann.

Gertz, M., and U. W. Lipeck. 1995. "Temporal" Integrity Constraints in Temporal Databases. In *Recent Advances in Temporal Databases*, ed. J. Clifford, and A. Tuzhilin, 77–92. Great Britain: British Computer Society.

Kimball, R., L. Reeves, M. Ross, and W. Thornthwaite. 1998. *The Data Warehouse Lifecycle Toolkit—Expert Methods for Designing, Developing, and Deploying Data Warehouses*. New York: John Wiley & Sons.

Kimball, R., and M. Ross. 2005. Slowly Changing Dimensions Are Not Always as Easy as 1, 2, 3—How Do You Deal with Changing Dimensions? Hybrid Approaches Fill Gaps Left by the Three Fundamental Techniques. http://www.informationweek.com/news/software/bi/showArticle.jhtml? articleID=59301280 (accessed March 4, 2011).

Silvers, F. 2008. *Building and Maintaining a Data Warehouse*. Boca Raton: Taylor & Francis.

Index